Advance praise for *ALEXA!*

"I never had the opportunity to know or to work with Alexa McDonough — but I really wish I had. Her story is a rich piece of Canada's political story. Her heart, her compassion, and her commitment to politics connected to real people are a profound counterbalance to the prevailing cynicism that threatens the very foundations of democracy. And we need more women's stories. It was such a pleasure to read the story of this feisty, principled, brilliant woman who persevered through highs and lows, who defied the odds and the men who tried to bring her down, and who always found the light in the moment. Alexa touched the lives of millions of Canadians. I owe her a particular debt of gratitude for blazing a trail for women in leadership. This book is a delightful, important read!"
— Kathleen Wynne

"Alexa McDonough tackled important issues for Canada at a time when even talking about these issues would result in anything from laughter to sneers to threats. I'm thankful that this book is written so that a record of her work exists and won't be taken for granted. It is a gift to those of us who have followed in her giant footsteps and to those who may be inspired yet to do so. Kimber candidly covers her journey but treats her story with great care. Her humanity shines through."
— Megan Leslie

"A powerful and beautifully written biography of an important Canadian activist, feminist, and trailblazing politician. Her inspiring story, illustrating Alexa's genuine motivation to make real change, is what propels women to run for public office. We are so grateful for Rosemary Brown's advice 'You Should' when Alexa was asked to run for office. 'You Should' would be my advice to all young women in Canada. Read this book to better understand that when you add women, politics changes for the better."
— Hon. Carolyn Bennett

"A moving and delightfully descriptive account of Alexa McDonough, who successfully navigated the testosterone-fuelled world of elected office, winning the leadership of both the Nova Scotia NDP and the federal party. As a former political journalist who spent years covering women in politics, I had the opportunity to watch McDonough in action. Kimber's account is spot on. He sugar-coats nothing, and McDonough, a private person, who was under a spotlight for most of her career, helps him tell the story. "
— Jane Taber

STEPHEN KIMBER

ALEXA!

Changing the Face of Canadian Politics

Edited by Susan Renouf.
Cover and page design by Julie Scriver.
Cover image detailed from NDP Leadership Convention 2003 at Exhibition Place. Former NDP Leader Alexa McDonough waves goodbye after giving her farewell speech. January 23, 2003 Photo by Louie Palu/ The *Globe and Mail*.
Printed in Canada by Friesens.
10 9 8 7 6 5 4 3 2 1

Library and Archives Canada Cataloguing in Publication

Title: Alexa! : changing the face of Canadian politics / Stephen Kimber.
Names: Kimber, Stephen, author.
Description: Includes bibliographical references and index.
Identifiers: Canadiana (print) 2020031825X | Canadiana (ebook) 20200318268 | ISBN 9781773101958 (hardcover) | ISBN 9781773101941 (EPUB)
Subjects: LCSH: McDonough, Alexa. | LCSH: Politicians—Canada—Biography. | LCSH: Politicians—Nova Scotia—Biography. | LCSH: Women politicians—Canada—Biography. | LCSH: Women politicians—Nova Scotia—Biography. | CSH: Canada—Politics and government—1993-2006. | CSH: Canada—Politics and government—2006-2015. | CSH: Nova Scotia—Politics and government—1978-1993. | CSH: Nova Scotia—Politics and government—1993-1999.
Classification: LCC FC636.M38 K54 2020 | DDC 971.064/8092—dc23

Goose Lane Editions acknowledges the generous support of the Government of Canada, the Canada Council for the Arts, and the Government of New Brunswick.

Goose Lane Editions
500 Beaverbrook Court, Suite 330
Fredericton, New Brunswick
CANADA E3B 5X4
gooselane.com

CONTENTS

Alexa McDonough, flanked by her sons Travis (left) and Justin (right), receives applause during the NDP's federal leadership convention in October, 1995

(courtesy of McDonough Family Collection)

PROLOGUE

You should.
I can't.
What do you mean, you can't? Of course, you can.
But I'm a social worker.
I was a social worker.
I have two young kids.
I had three young kids.
But if I ran, I'd have to run against my husband's law partner.
*That's okay. I ran against my husband's medical partner for my
nomination. And I beat him.*
But I don't know enough.
Not good enough.

This conversation happened in Halifax in the spring of 1977. The You–Should in this conversation was Rosemary Brown, a forty-seven-year-old Jamaican-born Canadian then serving as a New Democratic Party (NDP) member of the British Columbia legislature. She was the first Black woman ever elected to any legislature in Canada. Two years earlier, she'd been the first Black woman to run for the leadership of a Canadian federal political party.

That was how she and I–Can't came to be in Halifax having this conversation.

I–Can't was Alexa McDonough, a thirty-three-year-old Nova Scotian woman on the last legs of her long, unsuccessful run to escape what writer Harry Bruce in *Atlantic Insight* magazine would later call her "invisible hound of destiny." She still seemed more constrained by the sum of all the moving parts of her life — the silver-spoon daughter of the millionaire socialist, the wife of the corporate lawyer, the mother of two young sons, and member in awkward standing among South End Halifax's conservative elite — than freed by the scope of her personal possibilities. But she was already chafing at the limitations of the traditional values of her place and time, seeking ways to integrate her own evolving feminism and increasing political activism into a future she couldn't yet imagine for herself.

At her mother's urging, she'd read *The Feminine Mystique*, Betty Friedan's landmark book that challenged the still-prevailing 1950s presumption that truly "feminine women" preferred domesticity to a life of the mind, or a career, or, certainly, political activism. The book's influence on the young Alexa was seminal.

After her 1966 marriage to lawyer Peter McDonough, she had found a satisfying career in social work and, while pregnant with her first son, also negotiated with her employer, the City of Halifax, the municipality's first maternity leave with the guarantee she could return to her old job. And she'd become politically active. After a brief, disillusioning flirtation with the Nova Scotia Liberal Party, she'd returned to the Co-operative Commonwealth Federation (CCF)/NDP politics of her parents.

In 1973, her father, Lloyd Shaw, bought her a plane ticket to attend a conference on democratic socialism at the University of Regina. But it was her mother, Jean, who sagely suggested she share a dorm room with Grace MacInnis, a family friend, the daughter of one of the CCF's founding fathers and the only woman, among 263 men, elected to the House of Commons in 1968. Alexa McDonough was impressed — and inspired, "exceptionally inspired," by MacInnis. But she was still a social worker with a husband and two small kids. What was she supposed to do with inspiration?

In 1974, she had served as campaign manager for social activist Muriel Duckworth's unsuccessful NDP bid for the Nova Scotia legislature and had become the president of her local constituency association. She was selected — along with her mother and father — as a delegate to the 1975 NDP national leadership convention.

The front-runner was Ed Broadbent, a former university professor who'd been a Member of Parliament (MP) since 1968. Alexa's father supported Broadbent, the party establishment's candidate. Alexa did not. She'd served on the federal party's participation of women committee with Rosemary Brown, who had helped found the Vancouver Status of Women Council and championed the notion that women's rights were human rights. "Rosemary emerged as a rock star," Alexa would recall years later. "She galvanized the women's movement."

Once Brown announced her leadership bid, Alexa informed her father she'd be voting for Brown; he wasn't thrilled. He was less happy when his wife, Jean, declared: "You can support Broadbent, Lloyd. That's fine, but I'm supporting Rosemary Brown."

"There was upheaval in my household, the likes of which I don't remember before or since," explained Alexa, who noted her mother's decision to strike out on her own after so many decades of walking in political lockstep with her husband marked a "clenching of the sisterhood between me and my mother."

Brown came second but closer than expected, taking 40 per cent of the vote. Two years later, she called Alexa, whom she now knew through NDP and various feminist circles as well as through Alexa's friendship with Brown's brother, Gus Wedderburn, a respected Halifax social justice advocate. "Can I come and stay with you and Peter?" Brown asked. "I'm just totally exhausted."

Of course. The McDonoughs had a small basement apartment in their house where she could "hide out." And, of course, she and Brown talked. And talked. About anything and everything. Including the notion Alexa should run for office herself. Brown parried every Alexa "I can't" with her own "you should." McDonough soon ran out of defences. "If you run," Brown added by way of sweetener, "I will come and speak for you."

And the rest, as they say, is history.

Well, not exactly.

•

I didn't know Alexa McDonough then, but I'd known of her for a long time. We're both from Halifax, where you couldn't help but be aware of the Shaws. Still, we grew up five years and five kilometres apart, unbridgeable divides in that time and place.

In the late 1970s, my wife became close friends with one of Alexa's best friends, but Alexa and I only met during the 1980 federal election. After finishing third as the federal NDP candidate in Halifax in 1979, she was reprising that role, and its result, in the February 1980 electoral rerun. *Today* magazine had assigned me to follow her around for a cheeky "losers' round-up." The magazine's lead-in to the article went like this: "As the hopeless losers pick up the pieces, bandage the wounds, and return to the private lives that only saints, crazies, or political animals would have left in the first place, we might remember that to keep the democratic process going, someone has to pay."[1]

Given our premise, Alexa was remarkably gracious. She cheerfully acknowledged she didn't expect to win but hoped to garner at least 25 per cent of the votes cast in the three-way race. Her actual share barely nudged 20 per cent. "It will be a slow process," she told me without resignation on election night. "But given time and effort, we will win this riding."

Neither of us would have guessed that it would take seventeen years, or that the NDP candidate who finally won the riding would be Alexa herself, by then the battle-hardened leader of the federal New Democratic Party.

After the 1980 election, Alexa switched to provincial politics, won the no-prize Nova Scotia NDP leadership, and then its lone seat in the legislature. Because the NDP didn't qualify for public funding to hire staff, she hired me to write freelance press releases and occasional speeches. She impressed me with her intelligence, her determination, and her passionate positivism in the face of daunting reality, which was even more daunting than I knew. I didn't realize, because she never mentioned it, that she faced unrelenting bullying and harassment from many of her male colleagues in the provincial legislature. Three years later, the NDP won three seats in the legislature (another "slow process"), Alexa finally had public funding to hire staff, and we went our separate ways.

Most of my memories of her between then and when I began working on this biography are fragmentary. A dinner party in the mid-eighties when Alexa's then husband, Peter, silenced the room by demanding loudly of the flustered hostess: "Are you trying to kill the leader of the NDP?" The hostess had unknowingly served a shellfish appetizer. "Can you imagine the headline?" Peter leaped into the silence with his typical tension-deflating smile. "A Nova Scotia politician with a deathly allergy to seafood?"

Another night in the winter of 1992. I'd gone to Alexa's house to interview her about something or other, but she seemed in an unusual hurry to shuffle me back out the door. I discovered why when, as I was leaving, John Savage, the mayor of Dartmouth, arrived for a private tête-à-tête. Alexa was trying to woo Savage, a left-leaning Liberal, to run for the NDP. As I later learned from others, she was convinced — or convinced herself, as she often did — he was on the edge of agreeing to join her team. Instead, a few weeks later, Savage announced his own candidacy for the provincial Liberal leadership.

And then, a few months before Alexa resigned as provincial NDP leader, she contacted me looking for advice. She'd been offered a job in Africa with the Inter Press Service, a progressive global news agency. Would the job be a good fit? I had no idea. I don't remember what I advised; I am certain I wouldn't have suggested she run for federal NDP leader. Which she did soon after.

•

When I was approached to write her biography in December 2018, I confess I wasn't sure there was much that wasn't already known — or that we needed to know. If you were to employ conventional political metrics, it would be simple enough to stick an asterisk at the end of Alexa Ann Shaw McDonough's name and discreetly move on to other, more significant figures in Canadian political history. After all, she was never a premier or a prime minister. Although she led both the federal and provincial New Democratic Parties, electorally she led them almost exactly nowhere.

But a bald recitation of un-winning numbers misses much of what is most significant about Alexa McDonough and her nearly thirty-year career in Canadian politics. Her more important — most important, in fact — contribution to Canadian political life has not been her electoral successes so much as her seminal role in changing the face of Canadian politics for the better. And for women. In the process, she transcended both her party affiliation and the bias against her gender to become known among Canadians simply as "Alexa," no last name needed, a beloved, respected, and significant player in Canadian public life.

McDonough deserves much more credit than she has been given for the fact that the then newly minted Canadian Prime Minister Justin Trudeau could respond to a reporter's question about why he'd decided to appoint Canada's first-ever gender-balanced cabinet with an almost flippant, "Because it's 2015." It became 2015 in no small measure because of Alexa McDonough.

And yet, that is not the entire story either.

•

There are many, often contradictory, sometimes confounding, Alexa McDonoughs.

Start with all those elitist stereotypes, beginning with the silver spoon. They are all factually true. But she was also, by upbringing and inclination, acutely aware of and genuinely committed to changing the social inequities that bestowed untold advantages on her while handing less-fortunate others rock-filled backpacks and mountains to climb. She came of age more the dutiful daughter of the fifties than the rebellious child of the sixties. But, during the seventies, she underwent a metamorphic transformation from the young bride who dreamed of nothing more than becoming "Mrs. Peter J.E. McDonough" to the ambitious woman, a steadfast and vocal champion of all manner of feminist causes.

At the same time, she was, and is still, a hopeless romantic, a lover of all manner of men, and a woman loved by many men. But she is also best-friends-forever with concentric circles of women, many of whom she has known since childhood. As a political leader, she could be a driven, demanding, Sharpie-wielding boss but also an understanding, generous friend, sometimes with the same person in the same moment. She could be seriously shocked and appalled but also, often, seriously silly-funny. Though she has lived much of her private life in the open — her marriage, her separation and divorce, her relationships with men, even many of her most intimate health issues — there are some doors, like the one that led to her Alzheimer's diagnosis in 2011, she has kept closed, even to members of her own family.

If you're going to connect all the disparate dots that make up her life, it's best to begin with family, to a time before Alexa Ann Shaw McDonough was born when those who would come to shape her life were still being shaped themselves.

BEFORE

1

The marriage of Alexa McDonough's maternal grandparents, Donald Laughlin MacKinnon and Winnifred Cruikshank, had been tumultuous, chaotic. Their 1922 divorce would be rancorous and—at a time when divorce was still rare in Nova Scotia—a public scandal involving a prominent small-town doctor and his young wife. Worse, wrote James J. Ritchie, the judge for Nova Scotia's Court of Divorce and Matrimonial Causes, "One sad result of this most unhappy marriage is the effect upon the four little girls who are the children of the marriage."

None would be more scarred than Alexa's mother, six-year-old Jean, the third of Donald and Winnifred's four daughters, who would grow up to become, in the words of family members, a "vulnerable" woman, wife, and mother, a person who "lacked confidence in herself."

There must have been happy moments in Donald and Winnifred's relationship, but you won't find them described in any of the official documents from their divorce proceedings.[1] There is much we may never know. We know Donald was born in Lake Ainslie, Cape Breton, on August 15, 1873, one of seven sons in an over-achieving family. Every one of the sons would graduate from Queen's University in Kingston, Ontario. We know Donald was a Liberal. He even carried that party's colours in the 1928 provincial election though he lost. We know Donald Laughlin MacKinnon had, as a 1942 obituary would note without comment, "a forceful personality."

Following graduation as a doctor in 1905, Donald began his surgery residency at Boston City Hospital. There, he met and married Winnifred Cruikshank. She had been born in Nova Scotia too, in Salmon River, a rail yard community on the outskirts of Truro. In 1904, when Winnifred was thirteen, her father—like plenty of other Nova Scotians of his time and circumstance—moved his wife and family of six to the "Boston States" in search of greater opportunity. For him, that became a job as a porter.

Winnifred was her family's third youngest child, its oldest daughter. On March 23, 1909, Winnifred's eighteenth birthday, she married Donald, a man twice her age. Children followed quickly: Catherine, known as "Kaye," less than a year after the wedding in February 1910, then Alexa Margaret in 1911, and Donald Duncan in 1912. Their only son died when he was just two. A year after that, on March 21, 1915, Jean arrived. A little over a year later, on December 24, 1916, Winnifred, the baby of the family, was born.

By then, it appears the MacKinnons had decided to return to Nova Scotia. Donald wrote his Canadian medical exams in 1915 and, a year later, bought the residence and practice of a retiring Truro doctor. While the incomplete divorce records do not shed much light on the roots of the conflict between Donald and Winnifred, it seems the difficulties in their marriage were long-standing; some allegations date back to their days in Boston. Judge Ritchie himself tried to read between the lines, pointing to the gulf in their ages and noting, "from the early days of their marriage, [Donald] was, without cause, very jealous of his wife."

Winnifred accused Donald of carrying on an affair with Lavinia Adams, the superintendent of nurses at Donald's hospital. "The acts of adultery were committed at various times since the said Adams became the said superintendent," Winnifred's petition declared, "particulars of which are well known to the respondent." For his part, Donald denied the adultery, and Lavinia herself testified there was nothing going on between them. (Those denials seemed less than credible when, not even a year after the divorce, Donald and Lavinia married.)

Much of the evidence in the court documents is a ping-ponging *j'accuse/je refute*, with Donald's inevitable, for-good-measure caveat that, if any of the things Winnifred accused him of saying or doing were true, they were "in all and every instance, the result of [Winnifred's] provocation." They argued over family. There were disputes about money. She claimed he refused to give her money for personal expenses. He claimed he'd supplied her with "all spending money reasonable for her station and condition in life," but he also claimed she'd used his money to travel "clandestinely" to Halifax for her "whoring excursions," or for "meeting men by appointment."

According to Winnifred, who denied those allegations, their marriage was also physically violent, their home a dangerous battleground. She claimed he'd once bodily thrown her out of their house, bruising her, and, on another occasion, forced her to seek shelter at her mother's home. Still another time, he'd "bodily dragged her back to the house in the presence of passersby." She described incidents in which he threw her "violently" on the bed, dumped a pitcher of water over her while she slept, tore her dress, smashed a telephone, overturned a table, broke dishes. During yet another altercation, Winnifred said he ripped the decorations off the Christmas tree.

More than once, Winnifred told the court, Donald threatened her life, telling her "she had so many minutes to live," or "this was but the beginning of what was coming to her."

Donald denied everything.

Perhaps not surprisingly, the children, including Alexa's mother Jean, were dragged into their parents' disagreements. Donald recalled an evening when Winnifred disappeared and "the young child," who isn't identified further in the documents, "was home very ill and greatly needing care and ministration." Donald said his wife's absence was "reasonably calculated to lead the respondent to believe [she] was out with men." After Winnifred returned from a trip to Boston to visit her family, Donald accused her — in front of one of their daughters — of having gone there to get an abortion. He told the little girl her mother "had gotten diseases from men." Winnifred also claimed at least one of Donald's physical assaults against her happened in the presence of a daughter, again unnamed, who'd intervened, allowing her to escape. Worse, Winnifred accused Donald of committing "acts of indecency" in front of the children.

After a four-day hearing in which Donald acknowledged his wife was, in fact, "a pure woman," and he had lied to "hurt her," Judge Ritchie rendered his decision on August 11, 1922. Perhaps surprisingly, he refused to grant the divorce for adultery. While there was cause "for very reasonable suspicion," Adams denied the affair and there was "no clear evidence" to contradict her.

That said, Ritchie was unequivocal about whose evidence he accepted. "I believe the evidence of the petitioner and accept it without reservation... I have never heard evidence given of anything approaching such unspeakably vile and filthy language as that which the respondent used to his wife," the judge declared, noting he would not "pollute" the pages of his decision by

repeating it. Worse, "there was actual physical violence.... Based on both
the evidence and my observations of him in the witness box, [Donald
MacKinnon] is a man of absolutely uncontrollable temper." Of Winnifred,
he said: "There is a limit to a woman's endurance."

Judge Ritchie put off to a later hearing issues of alimony and child
custody. This is where the record gets murky. We know from Winnifred's
petition, filed that October, she was "desirous of securing the custody of my
four infant children." With reasonable alimony, "I would be in a position
to properly maintain and educate" them. As for her ex-husband's parenting
abilities, "I crave leave to refer to the said decision" concerning their divorce.

There is, unfortunately, no remaining record in the official file to show
what transpired during the hearing to determine alimony and child custody.
We are left only with Judge Ritchie's stunning final decision, delivered
on November 3, 1922. After declaring the marriage "hereby dissolved and
declared henceforth null and void," he ordered Donald to pay $125 a month
for the "maintenance" of Winnifred, their oldest daughter Kaye, and their
youngest daughter Winnifred. "It is further ordered adjudged and decreed
that the respondent [Donald MacKinnon] shall have the sole control and
legal custody of ALEXA MACKINNON and JEAN MACKINNON, two
of the infant daughters of the said marriage." There is no explanation in the
decision about how or why Judge Ritchie came to the determination that
custody of the four daughters should be split between the two parents, or why
the children were divided as they were.

The story that has survived inside the family is that the judge decided
either Donald was not "responsible" enough to parent all the children, or
Winnifred, who planned to return to Boston to live with her parents and had
no marketable skills or immediate job prospects, would not be in a financial
position to care for them all. In any case, he instructed Winnifred to choose
just two of her daughters to take with her. It was an awful kind of Sophie's
choice. Why did Winnifred decide as she did? The presumption in the family
is that Winnifred chose Kaye, the oldest child, and Winnifred, the youngest,
to accompany her because the oldest would be able to help her care for the
youngest while she looked for work and re-established herself in Boston.

Seen from the outside, there is a certain coolly intellectual logic to the
decision. Seen from the inside...well, that was a much different matter. The

image would remain seared in Jean MacKinnon's memory for the rest of her life. On Christmas Eve 1922, Jean's mother and two of her sisters walked out of the family home in Truro and disappeared from her seven-year-old life. Jean had been abandoned. Left. Not chosen. This would colour and cloud Jean's later perceptions, lead her into depression, breakdowns, hospitalizations, even a suicide attempt. And it would also, in perhaps surprising, and surprisingly positive ways, affect the mother she would become to her own daughter.

"My mother would recall with horror that her earliest childhood memory was of her mother walking out of that house on Christmas Eve," Alexa recalled. What Jean remembered more clearly than anything else, Alexa explained, is that her own mother "'never looked back.' I said, 'Mom, of course, she didn't look back. How could she look back and not just be broken-hearted?'"

•

Family stories are endlessly fascinating. What gets told? What gets left out? Growing up, Alexa and Robbie—her older brother by two-and-a-half years—were well aware of their grandfather's adultery, their grandparents' divorce, the division of the children that followed, and, of course, intimately understood their own mother's lifetime of suffering that followed. But what they didn't know—until I shared the long-lost divorce court records with them—was the backstory of their grandfather's cruelty and the domestic war zone in which their mother had spent her earliest years.

At one level, that probably makes sense. Donald MacKinnon died in 1942, the year Robbie was born. In death, he'd been eulogized, and then gauzily remembered as a family doctor in Truro, giving residents their first real hospital, being a "doughty champion" of civic causes and, of course, his "skill and care as a surgeon." As is often the case, Donald MacKinnon's darker side was buried with him.

Alexa and Robbie grew up with two loving maternal grandmothers. There was Lavinia, who preferred to be called Vinnie, their mother's kind and generous stepmother. As children, Alexa and Robbie would often stay overnight with her in Truro. At least twice a year, Robbie and Alexa would also make the long drive with their parents to Boston to spend time with their mother's biological mother, Winnifred, whom they knew as Nonnie.

But the backstory of their grandfather's cruelty wasn't the only one Jean excised from her family stories. There was also the tale of that night in Boston when she was seventeen and decided life was no longer worth living.

2

Fritz Grob couldn't have had any idea his actions on the night of March 12, 1933, would change the course of Canadian political history. Grob was a Harvard University graduate student from Zurich, Switzerland. On that chilly evening in Boston, as he hurried along Cambridge's Memorial Drive seeking the warmth of his residence room, Grob noticed someone in distress in the middle of the Charles River. He waded into the icy water and swam seventy-five feet to the middle of the river to where a young woman struggled to keep her head above water. He wrapped one arm around her shoulders and dragged the woman with him toward the shore. According to the Carnegie Hero Fund bronze medal for bravery he received the next year, Grob "became weak from the cold water, drifted somewhat with the current, and was doubtful whether he would reach the bank. With great exertion, he finally reached wade-able water."[2]

The young woman whose life Fritz Grob saved was Jean MacKinnon, then just eleven days short of her eighteenth birthday. She had jumped into the middle of the Charles from the Anderson Memorial Bridge.[3] For Jean, the decade between her abandonment by her mother and her rescue from the Charles River had not been easy. Although she came to love her easygoing stepmother, she deeply missed her own mother and two sisters. Jean's relationship with her father was complicated. She did her best to get along, looking for ways to placate him, to accommodate herself to his mercurial ways.

The war of words between Donald and Winnifred hadn't ended, even with their divorce. Two years later, in 1924, Donald returned to court to ask Judge Ritchie to reduce his alimony obligations because his medical practice had "decreased very materially" and "I have had to use my principal for the maintenance of my present wife and the two children whom I maintain. . . . I will be bankrupt in about four or five months at the rate I am going now, possibly less." Some of his financial problems, he claimed, had been the direct result of a beating he'd received at the hands of Winnifred's brother, who had apparently punched Donald in the face, breaking his glasses and a blood vessel in his eye, making one eye "dim and weak and painful." That, coupled with another blow that had wreaked permanent damage on his thumb, made it impossible for him to continue to perform "fine surgery," one of his significant sources of income.

Judge Ritchie wasn't buying. "Every man has to exercise strict economy if that is necessary to meet his obligations," he wrote. Two years later, Winnifred herself returned to court, this time seeking an order to force Donald to pay her $700 in back alimony.

By that point, Winnifred was living permanently in Boston. She had gone back to school and, after graduating from the Burdett College of Business, landed what would become a twenty-five-year career as private secretary to Adrian Bessey, the treasurer of the Brookline Savings Bank.

Just before the 1931 school year, Jean arrived in Boston to join her mother and sisters. There is nothing in the record to indicate how or why this decision was made but the transition must have been difficult. Jean was fifteen and suddenly sharing an apartment with sisters and a mother she hadn't lived with, and had rarely seen, for nearly a decade. She was also transferring to high school in a new city where she had no friends.

We'll never know what combination of experiences and emotions led Jean to the Anderson Bridge that March night in 1933. What we do know is that Jean appeared to recover quickly. In fact, less than a year later, the *Boston Globe* reported on a new play called *Anybody's Game* staged by the Belmont High School Dramatic Club. The newspaper featured a charming head-and-shoulders photo of a smiling Jean, the leading lady, with her head slightly tilted to one side.[4] In June, Jean graduated from grade 12 as the winner of the school's Beaton Art Prize.[5]

She returned to Nova Scotia to attend Acadia University that fall but, after two years, returned to Boston to pursue her passion, and talent, for art and the arts, enrolling as a student at the Massachusetts School of Art. She loved the school, loved making art, playing with design. It seemed life couldn't get better.

•

On January 5, 1937, Jean MacKinnon and Lloyd Shaw met aboard the SS *Yarmouth*, a steamship bound for Boston from Yarmouth, Nova Scotia. Jean, twenty-one, was on her way back to Boston for winter term; Lloyd, a year older, was heading to New York to continue his master's degree in economics at Columbia University.

It was love at first sight, though it was not really the first time they'd met, as Jean pointed out in a letter to Lloyd that spring. "Looking through my scrapbook, I happened to glance over some Acadia dance programs," she wrote. "And lo and behold! I've discovered the very date on which we met. March 23, 1935. We danced together! A very important day, young man. Please bear that in mind."[6]

Lloyd may not have remembered their first encounter, but he certainly understood the significance of their second. Within a month of their shipboard encounter, Lloyd wrote to ask to see her again. For the still insecure Jean, his letter landed as a welcome surprise. When she hadn't heard from him immediately after their shipboard encounter, her anxieties led her to suspect the worst. "I had every reason in the world to believe you were engaged to another girl...I was the unhappiest person thinking I should never hear from you again."[7]

"Of course I'd love to see you," she wrote back immediately.[8] Lloyd boarded the train for Boston the next weekend. Their time together was delightful. Two months later, she visited him in New York. "Honestly, Lloyd," Jean wrote after returning to Boston, "it feels like a century since you kissed me goodbye and I've not yet used to awakening mornings without you beside me or going to bed at night without being held so closely and kissed first. You'll never know how much you mean to me. I hope though that since my visit I made you realize that there was never before anyone like you — and there never will be. I am confident of that as the days are long."[9]

It was the beginning of a grand love affair that would last for fifty-six years.

3

Lloyd Robert Shaw's family history was as rooted and rigid as Jean MacKinnon's had been rootless and random. The Shaws could map their Nova Scotia roots back six generations to 1761, when David Shaw, a sixteen-year old from Rhode Island, landed in Falmouth, Nova Scotia, with his father and brother. For most of the next four generations, the Shaws stuck close to their landfall on the Valley's eastern fringes, settling along the Avon River, birthing large families and carving out modestly successful lives as farmers or seafarers.

That changed in 1861, when twenty-one-year-old Robert Shaw decided to go into business. According to family lore, during a trip abroad he had become fascinated with a small brickyard. Back home, he serendipitously discovered a significant concentration of red clay near Hantsport, a small shipbuilding, shipping hub a few kilometres from his home, "grasped the opportunity and set up a small, crude plant...entirely handmade."[10]

Robert's son, Lloyd Ethelbert, Alexa's paternal grandfather, transformed Robert's small business into what would ultimately blossom as the Shaw Group, "one of Canada's leading natural resource manufacturers and community developers." The path was not straightforward. At one point early in the twentieth century, L.E., as he was known, had a falling out with other investors in the region's largest brickmaker, sold his stock, and invested the proceeds badly. To complicate matters, L.E., who had a history of undiagnosed stomach maladies and had "not been feeling well" for some time, was ordered to bed by his doctor in September 1914. "It was March of the next year before I was able to sit up in bed." The only positive note in that dark time, L.E. noted in his memoir, was the birth of his and wife Lillian's fourth child and second son, Lloyd Robert, on February 7, 1914. "That proved to be a God-send."

Three years later, L.E.'s relaunched brick business, now L.E. Shaw Limited, received an unexpected business bonus from a human tragedy. In the early morning hours of December 6, 1917, as L.E. and a helper were preparing for the winter slowdown, "We heard faintly the rumble and knew that something must have happened." That something was the Halifax Explosion. "The next morning," L.E. wrote, "I took the early train into Halifax, only to witness the saddest sight that the human eye could imagine." But, of course, that saddest sight — a flattened city, its mainly wooden structures destroyed — also, ironically, offered an unprecedented business opportunity for a man who made sturdy, dependable bricks. L.E. left the city that day with an order for one million bricks, "the largest single order ever to come out of Halifax."

4

"Lloyd, darling, everyone simply raves about my ring," Jean wrote to Lloyd on January 15, 1938, soon after they'd both returned to their separate schools, still basking in the warm afterglow of the public announcement of their engagement. "For a few days, I had such a hard time getting used to it. Now it's like you — it's part of me."

Jean spent much of that winter and spring planning her wedding, including writing her college thesis on bridal fashion. "Do we hear wedding bells in August?" asked the upbeat entry in her college yearbook.

In the years following her suicide attempt — in particular since she'd met Lloyd — Jean had indeed seemed to come into her own. But the tangle of family was never far from her mind, even, or perhaps especially, as she organized their nuptials. Jean's father was "anxious" for them to be married in Truro at his and her stepmother's church. Although she and Lloyd had already agreed Halifax offered the most neutral location for the marriage given her parents' divorce, she was, as usual, eager to placate.

The next complication was the wedding reception. Donald wanted the reception to take place at his and Lavinia's home, at which "he thought Mother should not be present. At first," Jean wrote, "I thought he was a trifle peeved that I should take it for granted Mom should be at the reception, and then I realized I was very stupid not to see that he knew he could never go through with it. He as well as admitted it, and I'm positive Mom would be the same — the only difference is she would never admit it."[11]

While Jean's "one-in-a-million" stepmother, Vinnie, "will do absolutely anything we want her to — she made that very emphatic without my even consulting her" — Jean ultimately decided she could not upset her father. She felt "terribly about Mom not being at the reception," she told Lloyd, but she had a fallback strategy. "We plan to have a little luncheon in

Halifax — possibly at the Lord Nelson Hotel — for the girls in the bridal party, your mother, sisters, and Mom. That's quite customary," she assured her husband-to-be.

And so, on August 12, 1939, in the Presbyterian Church in Truro, Lloyd Robert Shaw, twenty-five, the recently appointed boys' work secretary of the Halifax YMCA, took Marjorie Jean MacKinnon, twenty-four, to be his lawfully wedded wife. In what would be a harbinger of the life they would lead, the happy couple spent their honeymoon attending a CCF political convention.

5

"Pack up the kids, Jeanie," Lloyd Shaw announced as he breezed in, through, and out of their cramped Ottawa apartment on an early fall day in 1944. "We're moving back to Halifax."

Those may not have been the exact words Lloyd Shaw spoke to his wife that day. But they have become embedded as fact in the family stories, in part because they capture Lloyd's restless energy and enthusiasms and, in part, because they embody the unspoken, fathers-know-best assumptions that fit so neatly with the times. They fit too with Jean's unspoken understanding of her place in the family decision-making firmament. Her husband was on his way home to Nova Scotia. Jean and the family — now including two-year-old toddler Robbie and infant daughter Alexa Ann — would follow. Lloyd was going to run for a seat in Parliament. Lloyd was going to win. And the universe would unfold as it should.

None of it unfolded as planned.

Much of moment had taken place in Lloyd's and Jean's lives during the first five years of their marriage, starting just three weeks after their wedding day when German troops invaded Poland, officially triggering the world war everyone knew was coming.

The YMCA's national board of directors, of which L.E. was then the chair, understood the challenge and opportunity. During the First World War, the Y had played only a modest role in serving the needs of the country's servicemen and their families, "and it was determined not to make that mistake again."[12] But how? Other organizations like the Salvation Army had quickly taken the lead in establishing servicemen's canteens in major cities. What could the Y do?

During the years leading up to the war, the Ottawa YMCA board had toyed with a seemingly unrelated idea of sponsoring college courses for Ottawa's 75,000 non-Catholics, many of whom did not feel welcomed by the city's existing, predominantly Catholic universities.[13] That scheme had now been resurrected as a wartime way for the Y to meet the educational needs of all the young men and women who normally would be attending universities across the nation,[14] but were doing war work in Ottawa instead. Why not create a new college, with professors drawn from the eclectic array of academics and experts gathered in the capital for the war's duration, and with night classes to accommodate the young public servants' workday needs? And who better to spearhead such an effort than Lloyd Shaw? Shaw not only boasted a master's degree and his all-but-dissertation PhD from one of North America's most prestigious universities, but he could also claim teaching experience, having spent several years before Columbia teaching at schools in Nova Scotia's Annapolis Valley.

In September 1940, Lloyd and Jean relocated to Ottawa, where Lloyd took up his new role as secretary of the local Y. The Y allowed Lloyd to devote most of his time to the college project. Operating out of a cramped office on the Y's second floor, Lloyd began assembling the administrative structure of what would eventually become today's Carleton University. In the spring of 1942, the committee appointed him Carleton College's first registrar.

David Lewis, the thirty-two-year-old national secretary of the CCF, was on Carleton College's board. The two men had met through CCF events and volunteering. "He seemed to approach people with diffidence and his demeanour suggested hesitancy and uncertainty," Lewis wrote in his memoir, *The Good Fight*, but "first impressions had misled me. I could not have been more wrong. Behind the apparent diffidence was a strong will and uncanny ability to persuade people to do things before they realized they had undertaken them."[15]

That may explain why, later that fall, Lewis recommended the CCF appoint Shaw its Ottawa-based national research director, the party's second full-time employee. At the time, the CCF seemed on the precipice of a national political breakthrough. Canadians were still struggling with the effects of the Great Depression and had experienced first-hand the traditional parties' failures to come to grips with it. The war had only exacerbated what Lloyd Shaw saw as capitalism's contradictions and the CCF's better solutions: unemployment insurance, public health insurance, public housing, farm price supports, laws to protect farmers from their bankers, public ownership of major industries and financial institutions. Those seemed more relevant than ever as the CCF morphed from a social movement into a legitimate and competitive national political party.

In 1943, CCF support topped 30 per cent nationally. That year, the Ontario party captured enough seats, including most of the industrial working-class ridings, to claim provincial opposition party status. In Saskatchewan, the party was on the brink of forming North America's first socialist government.

Although technically Ottawa-based, Lloyd Shaw spent much of his time on the road. "We expect to form the next federal government at Ottawa," Lloyd confidently told the *Vancouver Sun* after a party meeting there to plot plans for governing after the war's end. "And we want to be prepared with our policies."[16]

In December 1943, Lloyd Shaw made a speech in Halifax about one of those policies. After slamming the country's monopolistic insurance industry for peddling insurance at two-to-three times reasonable rates, he declared the CCF would launch an investigation into the industry after it won power. By then, the surging CCF had the undivided attention of the country's business class, including its powerful newspaper publishers. A *Vancouver Sun* editorial, typical of the response to Shaw's broadside, thundered, "Anyone who seeks to undermine confidence in [the insurance industry], and thus reducing the amount of insurance sold, is damaging the nation at large."[17]

The newspapers' criticism quickly became an echo chamber, with the president of an underwriters' association distributing copies to their employees and agents. When CCF leader M.J. Coldwell complained of the vehemence of these attacks, the newspapers piled on to that too. "Under socialism, no such editorials would be allowed to appear, so there would be none to pass on."[18]

In the middle of the raging controversy he'd triggered, Lloyd resigned to join the Royal Canadian Air Force as a flight sergeant at its new training school in Gimli, Manitoba. There isn't much in the public record to explain his decision so late in the war, but there is no question he brought his politics with him. Harry Brumpton, who bunked with Lloyd at the base, recalled the "Shaw side" of their room "had shelving attached, which contained rows and rows of Hansards."[19] Because the base was less than a hundred kilometres from Winnipeg, Gimli was politically convenient. Lloyd spent weekends with key CCF operatives like Stanley Knowles, already a federal MP, and David Orlikow, an up-and-coming young activist. And he was also able to keep in closer contact with Tommy Douglas's new socialist government in Saskatchewan.

At some point that year, with the war grinding to its conclusion, Lloyd Shaw took stock of his options. "My interest had gone from economics to politics because I decided that these basic questions were not so much economic as political," he would explain later, "and the economic problems could be solved provided the political will was there to solve them."[20]

Lloyd Shaw would stand as a candidate for the CCF in the 1945 federal election. Where better to run than Halifax, where his father had recently relocated the head office of his brick and construction business and where the Shaw name already carried the weight of business success? All that remained was to stop into their apartment in Ottawa on his way to Nova Scotia to let Jean know his decision.

6

On her marriage certificate in 1939, in the space for "trade, profession, kind of work," Jean MacKinnon had written simply: "Artist." But Jean didn't make much art during the couple's years in Ottawa. Like many women, she became, instead, an unpaid helpmate in her husband's work. After Lloyd added Carleton registrar to his Ottawa job titles, Jean became one of its first students, was elected to its first student council, and became president of the campus Latin American Club.

Jean's interest in Latin America—she didn't speak Spanish—may have had something to do with the fact that her older sisters, Kaye and Alexa, had recently settled in Peru. Jean's relationship with her "brilliant" older sisters was complicated. By 1931, when Jean moved in with her mother and youngest sister, Win, in Boston, Kaye and Alexa were finishing undergraduate degrees at Jackson College for Women, a Boston college affiliated with Tufts, then one of the most prestigious small colleges in the United States.

Kaye graduated in 1931. A trained ballet dancer, she made her international professional debut soon after her graduation with the Ballet Russes of Bronislava Nijinska in Paris.[21] Meanwhile, trilingual Alexa, who graduated from Jackson a year later, did graduate work at the Sorbonne in Paris, taught at the MacJannet School for Young Americans near Paris and landed a full-time position at the International School in Geneva, Switzerland. There, she met her husband, Jorge Payan Herce, a wool merchant from a wealthy Peruvian family. They moved to South America, where Alexa soon added a new swashbuckling career — roving international journalist — to her resumé.[22]

Kaye, who had married Jorge's half-brother, Luís Pacheco de Céspedes, an internationally acclaimed contemporary Latin American composer, decamped to Lima just before the Second World War. Luís became musical director of Radio Nacional del Peru before founding the Peruvian National Symphony; Kaye laid the groundwork for what would become Peru's national ballet.

All of that must have seemed wildly exotic to Jean, stuck in backwater Ottawa, her own artistic ambitions on hold. "My mother was a very loving mom and she had a lot of artistic talent," her daughter Alexa would note many years later, "but she was a stay-at-home, a-lot-of-time-in-the-kitchen kind of mother.... And then there were my Tia Alexa and my Tia Kaye, out there soaring on the international stage."

"There were always tensions among the sisters," added Alexa's brother, Robbie. "They were all difficult with each other. Aunt Kaye, in particular, who travelled the world and had no kids of her own, seemed to have a superiority complex when it came to the rest of the family."

"Kaye was always — we'd say in today's terms — a princess," agreed his sister. "She was very exotic, an artist, and she thought she was on the stage all the time."

But her sisters' reality didn't live up to Jean's imaginings. Kaye's "turbulent" letters to family back in Canada were filled with what Robbie remembered as "constant references to financial ups and downs and all the political turmoil in Peru." Alexa's wool-merchant husband became a gambler and an alcoholic who lost the family fortune.

What Jean had that Kaye didn't was a growing family: son Robbie had been born on March 23, 1942, just five months before the MacKinnon

Jean Shaw with Alexa and her older
brother, Robbie, c. 1944
(courtesy of McDonough Family Collection)

family's complicated patriarch, Donald MacKinnon, died after a brief illness.
Two years later, at 12:05 pm on August 11, 1944—the day before Lloyd's and
Jean's fifth anniversary and, coincidentally, in the middle of the hottest day
on record in Ottawa—Jean gave birth in the Ottawa Civic Hospital to a
healthy seven-pound-five-ounce daughter, Alexa Ann.

The next day, a delighted Lloyd sent a punctuation-free but heartfelt
telegram of congratulation: "OUR LITTLE ALEXA BEST ANNIVERSARY
PRESENT EVER ALL MY LOVE DEAREST WIFE ON THIS OUR
DAY OF DAYS AS ALWAYS YOUR HUSBAND."

7

Alexa was still an infant sleeping in a hanging wooden cradle in the living
room of their crowded apartment when Lloyd passed through Ottawa that
early fall day in 1944. While he sought the CCF nomination in Halifax
in Canada's first postwar federal election, he would stay with his parents.
Halifax was then one of the country's handful of dual-member ridings,
created largely to ensure voters in a constituency where religious affiliations
still mattered could elect one Protestant and one Roman Catholic to represent

their interests. On October 1, 1944, Catholic Leo Rooney, Halifax's assistant city solicitor, and Baptist Lloyd Shaw were chosen to represent the CCF.

Although Lloyd was, as always, upbeat about his party's chances, the political ground had shifted tectonically since the party's high-water polling numbers the year before. Historians disagree about why that happened — but it did.

Ottawa had already stepped into the wartime breach, assuming, of necessity, an ever increasing role in the economy and laying the groundwork for the postwar social welfare state. Thanks to the war, there was now full employment; thanks to federal wage and price controls, prices had been held in check. The wily Liberal prime minister William Lyon Mackenzie King sensed political sentiment in the country drifting to the left and, as he wrote in his diary in 1940, was "anxious to keep Liberalism in control in Canada.... [and] not let third parties wrest away from us our rightful place in the matter of social reform." Soon after, he introduced unemployment insurance, a bedrock promise from the Regina manifesto, followed by family allowances. By 1945, the Liberal campaign slogan was a CCF-sounding "Build a New Social Order."

There were other reasons for the CCF's fall from voter grace, including what appeared to be a massive, well-funded conspiracy to discredit the party and its leaders. "As one saw more of life," David Lewis allowed in his 1981 memoir *The Good Fight*, "one began to doubt the existence of an actual conspiracy, because one could not find direct evidence to support it, but the phenomenon remained and was never more striking in its effect on the CCF than in the years 1943 to 1945.... The anti-CCF barrage began from every direction and every medium."[23]

If not a conspiracy, it seemed at least a concerted, coordinated effort to undercut the party's growing popularity by linking the CCF to Stalin's Soviet Union or Hitler's Germany. The Canadian Chamber of Commerce's executive board dispensed its planned agenda and spent a full day strategizing "to combat the menace of the CCF." Employers threatened employees. "You may vote CCF against my advice. This is your privilege," explained one. "I cannot, however, accept the responsibility of maintaining employment for you and the other members of our organization for any length of time under a CCF-controlled government." The press, as usual, cheered from the sidelines: The goal of the CCF, declared the Ottawa *Journal* in a January

12, 1944, editorial, was to level society "so that the intelligent, energetic, and industrious people will get less, and the lazy, the idle, the inefficient, and the unintelligent shall get more."

Perhaps the most egregious attacks on the party came from a mysterious Toronto man, B.A. Trestrail, whose innuendo-filled screeds were quietly underwritten by executives from some of Canada's major banks, insurance companies, publishers, oil companies, and even popular retailers like Simpsons. With their financial support, Trestrail printed and distributed a series of anti-socialist pamphlets in the lead-up to the 1945 general election, including mailing out three million copies of one twenty-four-page tabloid called *Social Suicide,* which painted "the CCF goal of a cooperative commonwealth with a striped pattern of red communism and brown fascism." Frank Scott was "an intellectual who had never met a payroll," while David Lewis was that "Polish Jew whose family changed their name."[24]

Years later, Lloyd Shaw could still remember walking down the street in Halifax the day after Trestrail's pamphlet showed up in voters' mailboxes. "It wasn't just imagination, the whole atmosphere changed just that quick. . . . It was one of the most shattering experiences."[25]

The election result was a bitter disappointment. King's Liberals may have only eked out their victory, officially winning a minority of 118 seats in the 245-seat House of Commons, and the CCF did win 28 seats, 20 more than it had in the previous election—or ever—but expectations had been that the party could take 70–100 seats.

One of the many ridings that did not go the CCF's way that June day was Halifax. Despite campaigning in uniform as a patriotic RCAF flight sergeant with his jaunty "wedge" cap, the voters crushed Lloyd Shaw's electoral dreams. The Liberal incumbents didn't just defeat their CCF rivals; they tripled their vote. The two CCF candidates ended a distant, dismal third behind the Liberals and the Progressive Conservatives.

No matter. Undaunted, Lloyd Shaw determined to stay in Nova Scotia, raise his young family, and build his socialist tomorrow. He accepted a new full-time position as the party's provincial secretary.

8

They'd gotten her name wrong. Again. "This dress was designed by Mrs. Margaret Shaw of Halifax," read the caption beneath a photo of a woman modelling the garment at the first annual Halifax *Chronicle* and *Daily Star* Canadiana fashion show in November 1945. If the newspaper wasn't referring to her as Margaret instead of Jean, the *Halifax City Directory* was identifying her by her rarely used first name, "Marjorie." Jean could count herself lucky just to be called Mrs. Lloyd Shaw.

In September 1945, however, just two months after Lloyd's ignominious electoral defeat, Jean — by her right name — had been among thirty-two finalists honoured by the Montréal Dress Manufacturers' Guild at a gala dinner in that city. "Everyone who was anybody in fashion circles attended," according to the newspapers.[26]

Jean's award-winning entry from among 10,000 entrants and 60,000 sketches was for a "smart dress that could be made with apron or with double peplum" that created "much interest" among the judges. The Montréal competition had been part of a national talent hunt for Canadian postwar fashion designers. During the war, Canadian "dress designers were forced to draw on Canadian talent — and found there was such a thing as Canadian taste and that Canadians had something to say about it." Noted the marketing promotions manager of *Women's Wear Daily* in New York, "You have shown yourselves to be an aggressive force that is going to awaken a dormant talent throughout your country."

Could Jean Shaw be part of that aggressive force?

Although Jean told a reporter for the Halifax *Chronicle* that one of her personal ambitions was "to assist in the promotion of designing and illustrating in Canada," even the news story about her award-winning design seemed to give short shrift to her talents, devoting more ink to her "successful sisters." For one whose confidence was fragile, finding herself measured up against her older sisters, even in a story about your own accomplishments, must have been difficult.

Since the family's move to Halifax the year before, Jean had done her best to juggle the competing needs of her young family and her continuing role as unpaid helpmate in Lloyd's new position as the CCF's provincial secretary.

Jean edited the party's provincial newsletter and organized its women's auxiliary. None of which left much time for her own artistic work.

That made that November fashion show in Halifax all the more significant. The well-publicized and eagerly anticipated event was sponsored by the city's two leading newspapers. The ballroom of the Nova Scotian Hotel, the city's largest, was "overflowing" with more than 2,000 "fashion-conscious people" taking in the "parade of the exciting and beautiful yet extremely practical new fashions displayed by the lovely Canadian models."

Among those "exciting and beautiful yet extremely practical new fashions," of course, was Jean Shaw's award-winning dress. It should have been a great coming-out moment.... Margaret? She clipped the photos and carefully drew a line through the offending name in blue pen, replacing it with "Marjorie Jean Shaw."

9

On December 14, 1948, six-year-old Robbie Shaw ran home from school at lunch, eager to learn exactly how many votes his father had received in a federal by-election the day before.

Lloyd was again running against formidable opponents. John Douglas McKenzie, the Liberal, was a local businessman who had served as mayor of Middleton and as the patronage-dispensing provincial minister of highways and public works during the Second World War. George Nowlan, the Progressive Conservative, had been a gunner during the First World War who had returned home to Wolfville to become a prominent lawyer. He, too, had served as a member of the provincial legislature.

While Lloyd may have had personal roots in the deeply conservative Annapolis Valley, his party did not. By the late 1940s, it was clear a CCF nomination there was not so much a prize as a burden to be borne by the party's paid full-time provincial secretary. Not that ever-optimistic, upbeat Lloyd ever treated it as the losing proposition it was. He threw himself into the campaign with his usual enthusiasm, which had rubbed off on his children.

The night of the election, while Lloyd waited for the results at party headquarters, Robbie and Alexa climbed into bed with their mother in Halifax to listen to the radio election broadcast. Jean had drawn three columns on a pad. At the top of each column, she wrote the names, in alphabetical order, of the candidates — McKenzie, Nowlan, and Shaw — and began filling in the votes as they were announced.

Jean later noted: "Robbie, with each announcement, became more and more excited, exclaiming: 'See, Mummie, Daddy's getting more and more all the time — just look.' He was watching the numbers increase in the third column and was just ignoring the first two, doubling and tripling Lloyd's as they were!" The final outcome (between McKenzie and Nowlan) was still in doubt when Robbie and Alexa finally trundled off to their own beds for the night, with Robbie, as optimistic as his father, insisting, "Daddy is winning third."

In the end, Daddy did "win" third with 1,992 votes, 10,477 votes behind McKenzie and 12,135 short of the winner, Nowlan. His vote count was so low, he lost his deposit.

"Mr. Lloyd Shaw comes of a prominent Valley family," remarked the *Ottawa Citizen* in a by-election post-mortem, "but his activities have been elsewhere in recent years and, in its second campaign in the riding, his party had not the organization for a strong showing."

Lloyd, who'd finally arrived home at 2:30 a.m., was still asleep when Robbie left for school the next morning, so Robbie hadn't had a chance to talk with his father until the school lunch break. "Hi, Dad," he said, running in with a big grin on his face, "I hear you got a lot of votes in the election."

"Yes, Robbie," Lloyd answered. "We doubled the number we got in the last election. Next time we'll get 4,000, and by the third time, it'll be 8,000 and we'll win. Won't that be great?"

"No, Daddy," Robbie hollered in response. "*Next time*, we'll get 8,000 and win!"

At that point, four-year-old Alexa, who'd been listening quietly, piped up with her first — but far from last — recorded political statement. "Daddy, there must be an awful lot of dumb people." She paused then and turned to her mother. "Or is it Daddy that's dumb in the election, Mummie?"

Jean wrote, "We just hooted and right then and there decided we were anything but licked. And how could we be down in the mouth for very long with kids like ours, I ask you?"

•

"Kids like ours," however, would not be enough to alter the inconvenient political facts of life. In the June 1949 federal general election, Lloyd would run again — this time in Halifax — and lose again, finishing last with barely 5 per cent of the ballots cast. To make matters worse, the provincial party's fundraising efforts were — despite his best efforts — bringing in barely enough to pay his salary.

Given the growing needs of his family, Lloyd Shaw reluctantly came to the conclusion he could no longer "devote myself to furthering this people's movement." On July 29, 1949, he resigned as the CCF's research director and accepted his father's standing offer to join L.E. Shaw Limited as its personnel manager.

COMING OF AGE IN AN AGE

1

Though photos from the day belie her self-image, a grown-up Alexa McDonough would remember her child-self as a "chubby little kid who was a little bit clumsy and not at all graceful." She'd also been born with a "lazy eye," a condition called amblyopia, in which her left eye wasn't getting the correct messages from her brain and "wandered" on its own. As a child she had eye muscle surgery to correct it.

You would think this would not augur well for a future as a ballerina. And yet Alexa spent close to a decade deeply immersed in dance: learning, practising, rehearsing, performing. By the time she began high school, Alexa recalled, "I was going to dance classes four times a week." Why dance? The simplest answer might be opportunity. In the years after the Second World War, Halifax had become home for some of Europe's most talented classical musicians and dancers, refugees on their journey from displaced-persons camps to new lives in a new world.[1]

Alexa's dance career began as an eight-year-old in 1952, when she was cast as an "Icicle" in an annual recital production of *Four Seasons*. The next year, she graduated to the role of a "Black Card" in *Alice in Wonderland*. Under Mirdza Dambergs, once a Latvian prima ballerina, Alexa took on increasingly demanding roles, including solo dancer in a 1958 performance of excerpts from *Swan Lake*.

"I never had any illusions about being a professional ballerina," Alexa would say later. "I didn't think much one way or the other. It was just what I did."

As a teacher, however, Mirdza Dambergs saw classical ballet, which "combines mental and physical fitness on the highest level in the interpretation of music and story, and attempts to attain individual and co-operative perfection," as a way to develop young minds as well as bodies. "A child who has self-reliance about its movements," she wrote in an introduction to one of her students' recitals, "will rapidly grow in self-confidence, will become more active and later will adjust and find his or her right place in society."

Alexa Shaw, who would find her own right place in that larger society, was more prosaic. She said Dambergs, whom she described as her "biggest influence" as a young dancer, "taught me that, even though I wasn't destined to be a great dancer, I could take flying leaps and land on my feet. So when people would later sometimes come up and say to me, 'Where did you get the notion you could run for political office when you had no political science background and there were no women who ever did that?' I would tell them about Mme. Dambergs."

•

While the presence of a talented group of European ballet refugees in Halifax offered Alexa opportunities she might not have enjoyed otherwise, it was Jean who encouraged her to embrace them. In part, of course, that was just her mother being a mother. But there was more to it. Even as an adult, Jean remained the fragile daughter of a difficult divorce. Jean had mostly abandoned her own early artistic ambitions to become a mother and the full-time "wife of" one of Nova Scotia's most prominent business leaders.

As a mother, however, Jean was determined her own children — and particularly her daughter — would have opportunities she had not. "My mother lived through me in a weird sort of way," Alexa would allow years later. That's not to suggest Jean played the role of stage mother, pushing her daughter to become a professional ballerina like her own sister, Kaye, or the artist she still wished she had become. Instead, Jean was simply always there, nudging, supporting, enthusing, making her daughter believe she could do anything she set her mind to, and that she should always, at the very least, try.

"She was a tremendous cheerleader for her children, their champion," Alexa's lifelong friend Betty Muggah (née Crookshank) remembered. "Alexa and Robbie had confidence they could do anything. That early confidence came from Jean." Jean was "the consummate hostess," Betty remembered. She and their young friends would often stay over at the Shaws, "and she was always interested in us as young people."

Still, Jean paid a private price for her public face. "My mother had serious mental health issues," Robbie remembered. "She was in and out of the NS [the Nova Scotia Mental Hospital] when we were growing up, and she was often not in very good shape." While Robbie, who was two-and-a-half years older, knew where his mother went when she disappeared from time to time, Alexa did not, at least not at first. She believed — she thinks she may have been told — her mother was visiting family in Boston. But as she grew older, Alexa understood — without needing it spelled out — that her mother was insecure and vulnerable, and needed her care and understanding.

"Their mother's condition was a recurring theme and focus for the family," Betty explained. "Everyone was always adjusting and trying to assist Jean with her moods. But I think Alexa was the one who took on the burden most directly. Stepping back and analyzing now, you realize that, in trying to understand and figure out what she had to do to help her mother, Alexa became a strong, thoughtful, perceptive woman." In the end, as mother encouraged daughter, daughter supported mother. To the benefit of both.

From the time Alexa was a little girl, the Shaws had a housekeeper. That wasn't unusual among affluent South End Halifax families at the time, but it became essential to the smooth functioning of the Shaw household. When Jean was not in the hospital, she would sometimes spend two of every three days in her room, incommunicado.

For a time, Evelina Skeir, the wife of the Reverend Donald Skeir, a local Black Baptist minister who was a friend of the Shaw family, cleaned, cooked the family meals, and served as the children's primary caregiver. "She ran the house," remembered Robbie. "I loved her. She sometimes seemed more like a mother to me than my own mother."

This took a burden off Jean, not to mention Lloyd, who had been promoted to vice-president and general manager of L.E. Shaw Limited, and had become increasingly involved in the provincial business community.[2] Though Lloyd "adored my mother, just adored her in the fact that she was kind of vulnerable," Alexa would also acknowledge he was very much a man of his times. "No disrespect to my beloved father," she said, "but he was a very traditional postwar air force veteran." Despite his socialist roots and the CCF's official commitment to women's rights and equality, he, like many servicemen, "came back after the war and the women disappeared back into the home. My mother was one of millions who did."

In the late 1950s, after the children became teenagers, Jean would decide to join the paid workforce. She and a neighbour operated an interior decorating shop on Quinpool Road called Fabrics Inc. "My father was OK with it," Alexa recalled with a laugh, "as long as he could still come home every day for his lunch. He just couldn't really cope with the fact that it wasn't very convenient [for him] for my mother to be at work during that time."

Jean's foray into business did not last.

2

Jean Shaw couldn't help herself. As Rev. Donald Skeir began his benediction, signalling the end of that year's First Baptist Church's Christmas carol service, Jean "felt like weeping."[3] The night's carol service had been unlike any she'd attended for many reasons, not the least of which was the presence of Skeir, speaking from the pulpit of a church deep in the well-to-do heart of white South End Halifax. "May the God of hope fill you with all joy and peace by your faith in him until, by the power of the Holy Spirit, you overflow with hope," Skeir intoned.

On this night — December 23, 1960 — Jean's heart did overflow with hope, much of it thanks to the accomplishments of her sixteen-year-old daughter, Alexa, and Alexa's three best friends: Betty Crookshank, Nancy Hagen, and Cathy Isnor. Cathy and Alexa, who were the same age, had met as four-year-olds in Sunday school and became close friends in junior high. Nancy and Betty were a year older. Nancy was another church friend; Betty, the Anglican outsider, had slipped into their best-friend inner circle through Betty's school friendship with Nancy. The four friends, as Jean would later explain, had set out to show the children of Africville the real meaning of Christmas and, instead, "had found it for themselves."

Their journey had begun almost a year before with an explosive question Alexa posed one evening to the leaders of their church's Canadian Girls in Training (CGIT) group, including her mother: "Why are we talking about apartheid in South Africa when we have apartheid right here in Halifax?"

The CGIT was a church-based, Christian alternative to the Girl Guides. Members — girls between the ages of eleven and seventeen — wore distinctive white-and-blue middy blouses and pledged to "Cherish Health, Seek Truth,

Know God, Serve Others and . . . become the girl God would have me be."
The First Baptist CGIT girls had recently taken part in a Model United
Nations' discussion about Africa, after which they'd met to discuss what
they'd learned and how they could use that to "serve others." Someone had
heard about a nascent England-based Boycott Movement intended to pressure
the government of South Africa to abandon its racist apartheid policy.
Perhaps the girls could stop eating South African fruit, someone suggested.
Which had been when Alexa brought the conversation uncomfortably closer
to home.

She wasn't wrong. Halifax was a racially divided city. Most of its 1,750
Black citizens were clustered in two ghettos far from well-to-do white neighbourhoods, one near Gottingen Street in the city's North End, the other
even farther north at the fringe of the peninsula in a ramshackle community
known as Africville.

Truth be told, many — perhaps most — of the congregation at First
Baptist had never met a Black Nova Scotian socially, let alone counted any
as friends. They wouldn't have encountered them downtown; the banks and
shops were an almost exclusively white preserve, as were the universities,
the white-shoe and even scuffed-shoe law firms, and all government offices.
Thanks to educational streaming, which routinely shunted even the brightest
Black students into vocational training or out of school entirely, Alexa and
her friends would have had few Black classmates at Queen Elizabeth High
School. And fewer of them would have become friends.

For many of their white high school friends, Betty would explain years
later, Africville symbolized the Other, "a place of fear, separated out from the
rest of the community. Boys would get their fathers' cars and drive through
Africville at night, fast. That was a big thrill."

Africville might as well have been a foreign country. Originally settled
during the nineteenth century by a mix of freed slaves, Jamaican Maroons,
and refugees from the War of 1812, the community had been separated from
the rest of the city by facilities no one in white Halifax wanted in their own
backyards: a prison, a dump, a fertilizer plant, an animal slaughterhouse,
and an infectious diseases hospital. Although its 400 residents regularly
petitioned Halifax city fathers to extend them the same water and sewer
services, the same fire and police protection, the same paved roads as their
white neighbours, the city just as regularly ignored their requests. It would

be too expensive and, besides, local politicians and developers recognized the land they squatted on — many didn't have legal title — was prime waterfront industrial land.

Having never spent any time in Africville or gotten to know its people or understood their deep sense of community, most whites could not fathom why anyone there wouldn't be eager, even grateful, to move. As events would soon show, Africville's residents were neither eager nor grateful. But the other truth was that most of Africville's residents couldn't have relocated even if they wanted to. In 1960, it was still legal for landlords in Nova Scotia to turn away would-be tenants based on nothing more than the colour of their skin or for someone to refuse to sell their house to a Black person. To add one more insult to too many injuries of unwelcome, the national press reported that some local barbershops openly refused to even cut the hair of Black people.

Apartheid? What else would you call it?

That said, Alexa's pointed question might not have led anywhere except for the fact she was Lloyd and Jean Shaw's daughter. Although the Shaws, like some of their neighbours, did employ a Black housekeeper, they, unlike most of their neighbours, also had Black friends who were frequent guests in their home. Alexa would have learned some of what she knew about the state of race relations in Halifax from them. One frequent visitor was Rev. William Pearly Oliver, the pastor of Cornwallis Street Baptist Church in Halifax's North End. Oliver had been one of the founders of the Nova Scotia Association for the Advancement of Coloured People, a civil rights group that came to prominence in the late 1940s while championing Halifax businesswoman Viola Desmond's appeal of her conviction for sitting in the whites-only section of a theatre.

Lloyd knew the Rev. W.P. as "Billy." They'd grown up in Wolfville and attended Acadia University around the same time. When Lloyd heard what his daughter asked, he did what he usually did "when he liked something," as Betty put it. He breathed deeply and sharply, emitting a long sigh of satisfaction, then sought out ways to keep this interesting conversation bubbling.

"Alexa's dad always interacted with us," recalled Cathy Isnor. "He would tell us how important it was for us to contribute to the world, and to think about how to help others."

"There was no other father like him," agreed Betty. "He was curious about everything and everyone, including us."

Lloyd arranged for the girls to meet Reverend Oliver, who approved of their idea of a vacation Bible school for the children in Africville. With a second "all in favour" from Skeir, whose pastoral territory included Africville's Seaview Baptist Church, the girls prepared an official proposal that they then presented to First Baptist's elders, who blessed their plan.

The four girls took on all the organizational heavy lifting. Alexa became the group's "super-duper organizer; she really took charge of everything," Betty said. They plotted each day of their two-week camp—arts and crafts, games, Bible stories, singsongs, playtime in the yard behind the church. They approached local businesses for donations. Alexa and her mother filled the final few days before the camp opened "madly dashing" from supplier to supplier, picking up donated treats, even borrowing a fridge to keep the refreshments cool in the summer heat.

Their enthusiasm was infectious. "My dear Alexa," Garnet Colwell, one of the church elders and a prominent businessman, began one letter to her.[4] "In connection with the request you called me about last night, kindly be advised that I have spent the whole morning in trying to arrange transportation for the children of Africville." In the end, a dozen men from the church led by Lloyd made the daily crosstown trek to pick up the children, drive them to First Baptist, and then deliver them home to Africville again at the end of the day. The women of the church's auxiliary and missionary society pitched in to provide hot lunches, which were served by younger members of the CGIT. "There was hardly a church group that wasn't represented by time, effort, car, food, or money," Jean reported.

The camp proved a resounding success. Reverend Skeir initially told the girls to expect fifteen to twenty children; they ended up struggling to manage activities for fifty enthusiastic boys and girls ranging in age from six to thirteen. It was a learning experience for all of them. The girls discovered a Black community they'd barely known existed and discovered it was indeed a community. For many of the children, who'd spent their entire lives to that point inside their own insular world, "just the car ride and seeing other parts of town was a great novelty," Jean noted.

That one-off summer program spawned by Alexa's singular question had far-reaching ramifications. For starters, it became more than a one-off. By 1963, Alexa, then a university student and summer reporter for the Halifax *Mail Star*, returned to cover the camp's fourth annual closing ceremonies, this one at the church in Africville, "the first time that activity has been at Seaview."[5] Before the camp's second year, First Baptist's congregation fundraised $2,600 to transform the girls' initial volunteer adventure into summer jobs for the four girls. The city's recreation department noticed. After the girls' extended official seven-week camp ended, the department agreed to provide a bus for the rest of the summer so the girls could take their young charges to playgrounds in middle-class districts around the city. That finally shamed the city into promising to build a new playground "adjacent to Africville."

The adults in First Baptist's congregation even set up their own committee "to assist in the development of the Africville people spiritually, physically, mentally, socially and culturally," including providing funds to their fellow Africville church.[6] Although it would turn out to be a disaster for all concerned, the First Baptist Africville Committee also became one of a number of well-meaning liberal groups in the city and beyond urging Halifax's Housing Committee to "put Africville on its priority list for immediate attention." They called for the "abolition of the area to be replaced by a decent scheme for re-housing and relocation [of] those citizens."

Ironically, one of the children who participated in those early vacation Bible camps, Irvine Carvery, would become the most public and persistent spokesperson for Africville's dispossessed residents as the president of the Africville Genealogy Society. He and a few others from the early Africville Vacation Bible Camps, including Brenda Steed and Linda Mantley, would spearhead the long struggle to force the city to apologize for expropriating and razing their community. And, when the city did finally officially apologize, in 2010, Alexa McDonough — née Shaw — was among those in the audience to celebrate.

She and her three friends were all marked for life by their experiences with Africville. Alexa, Betty (Crookshank) Muggah, and Nancy (Hagen) Dickson would grow up to become social workers; Cathy (Isnor) Fry trained as a psychologist. "It was an important experience for all of us," said Betty. "It brought us together." They would remain best friends for life, one of a number of Alexa's vital women's friendship circles that would help sustain and support her through her three decades in public life and beyond.

But, on December 23, 1960, all of that was far in the future. Still flushed with their first summer success, the girls had decided to organize a Christmas reunion for the children. They decorated the church hall, put the Boy Scout troop in charge of rounding up tiny Christmas trees for each of the children to trim, got parishioners to contribute to a toy fund, arranged for the women's auxiliary to provide a turkey lunch, and coaxed a local transportation company to provide a free bus for the day.

After a day filled with games, movies, decoration-making, tree-trimming, turkey-eating, and gift-giving, the children settled into the church pews for this end-the-day Christmas carol service. Thirty-five years later, on the verge of her daughter's victory at the federal NDP leadership convention, Jean would recall that day again for a reporter from the *Toronto Star*. "It was the first time I ever saw her as a natural leader," she told Tim Harper. "I was never more proud of her."

3

Stanley Burke was drunk! It was pushing midnight on a Thursday night in early February 1961, and Alexa and Betty had borrowed Jean's car to drive to the Halifax International Airport to pick up their honoured guest. But the flight from New York had been delayed twice and now, finally, there was Burke, the last person off the plane, showing obvious signs of how he'd spent those extra hours in the airport and on the plane.

Alexa and Betty, along with Cathy and Nancy, were members of a student committee that had spent months organizing this weekend's Third Annual Halifax High-Y Model United Nations Assembly. They'd helped determine the issues, serious and less so, the students were to debate. And they'd even arranged to convince Burke, the CBC's handsome, cerebral thirty-seven-year-old United Nations correspondent, to be their assembly's star-power president, presiding over its sessions, and even make the opening speech.

Drunk? "That punctured a big hole in our idealism," Betty recalled with a laugh. "But luckily, he'd recovered completely by the next day and performed as we hoped he would. The Model UN was a complete success."

Given her later career, Alexa's involvement in a high school Model United Nations might seem a given. And, in a family way, it was. Lloyd was also a well-known anti-nuclear activist and internationalist humanitarian. The Shaws regularly hosted guests in the thick of global issues, and world affairs featured prominently in their family dinner table conversations. But for most of her high school years, with the exception of her leadership of the Africville summer camp, Alexa seemed content to hover in the background. While she was part of the UN Assembly planning committee, Betty played the role of the assembly's secretary-general, and their friend Nancy Hagen was its vice-president. In part, that may have been because Alexa was a year younger, and a grade behind most of her closest girlfriends, including Betty and Nancy. In a pattern that would repeat itself throughout her school years, Alexa felt herself, and appeared to others, more mature than her immediate peers.[7]

Most of her boyfriends were also older, seniors in their high school, even occasionally university students. "From the time I met her," recalled Betty, "Alexa really enjoyed the company of boys. There were always boyfriends. She was never without, and there always seemed to be a lineup. And she was always 100 per cent in love." Until, in the usual ways of high school romances, she wasn't. One reason her boyfriends were older, Betty suggested was that Alexa's brother, Robbie, "was a social animal and there were always lots of parties at his place." Robbie's vivacious, attractive younger sister was always welcome at such parties.

Robbie and Alexa were close. When they were away from one another, they would write regularly, often offering solicited, and unsolicited, advice on each other's love lives. They usually knew all the players in those dramas.

The siblings were also competitive, which might explain Alexa's seeming lack of interest in a student leadership role for herself because Robbie already fully occupied that space. He was the popular president of not only the six-hundred-member local Hi-Y organization but also its national president and seemed, at the time at least, to be the more natural leader. Not that anyone in those days could imagine any girl, even one of Alexa's obvious intelligence, aspiring to a prominent role, certainly never one as prominent as the leader of a national political party. At that time, "anyone" would probably have included Alexa herself.

She was still dancing—the *Mail Star*'s report on Mme. Dambergs's 1961 spring recital noted Alexa Ann Shaw had "strikingly presented...the brilliant and colourful Polish dance as proof that she has reached maturity as a ballet dancer"[8]—but other activities and diversions now competed for her time and attention.

She starred as Mary Skinner in their high school's drama society production of *Life with Father*, a popular Broadway play that had become both a film and TV series. During the winters, Alexa and her friends would attend Friday night hockey games to cheer on the QE boys—usually at least one of them a boyfriend, or potential boyfriend—before everyone hurried off to the YMCA in time for the last waltz at the weekly Twixteen dance. There were sometimes weekend ski trips to Wentworth, a ski hill two hours away by train, and Saturday night pre-socializing meetings of Sigma Rho, her Hi-Y club. Those YMCA-based groups were not as elitist as university fraternities and sororities. There was no "rushing," no secret handshakes. They were mostly just teenaged social clubs that mixed in Y-encouraged do-gooding.

But the clubs also reflected, in their own microcosmic way, Halifax's many religious, economic, and social cleavages. In religiously divided Halifax, Hi-Y (and the Y itself) was the preserve of students from nearby Queen Elizabeth, the city's Protestant and "other" high school. Roman Catholic students from St. Patrick's High School, QE's cross-street rival, hung out at the Knights of Columbus. But it was stratified in other ways too. Because there were only two high schools serving all of Halifax at the time, students from the richest white South End neighbourhoods ended up in the same school building as Black students from Gottingen Street and Africville—in the same building, perhaps, but not in the same world. With the exception of on the football field or basketball court, white and Black students rarely interacted. And Black students rarely joined—or felt welcomed by—the white students who hung out at the Y or became members of Hi-Y clubs themselves.

Unlike most of their peers, Alexa, Betty, Cathy, and Nancy were aware of that Black-white disconnect, thanks to their Africville summer camp. That said, they were also privileged young white girls whose loyalties were still more to one another than any larger world. "For three years," as Alexa wrote in a high school essay, "I have been a member of a so-called 'clique.' Many criticize that 'we' are snobs. [But] to me it seems inevitable that girls should group together in friendship circles."[9]

She and her friends spent countless hours together. When Alexa's parents were off on travels of their own, for example, the girls would often stay with Alexa. "There'd be a housekeeper during the day," recalled Cathy, "but at night we'd have the house to ourselves." She remembered the Shaws had a "wonderful sound system with music in every room. Before we went to bed, we'd stack the albums—all kinds, classical, dreamy choices—on the stereo," and listen and talk themselves to sleep.

But by the spring of 1961, the future of their circle was about to be tested by geography and circumstance. Betty and Nancy would head off to university, Betty to Queen's where Alexa's brother Rob was already a student. And although Cathy was in grade 11 with Alexa, she had decided to take advantage of a provision that allowed students to enrol in university after junior matriculation. Alexa wasn't quite ready for university, but she wasn't interested in spending another year at QE without her best friends either.

Enter Pop Shaw.

4

Robert "Pop" Shaw was Lloyd's first cousin. The family-history version is that Pop Shaw's father, Alfred—L.E.'s older brother—had landed in some kind of trouble as the result of "a bank scandal" in Nova Scotia during the late 1890s and had decamped with his family to New Jersey, where Pop had grown up.

Pop attended Harvard College and, later, Oxford. In the early 1920s, while working at a boys' summer camp in New Hampshire, Shaw and three fellow counsellors discovered they shared "a common interest in [creating] a different type of school for boys, much less regulated than the usual high school but rigorous in requiring high standards of achievement." In 1925, they launched Solebury, a boarding school in bucolic New Hope, Pennsylvania, a small town less than two hours south of New York. That first year, there were just four teachers and four students. By the early sixties, Solebury had become co-ed and, though its enrolment had increased substantially, it was still not unusual for a class to consist of a teacher and just two or three students.

Pop himself had become a larger-than-life figure, an academic pied piper with an inspiring personality who attracted young people to him. In the summer of 1960, he'd materialized out of nowhere in the Shaws' Halifax driveway. "He travelled in this beat-up old car," Alexa remembered, its trunk filled to bursting with books, its backseat festooned with clothes and toiletries. He was on his usual summer recruitment mission, and this time Alexa was in his crosshairs.

"You should come to Solebury," he told her.

At first, she remembered thinking, "Why would I want to go to school in Pennsylvania?" But then that fall, as it began to dawn on her she'd be without her best friends if she stayed at QE for grade 12, the idea became more appealing.

Perhaps more significantly, Alexa's mother was keen. "My mother was kind of the adventurer, the dreamer, the schemer who was kind of disappointed she hadn't chased those dreams the way Alexa and Kaye had." Jean also had a reverence, not just for education but for what she saw as quality education. "Our mother was American, a dual citizen, and she was also a big believer in private schools," Robbie explained.

After Pop's visit in the summer of 1960, Jean travelled to Solebury to see it for herself. "You should go," she told her daughter on her return. "We'll talk your father into it," she whispered. As usual, she did.

And so it was settled.

•

"You can stop pretending now," Alexa's cousin Jean began with a knowing smile. It was the night of June 9, 1962, and Alexa Ann Shaw had just graduated from Solebury School. To celebrate, Pop Shaw had organized a family dinner in New Hope, including not only Alexa's parents and brother who had come for the occasion but also his own son Eric and daughter Jean, both of whom had grown up on the Solebury campus and graduated about a decade earlier. Bill Berkeley, the school's assistant headmaster, was also a guest that night. It was, in fact, Berkeley to whom cousin Jean was referring when she breezily informed Alexa she could stop pretending.

"I assume you want me to invite Bill," Jean had said when she made the dinner arrangements.

"Bill Berkeley?"

"Oh, come on, Alexa, it's pretty clear you two are in love with each other."

Alexa was aghast. "Jean, you've got to be kidding me!"

"Well, do you want him to come to dinner with us, or don't you?"

Alexa did. Bill Berkeley had been kind to her. "He'd helped me through the year as my student counsellor, making sure I didn't freak right out and fall apart," she would recall years later. "I was just so enamoured, but he was, like, an old man. He was twenty-eight by then. So, I couldn't be involved with this guy, but I was just nuts about him."

For a serious, and relatively naïve young woman from conservative, still-living-in-the-1950s Nova Scotia, Alexa's year at Solebury—where the sixties were in full swing—had been an eye-opening, mind-expanding, mind-boggling, exhilarating, and sometimes frightening experience. Partly because of its proximity to New York, partly because it had an outsized academic reputation for excellence, and not least because of the individual attention its staff were able to devote to students, the school attracted a collection of the-best-and-the-brightest young people—plus more than a few troubled, complicated children of wealth whose parents were desperately seeking a last-chance pathway to higher education for them.

Alexa's roommate, Patricia, was among the school's best and brightest, but she was there because of her family situation. Her parents had divorced and remarried. She'd moved in with her father and his new wife, but then they got divorced too, and her father remarried yet again. She ended up at Solebury. She and Alexa shared a room under the eaves on the third floor of Appledore, a girls' residence. Patricia remembered Alexa as "a sparkling personality," but "she kept to herself."

Alexa was busy; as part of a scholarship arranged by Pop Shaw, she had to work one meal each day in the residence kitchen, helping with preparation or serving. But the more important reason she kept to herself was that she was frightened. She worried she wasn't smart enough to compete with Solebury's brightest American students. She was frightened too about what she, a Baptist from Nova Scotia, saw as the bacchanalian excesses of Solebury's students, not to mention its staff.

At one point, her residence's house parents separated after the husband had an affair with a student.[10] "I went to Pop Shaw," Alexa remembered. "I said, 'Pop, this is really shocking. I can't stay here because you wouldn't believe the drugs and the sex that are going on out behind the barn on my campus.'" Pop, who also taught her French, eventually calmed Alexa down. So did Bill Berkeley. Berkeley would recall many years later Solebury's "aggressive informality shook her up a bit. Alexa told me, 'We don't have schools like Solebury in Canada.'"

To cope, Alexa focused on academics. "When the other students were out boozing, and carousing, and sleeping around, I was studying." She was also overwhelmed by the school's free-wheeling classroom dynamics. "At the beginning of the term," she wrote in a post-term assessment of her fall English class, "I found it almost impossible to overcome shyness or reserve, no matter how strongly I felt about a certain subject, because of the disorder which prevailed. As time progressed, I learned to yell out, just like the rest, but I still maintain that the periods would be better spent if each, in turn, was granted the opportunity to voice his or her opinions!"

She soon gained confidence, in no small measure because of the responses of her teachers and her ability to get top marks. "This is an extremely well-written paper — and the fluidity of the style is a joy to read," noted one teacher on the cover of a paper that had earned an A. "Just beautiful, just beautiful," declared another about a short story she'd written fictionalizing her experiences of the Africville summer camp.

Alexa would later say the habits she developed at Solebury helped her "coast through university." As guest speaker at Solebury's commencement twenty-five years later, she told graduates no institution "had as much influence on me as Solebury had over the year I spent here . . . I am an activist, feminist, social democrat and politician . . . in large measure because of Solebury's philosophy of education."

Despite her obsession with doing well in her studies, Alexa was far from anti-social. She played basketball and took part in the school's drama club. For one school dance, she employed her dance skills to instruct her fellow students how to perform a can-can chorus line, although, as she confided to her parents, "they're a pretty uncoordinated bunch."

There was also a brief but bright flash of the grown-up Alexa who could never remain silent in the face of injustice. Some of the other girls at school had begun bullying her roommate Pat, a tall girl with an outsized, jealous-making stage talent.[11] Pat had somehow "bugged" a group of other girls, who taunted her, "engaging in such first-grade activities as name-calling, hair pulling, etc.," Alexa wrote to her parents. "At first, I decided to steer clear of it all but at dinner they started again. Pat left the table in tears and after I finished dishes, I went over to White Oaks [another residence] and gave them proper HELL." Because she'd "yelled at them for being so ruthless, childish and inconsiderate," the other girls "barely" spoke to her. "But perhaps in the long run they'll respect me just a little bit more for it. At any rate," she added, "I know I'll be happier and, if they disagree, they aren't the kids I thought that they were."

Alexa, recalled Bill Berkeley, was "very mature." She seemed like a college-aged student, a young woman among boys and girls. Everyone, he adds, "respected her a lot. You couldn't help but respect her."

Of course, there were more romantic entanglements. Although Alexa insisted she "didn't want to get messed up in those stupid Solebury romances where you dance with someone three times and everybody has you all tagged before you say a damn thing," she did keep in regular letter-writing contact with some of her former boyfriends back in Halifax, arranging and rearranging the seriousness of their relationships in letters over time.

And she found other older young men to mesmerize as well. During a weekend in Boston to visit her relatives, she had a date with a Harvard student named Keith Julian, whom she'd first met when he was a midshipman on a stopover in Halifax the summer before. "I can't seem to get last Wednesday nite out of my mind," he wrote of their date. "It had been a crazy week and I was tired and the whole night seemed like some cock-eyed dream. You *were* here, weren't you?"

During a visit to her brother at Queen's University in Kingston, Ontario, she was introduced to Mike Law, a popular college football player. They went on a blind date. "Blind dates never work," he wrote after. "You get a loser; she lives two blocks away. You get a winner — Where? Pennsylvania." Alexa had been "the first girl I hated saying good night to," he told her, adding, "it would be nice to have you around next year."

And then too, of course, there was her murky, mysterious relationship with Bill Berkeley. At one point in the spring, she'd mentioned to her parents she'd gone out to dinner with "Mr. Berkeley" and another student. "Remind me to tell you the story when I get home. It's much too complicated to try to relate now." In another later letter to Robbie, she wrote about attending the senior prom: "Tell Mom and Dad I danced a lot with Mr. Berkeley, and they'll tell you the story behind it."

Now, as Alexa sat at the graduation celebration dinner with her family and with Berkeley sitting across from her, Jean persisted. "Now that you've graduated," she said, "you don't have to pretend anymore." Alexa could only blush.

5

It began innocently enough, a teasing, post-graduation postcard later that summer after Bill Berkeley read news accounts about the Canadian army being called in to quell a riot at the Saint-Vincent-de-Paul federal penitentiary in Quebec. "Are you sure that's paradise north of the border?" Berkeley demanded of Alexa, who had spent much of her year at Solebury bragging that virtually everything he could imagine was better in Canada.

That postcard led to a letter in response, which led to a letter in reply, which led to... "I'm sure your casual invitation to 'bomb up' to Canada was a polite after-thought," Berkeley wrote on October 21, 1962, "but it so happens that I am just looking for an excuse to drive somewhere on a trip and try to jar myself out of this ever-deepening rut called Solebury. And, of course, a guarantee of instant rejuvenation sounds mysterious but welcome."

They eventually agreed he would drive to Kingston for the American Thanksgiving weekend, arriving late Friday, "ready to be wholesomely entertained." He kept his tone light. "During my stay, please feel free to sit me in my VW, point me in the direction of a local landmark of historical significance and let me fend for myself for a few hours while you 1) catch up on your studies; 2) try to placate those ten different guys who are wondering just *whatinthehell* is going on."[12]

Of course there was more to it, certainly on Berkeley's side. On Alexa's side, her feelings were complicated. She was infatuated, to be sure. Soon after she'd arrived at Queen's for her first fall semester, she and a friend had gotten drunk and giggly one night and called Berkeley out of the blue just to chat.

Bill Berkeley was handsome — "all the girls at Solebury said so" — smart, and thoughtful. He reminded her of her father. That was the problem, of course. He was "twelve years, three months and twenty-six days" older, as she noted in one letter home. Although she'd dated older boys and young men, this gap in age and experiences seemed much too big. Besides, she was just eighteen and having too much fun to contemplate settling down with one person.

Berkeley, on the other hand, was more than ready. When Alexa's match-making cousin, Jean Shaw, suggested he should wait five years then marry her, Berkeley replied, "I had no intention of waiting another five years before finding a suitable mate."

During their weekend together in Kingston that fall, Alexa and Berkeley had dinner Friday night at a local restaurant with Robbie and Betty Crookshank, his latest girlfriend and Alexa's high school best friend. The next day, they hopped into Berkeley's VW for a two-hour drive to Ottawa to see the Parliament Buildings. They even tried to visit the campus at Carleton College, the university her father had helped found, but after "asking seven times" and being sent off in a different direction each time, "we finally gave up." That night, back in Kingston, they went to a "lovely inn" just outside town for dinner and dancing.

Which was where Berkeley's hopes and dreams went awry. As he reconstructed his side of their conversation later, he'd told her: "'I've always had a grand crush on you, you cute Canuck, but before I say anything that might illuminate the situation, you commit yourself.' And damned if ole levelheaded Lex didn't come through again! Your position, as stated, is exactly as it should be."

The truth was Berkeley's forthrightness had been unexpected. As Alexa wrote later to her parents, "he was a little more serious about the whole situation than I had ever anticipated. I don't quite understand why I did this," she added, "but I told him I had to be in by 10:30 because I was going out with John." John McNeil was another suitor, a fellow Queen's student. But she had been confused by her own response. "I'm not just sure that I did what I most wanted," she conceded, "but I think that it's best . . . [Berkeley] was also so very understanding and realistic, however, and there are, I hope, no hard feelings."

There weren't. They resumed their friendly correspondence, writing each other about their lives and future plans. Her new goal, she wrote, was to become a social worker; he planned to take post-graduate studies at Harvard. Over time — as they found mates and married and created adult lives for themselves, she is politics, he in adult education — their letter writing became more sporadic, then sputtered out completely.

6

"Dear folks," Alexa wrote her parents on February 1, 1964. "I have at least twelve items that I must cover in this epistle." She had decisions to make. She was coming up to the end of the second year of her three-year Bachelor of Arts program at Queen's University, and she had come to a crossroads. Should she stay or should she go?

She hadn't so much chosen Queen's as it had chosen her. Queen's had been the family university for generations. By the time Alexa arrived in September 1962, "Robbie was the person with the microphone," as Betty Crookshank remembered, a "big man on campus," who was president of the Ontario Federation of Students. Alexa dated one of Robbie's roommates, John McNeil, and socialized with a group that included many of her high school friends. In many ways, Alexa's experiences at Queen's, which were more memorable for her lively social life than for any academic or political accomplishment, unfolded like an extension of her two years at Queen Elizabeth High School.

The tectonic societal shifts that would dramatically reshape Canada's university campuses by the end of the 1960s had not yet registered a blip on the Queen's Richter scale. Certainly, the fight for women's rights had not even been joined. When Alexa enrolled at Queen's, "Freshettes" were still required to display their name and telephone number on the back of their frosh uniform for the edification of upperclassmen. Engineering students openly rated the newcomers out of ten on the basis of their appearance. There is no record in any of her letters home to her family that Alexa objected to any of this. It was simply the way things were for her, and for most women on college campuses in the early 1960s.

Like every incoming female student, Alexa automatically became a member of the campus Levana Society. The society had been established in 1889 to provide mutual support among the university's small number of female students. While its official chant — "Arts Forever, Queen's Forever, Women's Rights or War" — might have sounded like militant feminism, the reality was much different. As Queen's historian Duncan McDowall explained it,[13] Levana "prepared women for 'societal life'" through formal dances, tea parties, and beauty contests. Its best-known rite of passage was an annual candle-lighting ceremony during which black-robed female first-year students were led into a dimly lit, locked Grant Hall by their second-year sisters. The second years would then convey secret oaths and traditions and cement their bond with the newcomers by lighting the first-year students' candles with a flame from their own. Conducted in what McDowall described as "an atmosphere of academic solemnity and Masonic secrecy," the wax droplets dripped from the candles onto a tri-coloured ribbon. According to Levana tradition, the colour of the ribbon on which the wax landed foretold the faculty — arts, engineering, medicine — of the Freshette's future husband, as well as the number of children they would have.

By the end of the 1960s, feminist students would describe the candle-lighting event as a "dehumanizing fertility ritual" and vote the Levana Society into extinction. But back in the fall of 1963, Alexa excitedly wrote home to her parents: "Wanted to let you know the election results — I got in! I'm quite excited about being on the Levana executive — it's a terrific experience."

Queen's, in many ways, was a terrific social experience for Alexa. She juggled myriad high-profile boyfriends. In one letter home, she wrote she had three dates for an upcoming Saturday night, "none of which I've been able to break yet." The weekend Bill Berkeley came to visit, she had indeed already committed to spending time with McNeil, the captain of the Queen's rugger team, in part because she'd snubbed him the week before to go to a "big bang-up" football party with her other boyfriend du jour, Mike Law, a star with the Queen's Golden Gaels' football team.[14] "It was a very convenient arrangement," Alexa would joke years later. "The rugger games were in the mornings on Saturdays, so I went to see John play rugger, and then in the afternoons, I always went to the big Golden Gaels' football games because my other boyfriend was a superstar."

There were ski weekends at Stowe, Vermont,[15] shopping expeditions to Montréal. "Jean and I shopped in Montréal practically all day," Alexa wrote to her parents after one such trip in January 1964. This Jean was Jean Little, by then Robbie's fiancée. After describing her failure to find just the right dress by the end of their day-long shopping spree, Alexa finished her account with a flourish. "Well, to make a long story short, I fell madly in love with a certain bathing suit," she told her allowance-providing parents. She acknowledged it wasn't the right season to buy a bathing suit and the price was a "little steep for our bracket, but I couldn't resist it.... I'm so weak!!!"

In truth, however, shopping was not the real reason for this particular trip. They had come to visit Ruth,[16] one of Alexa's high school friends who had recently moved to Montréal — to give birth. The father, a popular member of their Halifax social circle, refused to take responsibility for the baby, triggering a scandal among their friends and a dilemma for Ruth. After spending that fall and early winter cloistered at her family home, Ruth and her mother travelled to Montréal so Ruth could quietly have the baby and give it up for adoption.

In her report back to her parents, Alexa noted Ruth had been "looking forward to seeing us all week," as she phrased it elliptically, "to keep her mind off other things." They had also met Ruth's new boyfriend. "It's a great tribute to him," Alexa wrote approvingly but equally vaguely, "that he's been willing to stand by her at this time."

Neither do-gooding nor diversions, however, changed Alexa's essential dilemma. "It's no secret that I'm not enjoying life at Queen's at this point," she told her parents. "I just don't think I'm getting enough out of my life here to make the whole thing worthwhile."[17]

There were all sorts of reasons for her unhappiness, not the least of which was a recent failed relationship with yet another young man. For a change, Alexa had not been the one breaking this suitor's heart, but the one left heartbroken. And her plan to move into an apartment with several other women for her senior year had fallen through. Also, once again, most of her best friends at Queen's were about to graduate ahead of her. To make matters worse, she'd discovered the career she wanted and Queen's had limited courses in her field.

"I had discovered sociology," she explained many years later. Unlike other social sciences, sociology attempted to make sense of the dramatic changes that had reshaped their postwar world and opened a window on the political, economic, social, racial, and gender divides on the horizon.

She concluded that she would be better off finishing her degree at Dalhousie, where "sociology had really taken off" at the university's Maritime School of Social Work.

But before she returned to Halifax, she wanted to travel to England to take part in a United Nations Association volunteer summer work-camp program she had discovered. Six volunteers — "teachers or social work students especially welcomed" — were needed to run a two-week "racial tension project" in London, organizing summer activities for children at a local neighbourhood centre. She'd already written to the organizers, she told her parents, describing her experiences in Africville. "Your experience and interest in multi-racial problems would be of much value," came the reply.

While the organizers would provide her with full room and board, she'd still have to pay her own transportation. That would be prohibitively expensive for just a two-week program but what if she combined her volunteer placement with participation in the mind-and-geography-expanding Canadian Union of Students' whirlwind twenty-one-city Central European tour? It began in late June and ended in early August, conveniently bringing her back to London just as the summer camp was to begin. It would, of course, be more costly, but Alexa had a pre-emptive answer to that: because she would be saving them money by attending Dal, she explained hopefully, they would be able "put a good portion of that money, which I would otherwise be spending at Queen's, toward my passage" and travelling expenses.

In those days, it is fair to say, the silver spoon did not fall far from the mouth of the young Alexa.

7

It began on a warm summer afternoon near the tennis courts at the Waeg-woltic Club in South End Halifax. Lloyd Shaw and his neighbour, Dr. Robert MacDonald, were scouting for opponents for a doubles match when they spotted two young men coming off the courts. "Want to play doubles?" Alexa's father asked. Peter McDonough and Duff Waddell were keen. When it was over, Peter asked, innocently enough: "So, where's your daughter these days, Mr. Shaw?" Cutting to the chase of what is Alexa's version of those events, "Dad said, 'Well, she's come back home.' So he called and invited me out to dinner."

Or—and this is Peter's version—the story actually begins in the sweaty back of a Simpsons delivery truck. Peter and his best friend Duff Waddell had landed jobs that summer delivering furniture. "One day, we delivered a bed to Alexa's parents and we got to talking with them and I learned Alexa was back home in Halifax. I remembered Alexa as very attractive and I didn't have a date that night, so I thought, 'Why not? Let's give it a chance.' And I called her."

And that—whichever "that" you prefer—is how the romance between Alexa Ann Shaw and Peter John Ewing McDonough began.

Theirs did not seem, in the beginning, a match made in heaven. They'd emerged into young adulthood from very different social worlds. The McDonoughs were larger-than-life Irish Catholics. They liked their alcohol and their parties. Peter had been born in Galt, Ontario, where his father was a cinema manager and his mother a nurse. Peter was a teenager when his father landed a position as the Maritimes regional manager for the Famous Players theatre chain and the family moved to Halifax. They lived north of Quinpool Road, one of the many arbitrary social dividing lines between the "rich" South End and the rest of the city. Peter was two years older than Alexa, the same age as her brother, Robbie. They didn't so much know each other, explained Peter, as know of one another. That's not to suggest Peter didn't have what Betty Crookshank would remember as a "presence" in their high school. "I only knew Peter at a distance," she recalled. "But he was very attractive, and he always seemed to have a girl on his arm." At one point, he'd dated a beautiful fellow student named Joanna Shimkus, who would later become an international fashion model and film star.[18]

While Alexa attended Solebury and then Queen's, Peter studied commerce at Dalhousie, where he was known as a fun-loving "jock," a linebacker on the varsity football team, and a member of the Sigma Chi fraternity. Alexa's friend Cathy Isnor, who'd also remained in Halifax to study at Dal, remembered Peter as a student in her psychology classes. "He'd miss class and ask for my notes," she remembers, "but he was always charming."

After his commerce degree, Peter landed a job working on Nova Scotia's South Shore as an area sales representative for British American Oil. One day, while taking a break at a roadside ice-cream parlour, he encountered Ted Wickwire, who had been Dalhousie's star quarterback during Peter's years on the team. Now a lawyer, Wickwire and his wife were on their way to a bar society convention at Digby Pines. "You should think about law school," he suggested.

"I thought, 'Why not?' And I went home and applied," Peter recalled.

Though Alexa and Peter may not agree on the actual origin story of their relationship, they do agree on what happened next. That night, Peter and

Alexa, along with Waddell and his girlfriend, Nancy Parker, had a dinner date at the French Casino, then one of the city's most expensive restaurants. Peter ordered a bottle of Chateau Vieux Moulin, which was undoubtedly above his usual wine price point, but it impressed his date. Which seemed to be the point.

They also agree their first date soon led to another, and then another, and another. Cathy Isnor remembered seeing Peter and Alexa at weekend parties at the frat house and also double-dated with them for several semi-formal dances. By that winter, Peter had given Alexa his fraternity pin. They began to talk, tentatively, about becoming engaged. But Alexa had just been accepted for a two-and-a-half-year master of social work program at Smith College outside Boston while Peter was still in the middle of his law school studies at Dal.

8

Dalhousie University's undergraduate program had turned out to be the restorative elixir Alexa Shaw needed. And not just because she'd met Peter. She'd also rekindled her interest in academics and began to seriously consider career paths.

One of her most influential professors at Dalhousie, Dr. Barbara Clark, was an international pioneer in applied and developmental psychology whose research focused on ways to give disadvantaged preschoolers a head start on their education. Clark had teamed up with Geraldine Clarke,[19] a young Black woman who had taught at a school in North Preston and later opened up a preschool for inner-city children. Her preschool became a sought-after field placement for some of Clark's best students, including Alexa.

For George Elliott Clarke, Alexa's time at the centre was life-shaping. George was Geraldine Clarke's four-year-old son, who would become one of Canada's pre-eminent poets and authors. He often refers to Alexa in his public talks, with a slight exaggeration, as one of his first teachers. "She put me on the path to life," he said. "I had a precocious crush on her." At one point, he recalled, Alexa invited Geraldine and George for an afternoon at her parents' house on Armview Drive.[20] "I remember we went out in a canoe," he explained, "and then came back for lunch or a snack." At the end of the year, George even had an "exit interview" with Alexa. "She asked me questions and I gave her answers, and she gave me a little blue Matchbox car," He laughed. "I think every child got one."

Their paths would cross many times.

It would be no surprise to anyone who knew her that Alexa would also attend a major civil rights conference in Halifax that year. She remembered one of the speakers as "this amazing African American professor from Harvard who absolutely blew me away." After he spoke, she approached him. "I'm really interested in doing social change, community development social work, and I'd really like to go to New England because I've got all this family history there and relatives and..."

"Well, you should go to Smith College then," he said.

"Really?" She was nonplussed. "Smith College? Isn't that like a privileged white women's —"

He cut her off. "My dear," he said, "Smith College is the cathedral of social work education in North America."

9

Peter had made a vow to himself. He would not ask her that. It was unfair and presumptuous—and then he asked her anyway. "If the circumstances were different..."[21]

It was August 8, 1965, and they were at the Halifax airport awaiting the announcement of Alexa's flight back to the United States. It had been her first visit home since she'd left in June for her first ten-week course intensive at Smith. That would be followed by a full fall and winter of fieldwork at the Family Service Society in Hartford, Connecticut. After that, there would be yet another year of study and fieldwork, two years and five months in all before she earned her master's in social work, before they could finally get married. That wouldn't be until the summer of 1967! It seemed like forever.

Would he wait for her, she wanted to know? "I honestly believe I could wait twenty years as long as I always knew you were mine," he responded.

During their separation, they'd made do with almost daily, pining letters back and forth,[22] as well as occasional brief phone calls, mostly just to hear the sound of one another's voice. They'd learned things about each other.

"Honey," Alexa began one letter, "I don't very often say I disbelieve something you tell me."[23] But she was no longer sure he was telling the complete truth, she suggested, when he claimed he wasn't very good at writing personal letters. Was he sure he hadn't actually been "practising letter writing to persons of the female variety for the first twenty-three years of your precious life?" His letters had been "so beautiful I know they couldn't be a completely new venture."

There were also confessions. "I feel very strange telling you this," Alexa had written at the end of June.[24] For the first time in five-and-a-half months, "I've been out on the first date, [but] not with the man I love and have decided I want to spend the rest of my life with." Bill Berkeley had called and invited her out to dinner. He'd just accepted a "fabulous job" with the Independent Schools Talent Search Program, she explained, an organization seeking out "outstanding negro students from all over the USA" and then supporting them through preschools and universities, and he wanted to celebrate. "I sincerely like him as one of the best friends I've ever had, but it has never at any time been anything more than that," she was quick to add.

Peter wrote back to say he understood. And he had a confession of his own, he would write the day after she returned to Smith from her first trip back to Halifax. He had "acted dumb and confused" at the airport the night before just so she would say the words he so desperately wanted to hear. "'If circumstances were different' . . . I just had to know that that love was so all-consuming that if I gave the word, you would pack up everything, even your life-long desire to be the best possible social worker and come home to be my wife. I love you too much to make any such demand, be sure of that, Lex, but I had to know that if such a situation ever did arise, I'd come first above all else."

And she had said the words he wanted to hear. Then. And again later, and on several different occasions, unbidden, in person and in letters. "You can't imagine how wonderful I feel every moment of the day as I say over and over to myself, 'Mrs. P.J.E. McDonough.'" If she ever had to choose between being a social worker and being Mrs. McDonough, there was "no question" which she would choose.

10

Alexa was not normally given to cursing but she couldn't help herself. "It's all bullshit," she told Peter. "Freudian bullshit."

Smith had turned out to be less the cathedral of social work education and more a den of what seemed to Alexa like meaningless psychobabble. "I remember one of my professors, Dr. [Sidney] Wasserman,[25] who felt that everything was some kind of phallic symbol and the way someone held a knife was some sign of something else sexual." It wasn't that she wasn't learning anything. Unlike Queen's or Dalhousie, she told Peter, there were lots of foreign students at Smith, as well as Americans from a wide variety of ethnic and socio-economic backgrounds. That in itself, she wrote, made it "far easier to see how very, very many of our attitudes are white, Protestant, middle-class in origin."

By the time the ten weeks of academic courses ended, she was relieved — and eager — to begin her placement in a real-world, inner-city situation. Hartford's Family Service Society, she wrote to Peter, "is grossly disorganized, bursting at its seams with huge caseloads, with the result that our loads are heavy and we're therefore largely on our own . . . I think I'm going to be quite happy."

Except, of course, for Sigmund Freud. While "Freud couldn't have been further from entering my mind during the [client] interview," she wrote, she knew she would still have to find a way to incorporate him into her report to her Smith supervisor. Her Smith supervisors had told their students they needed to free themselves from "all culturally and socio-structurally-determined biases before trying to proceed with any diagnosis and treatment plan." Often, Alexa complained, "it seems they're trying to mould us into amateur psychiatrists or at least psychoanalytic practitioners."

In one long, bitter letter, she laid out what had happened during a meeting earlier that day with her Smith supervisor after she presented one of her cases: Mrs. B. was a twenty-four-year-old woman whose husband had muscular dystrophy, not a penny's worth of insurance, and couldn't find a job because of his disability. They had three children, the oldest just four-and-a-half, whom the mother admitted she spoiled. She was looking for advice on how better to discipline him. It seemed straightforward enough, Alexa explained, "not a pathological problem in itself."

"Can't you see what you're really being told?" her supervisor replied. "This is a totally unresolved [O]edipal complex stemming from incomplete identity with the parent of the same sex and unresolved erotic fantasies and desires toward the parent of the opposite sex — and all of this is being re-activated by the mother's erotic feelings toward her four-and-a-half-year-old boy. In short, she is scared she's going to seduce him."

Alexa wanted to laugh. She wanted to cry. "That's crap," she said. "Sheer crap."

"See how threatening you find it," the supervisor retorted. "Your defences of rationalization and denial against it are adamant." In short, Alexa reported to Peter, "I've now been diagnosed as having an unresolved [O]edipal complex."

She'd had it with Smith. She would not, could not, spend two more years putting up with such claptrap, she told him.

Peter had an easy and swift answer for that. "Why don't you come home and go to the Maritime School of Social Work."

"Okay," Alexa replied. "Consider it done."

11

They quickly decided Alexa should finish out her year at Smith so as not to lose any credits, then transfer to the Maritime School of Social Work for her final year. They'd finally be together again in the same city. So why shouldn't they . . . ? But they were both still students.

Alexa prepared a budget. "Tonight, your honey is all business," she wrote in a twenty-four-page handwritten letter on September 25, 1965, complete with two additional typed pages outlining a bare-bones sixteen-month budget that made perfect sense on paper: they would have a combined income of $5,000 against expenses of $4,410, even after setting aside six-dollars a month for laundry and twelve for recreation. Their income, she noted, included the cash her parents would otherwise have had to spend on another year at Smith, as well as her hoped-for-but-still-non-existent full-time job after graduation. But her calculations, she noted, didn't include other potential sources of income, such as "cash wedding gifts, (which I honestly think are terrible, but there are always a few relatives who do it so not to be bothered buying a gift)."

Cash wedding gifts? They had also decided to get married, though each kept asking the other in letter after letter if the other was certain. They reassured each other they were.

They decided Peter would visit her parents' Armview home to ask Lloyd and Jean in the traditional way for their daughter's hand in marriage. He'd keep their actual plans vague. They would decide on dates and other issues during the Christmas break, after which they'd announce it to their friends. They weren't expecting resistance. The Shaws, after all, had taken to Peter, made him feel part of the family, even while Alexa was away at Smith. Lloyd would call and invite Peter to play golf. He dined regularly at Armview with Lloyd and Jean. Robbie and Jean included him as a guest at their events. What could go wrong?

When I asked him that question more than fifty years later, Peter allowed diplomatically: "Her parents might have thought it a bit premature."

"A bit" hardly begins to cover it. Peter's visit to the Shaws triggered a full-blown family crisis. While Peter and Alexa talked about marriage themselves many times, Peter was saying the "wedding" word aloud to her parents for the first time. Alexa's parents almost certainly understood where Peter's and Alexa's relationship was headed, and they approved, but they had not expected something so definitive so soon. What was the rush, Lloyd wanted to know? Peter was still in law school; Alexa hadn't finished her schooling. Why would Alexa quit Smith now when she'd barely started, Jean demanded? And the wedding? It seemed to Jean as if the wedding plans had been finalized, without even consulting her.

Try as he might to reassure them, the conversation had veered off the rails into what seemed to Peter to be uncharted territory. Lloyd began to tell him about all "his activities, business and total lack of time in his life for a wife, except to have her wait on him at his beck and call."

After reading Peter's "Twenty-Page Volume on the Fateful Evening," Alexa quickly concluded her father's comments were "a pretty clear expression of the guilt he feels for mom's mental state. I love and admire and respect my father very, very much, but a person cannot play so many roles in life and fulfill them all to perfection. It really hurts me to admit that in many ways my father, for all his wonderful qualities, many of which I aspire to, is one hell of a husband, particularly for a woman so emotionally deprived in her childhood. I'm quite certain I could have understood exactly what's taken place this last week before I ever entered this Smith program, but now it's doubly clear."

When she hadn't heard from her parents four days after Peter's conversation with them, Alexa called home to ask directly their "initial reactions to the announcement that their daughter was seriously considering marriage in the not too distant future." Before she could even ask her question, however, the conversation "started off with Mom answering in a cool reserved voice and talking for about ten minutes about all Daddy's earth-shatteringly important activities. . . ." Alexa tried to interrupt, explain how "disappointed" she'd been by their apparent disapproval and their unwillingness to talk about it, "but I dissolved into tears."

That conversation ended when her father came on the line and promised he would call her right back. An hour-and-a-half later, he did. "Mom is on the verge of, if not in, the throes of a nervous breakdown," he explained. Their news had somehow tipped her balance.

Was this her mother's own long-ago abandonment issues bubbling back to the surface in a new form? "My mother lives vicariously through me," Alexa explained to Peter. Was Jean afraid her daughter was about to become a wife and no longer a daughter? And what about her father? Alexa's role in the family dynamic, as she saw it, was to act as a buffer between her father and mother, reminding Lloyd occasionally with a "great big kick in the you-know-what that he needed to redirect a little of his energy and attention to her." Was he resenting the idea Alexa was about to get married and hand back to him "the responsibility for his wife?"

It was messy. "We have suffered a bit more of a setback than either of us ever dreamed of," Alexa wrote to Peter. And yet, "out of this whole confused mess, it's only important that you get one thing, my darling, and that is my love and total commitment to you, which is a sound enough basis for any marriage, is it not?" The fact they'd had to deal with this crisis while hundreds of miles apart, she added, "may have served to help us get to know each other better. I can't help but feel that we would never have found it quite so easy to share some of our innermost thoughts if we'd been together, running into one another outside the (student) canteen or getting stoned at a law party!"

There was that.

•

"Ladies and gentlemen, Mr. and Mrs. Peter McDonough!"

They were wed on the afternoon of Friday, August 12, 1966, just one day after Alexa's twenty-second birthday and on the same day as her parents' twenty-seventh wedding anniversary. The family tensions of the previous fall had long since been forgiven, if not entirely forgotten. In the lead-up to the day Jean had recovered to become, as usual, her daughter's primary wedding advisor, helpmate, and cheerleader.

In many ways, the wedding was a neat bringing together of many of the strands of Alexa's life. The candlelight ceremony took place at First Baptist, the family church where Alexa had grown up and where, just six years earlier, she and her best friends had launched that summer camp for the children of Africville. Cathy Isnor, one of those friends, was Alexa's maid of honour; another, Betty Muggah, was a bridesmaid. So too was Robbie's wife, Jean. Robbie served as Peter's best man and the MC for the reception, which was held in the Commonwealth Room of the Nova Scotian Hotel where, twenty-one years earlier, Jean's dress design has been featured in a fashion show. Dr. Robert MacDonald, the Shaws' long-time neighbour, offered the toast to the bride. The Don Warner Orchestra played; everyone danced. "Please feel free to leave at any time," Robbie joked in his role as MC. "The bride and groom will be dancing into the night, although not too late as they have other things on their minds also."

Alexa and Peter with Justin (left) and Travis (right), c. 1980
(Nova Scotia Archives, NS NDP Fonds, 2014 - accrual, Box 2 [unprocessed])

RUNNING FROM HOUNDS

1

Alexa McDonough would long remember the dark night of April 5, 1968, in a parking lot of a shuttered gas station beside a highway somewhere between Dallas and New Orleans. It was one of the few moments she was ever "really scared for my life." But it wasn't because of the truckload of "yahoos" circling their camper truck, drinking, shouting, gun-toting.

Peter and Alexa, along with another couple—an Argentinian man from Peter's comparative law master's program at Southern Methodist University (SMU) and his Finnish wife—had decided to make the eight-hour road trip from Dallas to New Orleans so they could spend the long Easter weekend "enjoying the music and the sights and sounds."

But the day before, Martin Luther King Jr. had been cut down in Memphis by an assassin's bullet, triggering what writer Peter Levy, in his book, *The Great Uprising: Race Riots in Urban America during the 1960s,* would later describe as the United States' "greatest wave of social unrest since the Civil War."[1] News of King's murder had led to a night of "rioting, looting, and burning"[2] in Washington, DC, and there were well-founded fears the violence would spread to other cities, including the American South.

Louisiana state police had noted the Nova Scotia licence plate on Peter's pickup and pulled their vehicle over to the side of the highway several times. "They said, 'Where do y'all think you're going?'" Alexa recalled. "They didn't know where Nova Scotia was, but they knew we weren't southerners and that we could be troublemakers from the north on our way down to cause riots." Although the encounters themselves were benign—"I never knew this road went to Nova Scotia," one officer joked before sending them on their way—they couldn't help but be rattled by such unexpected, unwanted attention.

When they didn't find a suitable campground for the night, they'd pulled into the gas station parking lot and settled in until morning. They were all asleep when the commotion outside woke them. "There were two truckloads of them—or maybe one, I might be exaggerating, I can't remember now," Alexa said later. "But it felt like a whole army." She stopped, considered. "They probably were just hell-raisers, like young kids anywhere might be, only they had guns."

As frightening as that might have been, what really scared Alexa was what happened next inside the camper van. The Argentinian was already armed; he reached out and handed Peter a gun too. "It's a wonder Peter didn't have a heart attack," Alexa joked. Peter quickly waved away the offer of the weapon and instructed everyone to "just shut up, lie there and pretend we were all dead." It worked. "After a while, it must have gotten boring for them, and they just left.... Phew," she laughed.

Alexa and Peter definitely weren't in Nova Scotia anymore.

•

In his final year of law school, Peter had won a scholarship to spend the 1967–68 academic year studying comparative international law at SMU in Texas. While he would later joke his master's degree was like a Mexican divorce—"easy to get and not worth the paper it's printed on"—it provided an ideal opportunity for the recently married couple to nurture their relationship in a place far from friends and, perhaps more importantly, family. "It was a wonderful year for both of us," Peter would remember.

Peter had bought a half-ton pickup truck and equipped it with a slide-on camper van for the wandering adventures they planned to enjoy during their year in the United States. He drove it to Dallas in late August 1967. Alexa, who described herself as just "tagging along," flew to join him the next month. Thanks to Peter's advance work, she already had a job offer—as a social worker at the Dallas Legal Services Project, a War on Poverty–funded initiative run by Walter Steele Jr., who also happened to be the dean of SMU's law school.

Alexa's lawyer colleagues, "about the most radical people in all of Texas," saw their role as using legal channels to bring about social change. "You wouldn't think [Dallas] would be a likely breeding ground for a social democrat activist," Alexa mused years later, "but it worked, partly because I had a brilliant, brilliant boss, who taught me I could use the legal system to bring about change." Her brilliant boss, she also recalled, often didn't remember her name, so he just called her "'Sweetheart' in his Southern accent." He would buzz her on the intercom. "Sweetheart, would you just hustle on down here?" But he was quick to throw her into any project.

"I was so fearless," Alexa marvelled. "I would go on any adventure, do anything they asked." She remembered one early case involving a single mother in a wheelchair whose child was refused treatment at Parkland Hospital, the same hospital to which John F. Kennedy had been rushed after his assassination. "She didn't have any money and she was poor, so she was turned away. The child died on the sidewalk outside." The legal services project took the hospital to court for negligence. "I just couldn't believe that in a wealthy, wealthy place, there could be so many people living in pain with nothing and no prospects, no prospects at all."

Thirty years later, as leader of Canada's federal New Democratic Party, Alexa would revisit that incident in a speech, both as a tribute to what she saw as a more caring Canada "shaped by social democratic struggles," but also as a cautionary tale about the "horrific" dangerously unequal destination to which Jean Chrétien's deficit-slashing Liberal government was then hurtling.[3]

Their year in Dallas gave Alexa a new perspective on her homeland, and her own nascent desire to play a role in it. "I started to realize Canada was very different from the US, and the culture was different, and it challenged me to think about what are those valued issues that were big in our upbringing. I'd talk about how we had a social safety net that they didn't....I probably was just a pain in the ass, I mean, in terms of characterizing Canada in a completely inflated way as being a more compassionate, caring, egalitarian society. But it added to my sense of how much I cared about those things. It sent me back to Canada more fervently believing this is something worth not just hanging onto, but building on and trying to make even more true."

Alexa and Peter decided to cap their year in Dallas with a six-week, cross-continent vacation. In late June 1968, they packed up their apartment, said their goodbyes, and drove west to California. They took in iconic tourist attractions, then drove north along the west coast of the United States, and visited friends and relatives. After spending time on Vancouver Island, they turned east and spent midsummer getting acquainted with a Canada Alexa would come to know much more intimately thirty years later as the leader of Canada's NDP.

They were still in Las Vegas in late June, however, when they got their first hint the Canada they would be returning to might also be very different from the homeland they'd left nine months before. Las Vegas was a glamorous adventure, Alexa wrote to her parents.[4] She and Peter managed to catch "outstanding" performances by jazz singer Ella Fitzgerald and comedian Don Rickles. They'd "allowed" themselves ten dollars each night for gambling. "The first night, Peter won eleven dollars at blackjack, and the second I won $7.50." There was nothing in Alexa's chatty letter home to acknowledge she even knew what had just happened back in Canada, but Peter would later recall they'd picked up a newspaper one morning and noted a small Associated Press news item. "Trudeau Leads Liberals to Canada Election Win," read the headline.[5]

During their time in Dallas, little in the way of Canadian news had managed to seep through a wall of United States–centric media myopia. Even in April 1968, when Pierre Elliott Trudeau, a dashing, dynamic, Camelot-north-style political figure, emerged from relative obscurity to win Canada's Liberal leadership—news that might normally have piqued at least Kennedy-comparison curiosity among US journalists—Americans were still reeling from the assassination of Martin Luther King Jr. and its violent aftermath. So news that Trudeau had swept to victory in the June 25, 1968, federal election on a "tidal wave" of Canadian popular support, based partly on his promise to create a "just society" with expanded social programs, must have seemed intriguing to a young social worker who'd been raised to care about social justice and who had just experienced a society she considered especially unjust.

But the election result showed something else too. The federal New Democratic Party—the result of a merger between the old CCF and the Canadian Labour Congress in 1961 to create a worker-influenced social democratic party—had failed to find electoral traction. Again. Tommy Douglas, the former premier of Saskatchewan who'd become the leader of the NDP, had failed to lead the new party to any better result than the old CCF had achieved.

Could Pierre Trudeau's Liberals be the answer to Canada's progressive prayers?

2

Alexa McDonough wasn't certain if this was a job interview or just a friendly drop-by visit from an old friend of her father's and one of his employees. It was the early fall of 1968. She and Peter were back in Nova Scotia but still at loose ends. Peter was working at a Halifax law firm, although there were no guarantees it would lead to partnership. At one point, he'd written the department of trade and commerce in Ottawa inquiring about job prospects there. Alexa was in waiting mode: should she look for a job in Halifax or hold off until they knew whether they'd be relocating?

That weekend, as they often did, she and Peter decamped to the Shaw family's log cabin retreat on Shaw Island near Chester, about forty-five minutes from Halifax. The arrival of these visitors—Allan O'Brien was the mayor of Halifax, Harold Crowell his director of social planning—was both unusual and intriguing.

O'Brien and Alexa's father had been "close personal friends, close political buddies in the trenches." Like Shaw, O'Brien came of age in a family business. His father had run a wholesale fruit and vegetable business in Halifax. Like Shaw, O'Brien had been bitten early by the progressive politics bug. After the Second World War, he'd worked in Ottawa as executive secretary to CCF leader M.J. Coldwell. He'd also run twice—unsuccessfully—for Parliament. But in 1966, after ten years as an alderman, Allan O'Brien had been elected Halifax's mayor. An urbanist, an intellectual, a progressive, O'Brien arrived with ambitious plans.

Harold Crowell was one of his first important hires. Crowell had spent fifteen years as head of the Hants County Children's Aid Society, trying to bring its draconian welfare system into the twentieth century. When Ottawa introduced the Canada Assistance Plan in 1966, Crowell immediately pitched Ottawa to fund a community development program to create housing and recreation programs for low-income residents and to set up the first sheltered workshop in the province for disabled people.

Allan O'Brien hired Crowell as Halifax's welfare director but with a significant change in title and focus. As the city's first director of social planning, Crowell was responsible for transforming traditional notions of social welfare as a financial burden on taxpayers to creating community economic and social change that would benefit everyone.

To achieve that ambitious agenda Crowell needed help, and this was the reason he and O'Brien had come to Shaw Island. Setting aside her family connections that no doubt smoothed her way, Alexa McDonough was well and truly qualified for what she called her "dream job." She'd earned her joint master of social work degree at Dalhousie and her father's alma mater, Acadia University, and had spent the previous year mastering her trade in the challenging crucible of a troubled American city.

Crowell hired Alexa as his assistant. She remembered him as "a lot like my boss in Dallas. He just thought if he threw me off the deep end of the dock, I wouldn't end up doing too much damage when I landed."

Together, they "totally overhauled" the city's handout-based welfare system and transformed it into "a needs-and-rights-based model." Crowell began by eliminating the "humiliating, right-out-of-Dickens'" requirement that all welfare recipients—able-bodied, disabled, ill—must present themselves in person each month outside the city's poorhouse to collect their assistance payments in cash. Despite objections from city staff and council, they pushed through a program to pay the recipients by cheque. More significantly, they dreamed up everything they could think of to "convince the feds to let us take the damn welfare money, and turn it into opportunities for people to be trained, for people to be employed doing various kinds of community building work...."

Because Crowell was a shy man, he often delegated the outgoing Alexa to present their latest social re-engineering "schemes" to council. "I don't remember us having one scheme they didn't fund," Alexa said, "because, in the end, all those people were able to get jobs and decent housing."

Crowell and Alexa also shared the burden of finding a humane way to end a bitter standoff between the city and the last resident of Africville. By 1969, most of Africville's four hundred residents had been reluctantly relocated, some with their belongings in dump trucks, and the community razed in the name of "urban renewal." But Aaron "Pa" Carvery, a seventy-year-old who'd been born in Africville and insisted he would die there, refused to leave. Since his house stood in the way of plans for a new bridge across the harbour and contractors were threatening legal action over delays, city officials were desperate. Alexa and Crowell met with Carvery on several occasions during the summer and fall of 1969. Crowell even became an unwilling witness to an infamous meeting between senior city staff and Carvery, during which the elderly man was shown a cash-filled suitcase and told it could be his if he agreed to move. Later, Crowell went to see Carvery at his home with a different kind of offer. There was a house near the Africville site that Crowell had convinced the city buy and lease to Carvery for twenty dollars a month for the rest of his life. "He accepted the offer, which satisfied his needs."[6]

Crowell was "a huge influence," Alexa recalled. On his part, Crowell praised his young assistant for her big-picture thinking. "She was convinced that the focus of the helping professions should be to effect policy change rather than individual change," Crowell wrote in an undated endorsement. "She was largely responsible for setting the goals for the new department, and her commitment to this task surpassed in time and energy any expectations of her employer."

Then Alexa announced she was expecting a baby.

•

There had never been any question Alexa and Peter intended to start a family. The real question was whether city officials would allow her to take a leave to have her baby and return to her former position. There was no precedent for it. Women who became pregnant while working for the city, and most other businesses at the time, were considered undependable and almost guaranteed not to get their jobs back.

Harold Crowell, of course, wanted to keep his key staffer, so he badgered his bosses. He made the case that this was not the moment in history "to be seen to be slamming the door behind women as they go out to have a baby and then tell them they'll have to go to the end of the line where, if they're lucky, they may get back in." His stronger argument — the times had not changed that much! — was practical and personal. "Alexa's going to leave this really good work we're doing," he complained to Arthur Ward, the city's personnel manager, "and then we're going to have to start over again."

"Harold was like a dog with a bone," Alexa remembered. And he prevailed. The city finally agreed to allow McDonough to take a four-month leave — unpaid, of course — and return to her old job. "And that was the beginning of guaranteed maternity leave for women working for the City of Halifax."

Justin McDonough was born on November 12, 1969.

3

How did Alexa McDonough become, even briefly, a Liberal?

At the dawn of the 1970s, the *new* New Democratic Party registered barely a blip on Nova Scotia's body politic. The only New Democrat elected to the House of Commons from the province had been a blink-and-you-missed-him MP, sent to Parliament in 1962 and sent packing in the next election the next year. The last leader of the Nova Scotia CCF, and its only Member of the Legislative Assembly at its demise, had resigned soon after the formation of the NDP in 1961. He was succeeded by James Aitchison, the NDP's first leader, who failed to win his own, or any, seat in the House of Assembly. Worse, he was a Halifax-based university professor, exacerbating a growing split between the party's working-class Cape Breton base and what that base saw as the party's tweedy Halifax elite.

Through it all, of course, Lloyd Shaw never abandoned his dream of a socialist tomorrow. He continued to support the party, federally and provincially, financially and morally, as it morphed from social-movement CCF to labour-focused NDP.

His children were less steadfast.

During the sixties, the family's cottage on Shaw Island had served as the East Coast summer gathering spot of choice for what Robbie Shaw called "a who's who of the left in Canada." Allan Blakeney, for example, a Nova Scotia–born Rhodes Scholar who'd become an important Saskatchewan civil servant and, later, cabinet minister, and who would be elected premier there in 1971, was a regular visitor. Robbie remembered taking Blakeney and a number of prominent NDPers sailing off Chester. "There was beer consumed." Blakeney, "hanging off the bow," pointed to the summer homes of Chester's wealthy residents and shouted: "This is what all the houses are going to look like when Nova Scotia elects an NDP government!"

But did Nova Scotia, or Canada, really need the NDP?

Pierre Trudeau's new Liberal government seemed to have a progressive social, if not necessarily economic, agenda. Declaring "there's no place for the state in the bedrooms of the nation," Trudeau's 1968 omnibus Criminal Law Amendment Act set out to separate legality from morality, decriminalizing homosexuality between consenting adults, liberalizing divorce laws, legalizing abortion "under certain circumstances," and making it easier for women to access contraception. The Liberals introduced new restrictions on gun ownership and new laws against drinking and driving. Trudeau was a staunch defender of Canada's recently implemented universal health-care program and promoted regional development polices.

Meanwhile, Nova Scotia's tired, scandal-plagued Progressive Conservative government had imploded following revered Premier Robert Stanfield's ill-starred departure for the party's federal leadership in 1967. While the seat-less, seemingly hopeless NDP wasn't in any position to capitalize on that, the Liberal Party under Gerald Regan, a garrulous former sportscaster and labour lawyer, should have been poised to defeat the Tories. But the Liberals' private polling in the lead-up to the 1970 provincial election showed that "we were down by five or six points." As David Mann, the party's campaign committee chair, remembered later, "It was unheard of to pick up five points during a campaign."[7]

The party desperately needed help. "Perhaps the smartest thing Gerald Regan ever did politically," Liberal advertising man Ned Belliveau would recall in his 1984 memoir, "was to find a group of talented young people to handle the [1970] campaign."[8] That best-and-brightest inner circle included Mann, freshly returned to Nova Scotia after earning his master of laws in England; Michael Kirby, a coolly intellectual twenty-nine-year-old mathematics professor and technocrat; Gerry Godsoe, an Ontario-born Rhodes Scholar who'd been recruited to Halifax by one of the city's top law firms; Brian Flemming, a thirty-one-year-old, Halifax-born international law of the sea expert; James ("Jim") Cowan, who had arrived back from a stint at the London School of Economics; and Robbie Shaw, the lawyer-businessman son of Nova Scotia's leading socialist.

Robbie's conversion to the Liberal party had been gradual. His wife Jean's father, Walter Little, had been a prominent Ontario Liberal before his appointment as a judge. Robbie's best friend at Dal law school was Jim Cowan, the son of a prominent Halifax lawyer turned politician appointed judge, who became "like a second father to me." Robbie and Jim had worked together on Regan's 1965 leadership campaign, and the Cowans also boasted "a finished rec room, a first in our group, and it became a gathering spot."

The family Liberal Party connections also included Peter, who had described himself as "probably a Liberal" and had already volunteered to work on a Liberal lawyer colleague's campaign.[9] He and Alexa were friends

with many of the bright lights around Regan. So, it was no surprise that
Alexa would be recruited to help write what would become the Liberal party's
social policy plank for this election.[10]

But after the Liberal win, Alexa's progressive proposals were dumped
on a shelf to gather dust. "She was disillusioned," Robbie recalled. "The
government didn't follow through with what she thought was important."
Worse, she experienced Nova Scotia's patronage politics first-hand. At one
point, she was asked to represent Nova Scotia on a federal consumer council.
When she demurred, suggesting the name of a more qualified person, she
noted, "The response was, 'Oh, come on. It's just an opportunity to go to
Ottawa and meet some cabinet ministers and have a few days in a fancy
hotel.'...I was genuinely shocked."[11] She quit the party soon after. And began
to consider other ways to become involved in the world.

4

In the early seventies, Alexa and Peter created a pass-the-time, choose-your-
home weekend adventure. "If money was no object and we could have any
house we wanted," they would ask each other, "where would we live? Our
mission was to find our favourite house."

Since moving home from the United States, the couple and their growing
family — Travis was born in 1971 — lived in a comfortable two-storey
brick house in Clayton Park, a massive suburban development modelled
on Toronto's Don Mills that Alexa's father had conceived, and which her
brother, Robbie, now ran and continued to expand as the president and CEO
of Clayton Developments Limited.

The McDonoughs lived in the middle of this new upper middle-class
community that sprawled inland from Bedford Basin, just beyond peninsular
Halifax. That was the issue. The McDonoughs were peninsula people in
a city where living inside its constricting but defining foot-shaped old
boundaries, bordered on three sides by water, was a matter of both pride and
convenience. Peter was now a partner-track lawyer with McInnes Cooper, the
most downtown of downtown law firms; Alexa had become a lecturer at the
Maritime School of Social Work on the Dalhousie University campus in the

peninsula's leafy South End; and the boys were both enrolled in play school at the Halifax Ladies' College near her work.

One Sunday afternoon on one of their house-imagining expeditions, Alexa and Peter found what they instantly agreed was their dream house: a large, classic Cape Cod at the foot of Waegwoltic Avenue in familiar South End Halifax. The house was within walking distance of downtown for Peter, and conveniently a block and a half from Alexa's offices and the boys' child care. As a bonus, it sat cheek by jowl to a recreation park and baseball field, and just a two-minute walk to the Waegwoltic Club.

"We went up and knocked on the door," Alexa remembered, "and said to the person who answered, 'If you ever want to sell....'" The woman didn't but suggested that the man across the street might. He eventually did, and so, in 1974, the McDonoughs began a new stage of family life in a rambling, entertaining-friendly home on a large corner lot. There was even a basement apartment that became home to a rotating legion of "cellar-dwellers," usually college students who lived rent-free near campus in exchange for being there for the kids if Alexa or Peter couldn't be home. Most of the more than a dozen who would call the space home over the next few decades would not only end up as honorary members of the McDonough clan, but most, including those who arrived from other partisan traditions or no tradition at all, would come to identify as New Democrats. And Alexa-for-life supporters.

The McDonoughs hired "a really wonderful earth-mother, homemaker-type" named Mamie Penny to help maintain their busy household. The year she started, Penny's husband had drowned in a canoeing accident. The McDonoughs helped her adjust—she was from a rural Acadian community and "had never written a cheque in her life, didn't actually know what a bank account was"—and Penny "became a blessing in our life. She just turned her life over to our kids and she loved them dearly." Penny would arrive in late morning in time to make the boys lunch, then pre-prepare family dinners. While Alexa completed the final fixing after her day at work, Peter would drive Penny home to suburban Fairview. "She would talk your ear off," Alexa remembered, "but she very quickly became part of the family."[12]

The McDonoughs' new home soon became a social hub for an informal group of young professional couples, all with small children, most of whom lived in the neighbourhood. They were still largely identified—in the way of the times — by the profession of the couple's husband: the core group included Alexa and Peter, with Peter the lawyer; Mary and David Piggott (accountant); Carolyn and Peter MacGregor (doctor); Claudia and John Duckworth (engineer); and Joann and George Burpee Hallett (English professor).

The couples got together for weekend dinner parties and social events. "We partied hard, we drank hard," remembered Joann. For her own fortieth birthday, she "danced on a long table all decked out with crystal glassware." Every August, they staged their own "tennis classic" at the Waeg, during which everyone had to dress in costume and play "tennis rules on ping-pong tables."

They enjoyed occasional canoeing adventures together, disappeared for a winter week of skiing at the Cape Smokey resort in Cape Breton, spent summer weekends at Shaw Island, where Alexa and Joann would cook mass brunches in the kitchen of the Shaw log cabin, which Peter and Alexa had now made their own.[13]

Politics was rarely central to any of it.

5

Opinions differ on what Lloyd Shaw really thought when his two grown children turned their backs on the political party to which he'd devoted his adult life. Robbie recalled their father not only encouraged his children to discuss political issues while growing up but also, and more importantly, taught them to think for themselves. His decision to chart an independent partisan course, Robbie suggested, "endeared me to my father." Alexa, for her part, described Lloyd as "really devastated when my brother and I ran out and became Trudeau-ite Liberals." What they do agree on was that Lloyd never directly pressured either of them to return to the fold. "My father was smart enough to know you can't talk your kids out of something," Alexa explained, "especially after you told them to go and discover their own path."

Peter agreed: "I never recall Mr. Shaw trying to switch Lex back from the Liberals to the NDP, but you knew he was hoping she would."

Alexa's disillusionment with the Liberal Party offered Lloyd an opening. "My father had the smarts to invite me, meaning he'd pay my way to attend, a socialist conference in Regina." That December 1973 conference, a "collective soul searching about socialist principles as they should apply to Canada and its provinces,"[14] was the first organized by the new Douglas-Coldwell Foundation, established two years before to honour Tommy Douglas and M.J. Coldwell, two of the movement's founders, and to serve as "an instrument of research and education concerned with social planning in Canada."

The conference's keynote speakers included Gunnar Myrdal, the former leader of the Swedish Social Democratic Party, who would be awarded the Nobel Prize in economics the next year, and Michael Harrington, the former chair of the Socialist Party USA and author of *The Other America*, a seminal sociology book about poverty in the United States. They, along with recently elected NDP Premiers Ed Schreyer of Manitoba and Allan Blakeney of Saskatchewan, led discussions that focused not only on current hot-button topics — inflation, unemployment, energy, food supply — but also on larger philosophical issues like the place of socialism in society and the role of the private sector in a socialist economy.

While Alexa found the conference itself exhilarating, what would ultimately rearrange her thinking was rooming with Grace MacInnis in a university dorm. MacInnis, a long-time family friend of the Shaws, was the daughter of CCF founding leader J.S. Woodsworth, the widow of a CCF MP, and now a Member of Parliament in her own right. The only woman elected in the 1968 general election, she was that still rare thing in Canada, an unabashed feminist politician.

In a 1969 debate in the House of Commons on changes to the Criminal Code to make it easier for women to get abortions, MacInnis derided her male colleagues for their "inborn, inbred, uneducated" attitudes on abortion.[15] Later, she introduced a private member's bill to remove abortion from the Criminal Code entirely, then organized a committee to support Dr. Henry Morgentaler, the Montréal doctor accused of performing illegal abortions. She fought to include housewives in the Canada Pension Plan. And she publicly called out some of her parliamentary colleagues as "MCPs" (male chauvinist pigs) when they "tittered and talked" through the presentation of a progress report on the federal government's efforts to improve the status of women in Canada.

It had been Jean Shaw's idea to pair MacInnis with her daughter. Alexa would later describe it as "just Machiavellian. I was inspired just being around her and I began to see just how absolutely different the Liberal Party that I'd gotten swept up in" was from the NDP, as represented by MacInnis. "I had two small kids and I started to think, 'How does this fit with your values, and what you care about and the skills you learned as a social work activist, advocate, policy researcher, and community development worker?'"

Soon after returning to Halifax, Alexa signed on to manage the faint-hope campaign of Muriel Duckworth, the NDP candidate in Halifax Cornwallis in the 1974 provincial election. Duckworth, who was already a national legend in the women's and peace movements, had once worked on adult education issues with Lloyd Shaw, and was, coincidentally, the mother of Alexa's own good friend John.

The campaign proved complicated for Alexa's insular everyone-knows-everyone South End social circle. Before he knew Alexa would be running Muriel's campaign, Peter had offered to help George Mitchell, one of his law partners, who was the Liberal candidate. Muriel Duckworth's son, John, had also signed up to campaign for Mitchell. "I had to say, 'Sorry Mom, I'm already working for George,'" John recalled. It got even more convoluted in mid-campaign, when Tia Cooper, the pregnant wife of the Tory candidate, George Cooper—another couple in their social circle—was hospitalized. John Duckworth's wife, Claudia, stayed with Tia in the hospital while John campaigned door to door for Liberal Mitchell and Tory Cooper went door to door on his own. In the end, Mitchell won. Cooper came second. Duckworth finished a distant third.

If the family and friends' campaign conversations appeared ever so slightly awkward, "they weren't really," Alexa would explain. "We could all accept we each had our own lives."

That said, McDonough encountered plenty of awkward moments while campaigning door to door with Duckworth. If a woman answered, Alexa remembered, she would often say, "Oh, I don't do politics. I'll get my husband." The husbands tended to be dismissive. "Don't you think you should be home taking care of your children?" they would say to the sixty-six-year-old grandmother.

"Well, my children are all grown and gone," Duckworth would reply drily.

"Then shouldn't you be taking care of your grandchildren?"

"I would love to, but they've moved away," she'd answer ever so sweetly.

"That's why I'm campaigning now—to make life better for all of our grand-children."

Alexa learned plenty accompanying Duckworth. "It was like a training program for later in my life dealing with sexist views, trying to respond with humour in ways that weren't threatening but still made the point."

She learned other lessons too, including how to read between the lines of the reticence of some of the women they met. They'd hover a little behind their husbands, listening silently while the husband made his "very anti-NDP, anti-feminist comments," Alexa remembered. "And then you'd see them standing there, looking at you, rolling their eyes, as if to let you know they knew better. It just reinforced for me the idea that, yes, women do need to be in politics. There were a lot of women out there who needed some things to change, and politics was the way those changes would get made."

Despite that, Alexa still wasn't ready to put herself forward as a candidate. "I was pretty political," she allowed, "but still small *p* political, more in the civic context, focusing on community issues."

Which is why she became intimately involved with making A Woman's Place an actual space in Halifax.

6

It was one of those small, seemingly inconsequential gestures that changed a life. It happened sometime in the spring of 1976 in the ornate Women's Parlour of the Halifax YWCA. A group of women had gathered to flesh out a plan to create a women's centre in Halifax, a tangible follow-up to the success of 1975's International Women's Year.

The woman at the front of the room beside the flip chart and leading the discussion that morning was Alexa McDonough, chair of the YW's newly formed social action committee. Alexa was on the Y's board, and her committee had been established "to explore women's unmet needs to which the YW might be more responsive." At an earlier meeting, the women had agreed to split into two groups: one would work on the idea of opening up an emergency shelter for women facing abuse;[16] the other, the one meeting today, would develop a drop-in/resource/support centre for women.

At some point that day, Alexa pointed to Peggy Mahon, one of the young women sitting quietly in the middle of the audience. "Peggy," she said, "why don't you come up here to the flip chart and facilitate." When she saw Mahon's hesitation, Alexa added encouragingly, "You can do it."

Mahon could. And did. "That was a pivotal moment in my life," recalled Mahon, who would go on to become the first coordinator of the new centre, later overseeing all of Nova Scotia's eight women's centres, and eventually opening up her own community development consulting firm. "For the rest of my career, I became known as the flip chart queen."

At the time, however, she was "the new kid on the block," a twenty-seven-year-old mother of two small children who knew she did not want to be a stay-at-home mom. Unlike many in the audience that day, Mahon was also, as Nova Scotians put it, a "come-from-away." She and her husband had left Toronto to start over on the East Coast. Mahon's husband had been offered a job with a major architecture firm in Halifax but when they arrived in their new city, Mahon quickly realized they weren't in increasingly cosmopolitan Toronto anymore. Members of the firm took them on a car tour of the city, warning them never to venture into the city's North End, home to part of its Black community. "We bought a house there," Mahon said.

When they arrived in March 1975, Mahon was pregnant with their second daughter. Looking for opportunities to meet other women and "make a space for myself," she joined the YW's Parent-Child Centre. That was where she heard about a meeting to discuss establishing a women's centre in Halifax. She believes she must have met Alexa previously but she didn't know her well when she was invited to lead the discussion that day.

While the idea of creating a women's centre easily won support, issues around where it should be located, what kind of centre it should be and for whom, and by whom it should be run, were all more controversial. The fact that the YWCA building was located on Barrington Street—along the South End borderline between comfortable, old-Halifax neighbourhoods peopled with the sorts of women who used the Y's facilities, and blocks of rooming houses and down-at-the-heel apartment buildings near the waterfront filled with single mothers and poor families who *needed* the services the Y provided—only exacerbated the divide.

If anyone could bridge that yawning chasm of hope and expectation, it was Alexa McDonough. She had grown up in a privileged part of the city where the Junior League still represented the epitome of community volunteer do-goodism. At the same time, she was not only a Shaw to that manor (and manner) born, with all the social conscience and community activism it implied, but she now was also the field placement supervisor for students at the Maritime School of Social Work. This deepened her connections into communities where poor women were beginning to demand to speak for themselves.

And she was a young mother of two small boys and a Betty Friedan feminist who understood her own parents' traditional gender stereotypes should not, and would not, contain her. While her own mother "wasn't ready to take up the gauntlet herself," Alexa would explain later, she had been the one who'd introduced her to Friedan's *The Feminine Mystique*, and the radical sixties' notion that women could, and should, have and do it all.

7

The YWCA owned a large, rundown heritage house next to its main facility that it had no use for, could not afford to maintain, and did not want to pay to insure. The board decided to tear the building down and, at least temporarily, turn the land into a parking lot for downtown commuters.

The board had decided to do that until Alexa, her sister-in-law, Jean Shaw, and Peggy Mahon — "we were the three amigos," Alexa said — cajoled its members into keeping the wrecker's ball at bay long enough for them to put together financing and a plan to restore the structure as a women's centre. No one expected they would succeed. "And so we said, 'Oh yeah, well, just watch us.' And we did," Alexa remembered with a laugh.

They raised most of the funding they needed in "nickels and dimes." Because it was to be a women's centre, they were committed to the notion women should also restore the building. At the time, there were no women qualified to take on such specialized jobs, so Alexa went back to her former social planning department boss, Harold Crowell, and enlisted his help devising a job training scheme that they pitched to the federal government. "We said, 'Every city has these old houses that are going to be torn down for parking lots. We need to train women in these skills so they can restore those buildings and turn them into useful places.'" In the afterglow of International

Women's Year, Alexa recalled, Ottawa established "restoration workers" as a new job training category it would fund for women. The job skills program worked so well the Halifax *Chronicle-Herald* even published a cartoon depicting Premier Gerald Regan on the telephone to McDonough asking her for her "formula" for creating so many new jobs.

Restoring and renovating the three-storey building, however, was just the first step. There was then the central question of how to cover the monthly costs of what they had created. "I started to learn about real estate, which I had no interest in whatsoever and absolutely no knowledge about, but I realized I had to learn," Alexa said. She did understand the building would need an anchor tenant with sufficient resources to carry the mortgage but also with a sense of mission to complement what the non-profit women's centre was trying to accomplish. Which, of course, the women were still trying to articulate.

Although McDonough noted that many of the women involved in the Junior League at the time were "Junior-Leaguer society kids, and not much in my orbit," some had been her high school friends. She tapped into those connections to negotiate a long-term lease to have the Bargain Box, a Junior League–run used clothing outlet, set up shop on the ground floor. The Bargain Box wouldn't just be an important source of rental income, its clothing bins would also bring women into the building where they could then be encouraged to come up to the second floor to the women's centre's programs and services.

Which circled the conversation back to what the centre should be, what it should do, and, most importantly, who should make those decisions. Peggy Mahon, who had been charged with asking those questions across Halifax's social and political divides, remembered the process as exhausting and ex-hilarating, with philosophical tugs of war over whether the centre should be providing services to women or leading the charge for social change. *If you don't change women's circumstances, nothing will change. But if you don't help individual women who need it, how will they ever be in positions to make change?* The meetings, and the arguments, would often continue deep into the night. Mahon marvelled at Alexa's skill at keeping the conversations on track, "her ability to see both ends of the continuum and still bring people together, finding a way forward." Though Alexa was clearly the leader, Mahon said she was at pains to defer credit. "Oh, no, that wasn't me," she would say when someone thanked her. "The group did that."

In the end, the group came up with a two-page Statement of Philosophy that reads like a particularly progressive feminist manifesto. "A Woman's Place, as part of the Women's Movement, is committed to the full and equal participation of women in all facets of society," the typewritten statement began. The document then managed to highlight all the important touchstones: a woman's right to choose not only when and if to have children, but how many; universal, "affordable, high-quality, non-sexist" child care; universal, twenty-four-hour access to daycare facilities; the elimination of sexism in the "curricula, teaching methods, materials, and administration of all educational institutions"; an end to sexism in media and advertising; affirmative action in the workplace; equal, discrimination-free employment opportunities and equal pay for work of equal value, coupled with a recognition of "homemaking and child care as work of value to our society deserving of monetary reward."

To attain those goals, the statement declared, "A Woman's Place recognizes the need to work for legislative change."

•

In the five years since she'd attended the Regina socialist conference, Alexa McDonough had become more and more enmeshed in the backrooms of the New Democratic Party. She impressed everyone she met. "She was charismatic," recalled Colin Gabelmann, a British Columbia member of the party's federal council, who later became a provincial cabinet minister. At the time, he said, the party's next-generation leadership was finding its way to the federal council table from two different streams: a mostly male coterie, including future MPs Lorne Nystrom and Steven Langdon, whose views had been forged in university student politics, the anti-Vietnam war movement, and the party's own New Democratic Youth; and a mostly female contingent, including Alexa, who'd come of political age through the women's movement. Alexa, he added, had support from both groups. "You could see she had these innate leadership skills. She became a kind of pied piper for all of us, a little above and a little out of reach."

Alexa also served on the federal NDP's participation of women committee, which was encouraging women to take on leadership roles. Judy Wasylycia-Leis, a former executive assistant to Ed Broadbent who became the NDP's national women's organizer in 1976, acknowledged she "may have encouraged Alexa to run as part of my job," but added, "Alexa was ahead of the curve in terms of realizing the importance of women to be involved in politics, not on the outside knocking on the door all the time, but on the inside shaking things up."[17] Margaret Mitchell, another member of the committee who would later become the federal MP for Vancouver East, remembered one committee meeting in Toronto where everyone around the table tried to convince Alexa to run. "Of course, we all thought Alexa should run, but she was kind of shy at that stage."

During her flight back to Halifax after that meeting, however, as Alexa later confided to Mitchell, she finally began to take the idea seriously. In part, that was because her experiences as a social worker had convinced her "our real problems were embedded in our economic system. Governments just had to take a stronger social and economic role."[18] In part, too, there was another reality, which she'd discovered campaigning with Muriel Duckworth: Alexa McDonough came alive when she engaged people on their doorsteps, accepting the challenge of converting them, one voter at a time, to the cause she'd come to believe in.

She was still struggling through the conflicting permutations and combinations of whether to actually run for office — the pundits were predicting Pierre Trudeau might call an election at any moment — when she happened to meet Peggy Mahon on Barrington Street one day in the fall of 1978. Mahon, no longer the new kid on the block, was working full-time for the YWCA, thanks in part to Alexa's support. As they walked, Mahon remembered, Alexa mused aloud whether she could accomplish more as a social worker or as a politician.

"What if I ran and lost?" she asked. She knew this was Nova Scotia, a province where politics often trumped competence, and people still got fired for voting the wrong way. "Could I even get a job in this city?"

Peggy Mahon mostly listened, but she also believed — hoped — McDonough would choose to run. She had already decided that if McDonough did decide to seek office, Peggy Mahon would be first in line to volunteer for her campaign.

8

They agreed to meet for coffee at the soda fountain inside Coombe's Drug Store, an iconic landmark on Gottingen Street in Halifax's North End. Alexa McDonough was the New Democratic Party's freshly anointed candidate for the May 22, 1979, federal general election. The young Black man with the giant Afro sitting opposite her was George Elliott Clarke, who'd had a "precocious crush" on Alexa fifteen years before at his mother's child care centre when Alexa was a student on a university placement.

As with Alexa, much had changed in George's life. Like many young Black Nova Scotians, he'd become radicalized in the aftermath of the visit of the Black Panthers to Halifax in 1968. "I read Mao and Lenin," he recalled. He was currently in the midst of organizing what he hoped would be a militant Black youth organization to demand social change. Despite, or because of all that, Alexa had reached out to him. "She tried to convince me to help out with canvassing," he explained with a laugh. "At that point I was too far to the left, even if it was Alexa doing the asking." He paused. "Still, it meant a lot to me that she would ask."

One voter at a time.

•

"Halifax on election day," *Ottawa Citizen* political columnist Richard Gwyn informed his readers on May 3, 1979, "would be the best city to be a voter in, and the worst." That was because the three candidates in the riding were "just too good to be true." Knowlton Nash, the anchor of CBC's national news, who'd criss-crossed the country during the campaign, agreed. In a post-election column for the *Citizen,* he declared, "The single most impressive race in the country was in Halifax where three truly brilliant candidates, all friends, ran against each other."[19]

They certainly were an impressive lot. Forty-year-old Brian Flemming, a lawyer with one of Halifax's two biggest law firms, had spent the previous three years as Pierre Trudeau's assistant principal secretary and policy advisor. The *Globe and Mail*'s Geoff Stevens, in a May 1, 1979 column, described him as "intellectual, patrician, sardonic." George Cooper, a thirty-seven-year-old Rhodes Scholar who'd helmed PC leader Joe Clark's leadership campaign in Atlantic Canada was, Stevens wrote, "a down-to-earth successful city lawyer [with the city's other biggest law firm], not flashy but solid." While Stevens acknowledged that thirty-four-year-old Alexa McDonough, "the first woman to run in the riding since Confederation, is also impressive," he focused more on her pedigree than her professional accomplishments, noting that, "by blood and marriage," she was a member of the Halifax establishment.

Gwyn began his own description by placing Alexa in a soon-to-be equally familiar pigeonhole. Alexa McDonough, he wrote, "first strikes you by her fresh-faced Anne-Murray-by-the-sea look. But then," he added quickly, "you strike steel." When he'd referred to her during their interview as a social worker, she cut him off. She was, she said, "not one now. Social workers cope with society's casualties. My concern is with the causes of those casualties." When he noted her political patrimony, she made it clear she wasn't just her father's daughter. "My mother Jean sacrificed her career aspirations, sublimated them for the family," she said. "I'm as much her daughter as my father's. I've tried to get the press to report that, and they never will."

Alexa was, of course, also a woman running for office in what was considered an unwinnable riding. Women's presence on the ballot gave optics-savvy political parties bragging rights for encouraging women to become candidates without actually risking a potentially winnable seat.[20]

Alexa was ambivalent about how to position herself as a female candidate. "I don't believe in making an all-out pitch to get women to elect me, whether or not they believe in my basic political convictions," she told the *National Post*. "It's phony to appeal to them just on the basis of my being a woman."[21] On the other hand, she said many years later, she wanted to be "a change agent...a female, not an NDP candidate in the conventional sense."

While her campaign literature focused on issues that mattered to people—unemployment in Nova Scotia had almost tripled during the Trudeau years, food prices were escalating at close to 18 per cent a year—she did her best to translate those numbers into human terms on the doorstep. "Are you better off today than in 1968? 1978?"

Family and friends volunteered as campaign surrogates. Including Peter. "George was my law partner and Brian represented my party, but it was never a momentous decision for me. If Alexa wanted to run, I would support her." He and John Duckworth became stalwarts of the door to door. So did Lloyd, who'd retired from L.E. Shaw Ltd. earlier that year after selling the business to its managers. Peggy Mahon became "personal support," driving her to

Alexa with Lloyd Shaw (left) and Tommy Douglas (right),
during the 1979 federal election
(courtesy of McDonough Family Collection)

campaign events and debates. Still, Alexa canvassed mostly on her own. As a Canadian Press report explained: "She favours the personal touch as she goes unaccompanied door to door."[22]

Not that it mattered. When the ballots were counted, George Cooper won, barely, beating Brian Flemming by fifteen votes. Between them, they had vacuumed up more than 80 per cent of 41,000 ballots cast, leaving Alexa and the NDP far behind with just 7,590 votes, or 18.5 per cent.

She wasn't surprised. But she remained, like her father, relentlessly upbeat. "Every vote that got cast for the NDP," she said at the time, "was one more step in the process" of changing the world, one vote at a time. Although she couldn't know it then, Alexa McDonough had just set off on what would become a three-decade-long career in Canadian politics. To succeed, and survive, she would need all the patience she could muster.

•

Alexa returned to the campaign trail six months later, after Joe Clark's minority Progressive Conservative government was unexpectedly defeated on a confidence vote in December.

While Pierre Trudeau's Liberals won his 1980 mulligan election, and former Nova Scotia premier Gerald Regan, who'd replaced Flemming as the party's local candidate, defeated Cooper in the Halifax riding, little had changed for Alexa. Though she nudged her percentage of the popular vote up to 19.67 per cent, she still finished a distant third. She was, as *Maclean's* Ottawa bureau chief Robert Lewis described her, an "impressive" candidate who, Geoff Stevens added in the *Globe and Mail*, "belongs in the House of Commons." But she wasn't headed there soon.

"If you ask me if I have my bags packed," she'd joked to a reporter in mid-campaign, "the answer is no." That said, "You seize life's opportunities, or you get talked into chasing one thing at a time." She was about to talk herself—or be talked into—seeking yet another prize that seemed like no prize at all.

9

If you're going to understand the real value of the "prize" Alexa McDonough won on November 16, 1980, the Sunday afternoon she was elected leader of the Nova Scotia New Democratic Party, you might begin by rewinding seven months to May 16. On that Friday afternoon, without preamble or explanation, then-NDP leader Jeremy Akerman sent out a press release: "It is not my intention to seek re-election as leader of the party at its fall convention [and] I shall not seek re-election in [my constituency of] Cape Breton East at the next provincial general election." As if to emphasize that he was walking away without a backward glance, Akerman, then the longest-serving political leader in Canada after Prime Minister Pierre Trudeau and Quebec premier René Lévesque, underlined the following sentence in his resignation statement: "I shall make no further comment of any kind on this announcement."

And he didn't. Which, of course, made everything all the worse for the scrambling, disoriented party he left behind.

Akerman's decision to resign so abruptly, coupled with the reality that, after years of railing at the evils of the province's political patronage system, he had grabbed for a dangled Conservative government plum on his way out the door,[23] drove a stake through the heart of any future political career. But the manner of his leaving also seemed, and seemed intended, to shiv any future hopes harboured by the political party he had led for thirteen years.

To make sense of why he did that, and why so many inside and outside the party regarded his resignation as a flashing-neon sign the NDP's future was already in its past, it's best to start with the party's last best moment of new hope. That happened in 1967, when an energetic twenty-five-year-old Akerman—a British come-from-away, an archaeological draftsman turned fishermen's organizer turned radio talk show host—won the party leadership. In doing so, he wrested control of what seemed like, and often was, a Halifax-centric university debating society and turned it into a dynamic, electorally focused Cape Breton–based workers' party.

Although Akerman himself was "a bundle of apparent contradictions [who] identifies politically with coal miners, fishermen and the poor, yet has the deportment of an aristocrat,"[24] there was no denying either his hustings skills or his indefatigable energies. As Alexa herself would describe his accomplishments shortly before he announced his resignation, Akerman "brought the party from the wilderness with nothing but good will and hard work."[25]

In the 1970 general election, Akerman campaigned on what veteran political scientist J. Murray Beck described as a pragmatic brand of "softened socialism."[26] In truth, his approach hardly moved the provincial electoral needle in what became the closest election in provincial history. When all the votes were counted, Gerald Regan's Liberals had wedged their way into power, capturing twenty-three of the House of Assembly's forty-six seats and 46.9 per cent of the popular vote, barely edging out G.I. Smith's Progressive Conservatives, who mustered twenty-one seats and 46.1 per cent of the vote. Akerman's NDP pulled up a distant third, laying claim to only 6.7 per cent of the total votes cast, but the fact its support was concentrated among steelworkers, miners, and fishers in industrial Cape Breton earned the party two seats—Akerman's own and that of a schoolteacher named Paul MacEwan—and the balance of power.

Thanks to the Liberal's cliffhanger-close status in the House of Assembly and the fact Akerman "quickly distinguished himself as the best debater in the legislature,"[27] the NDP emerged as a significant if still minor player in provincial political life. In the 1974 election, Akerman leveraged that to double his party's share of the popular vote while adding one more Cape Breton seat.

By 1978, with Regan's scandal-plagued Liberals imploding, and the Tories, under new leader John Buchanan, still in disarray, the NDP seemed poised for its breakthrough moment. Akerman ran his best campaign ever, a province-wide affair for the first time. But the party still came up woefully short of its dream. It managed to increase its share of the popular vote by just 1.5 per cent. It did add a fourth legislature seat, but the House of Assembly had also expanded by six seats to fifty-two. Worse, the seats the party won were all still in Cape Breton; all but four of its mainland candidates lost their deposits and only one finished as high as second.

For Akerman, the result was a crushing, enthusiasm-sucking personal blow. "For twelve years," as columnist Parker Donham noted in his provincially syndicated column, "he has been pounding his head against the brick wall of Nova Scotia's ingrained conservatism.... He has defended more unpopular causes and more powerless people than any ten legislators in recent Nova Scotia history."

As he put it to an interviewer, however, Akerman had concluded "responsible, statesmanlike, mellow leadership" wasn't the path to electoral victory in Nova Scotia. "Voting here is an almost purely negative thing," he lamented in the May 1980 issue of *Atlantic Insight*, "to kick somebody out. The public doesn't say, 'We hate this government. Now let's see who has the best programs and the best leadership.' The public says, 'We hate this government. Let's see who has the best chance of winning.'"

Following that election, Akerman seemed to lose all interest in his job. He was out of the country during the failed re-election campaign for the party's only federal Cape Breton MP, Father Andy Hogan, a campaign Akerman had been expected to manage. Akerman shuttered his constituency office and told anyone who asked he would seriously consider other job offers.

Alexa McDonough was among many in the party taken aback. Even though she was now on the party's provincial council, she told *Atlantic Insight*, "You can't talk to him anymore. It's as if... [he] has turned on us."

Akerman's departure also brought into the open long-simmering tensions not only between Akerman and the party's mainland establishment, who had never quite warmed to him or him to them, but also between the party's executive and Cape Breton MLA Paul MacEwan. MacEwan, a bombastic populist with a narcissistic, paranoid streak, had first been elected with Akerman in 1970. There was an early dispute over $1,500 the party had loaned him until he got his first MLA's cheque that he had never paid back. That triggered the resignation of the party secretary. The party president also quit, accusing Akerman and MacEwan of having colluded with the Liberals by agreeing not to run candidates in certain mainland ridings in 1970 in exchange for the Liberals staying out of some Cape Breton constituencies Akerman believed the NDP could win. Three years later, MacEwan attracted national headlines when a Conservative MLA from Cape Breton punched him in the face on the floor of the legislature.

MacEwan's antics had been tolerated within the party largely because he was seen to have Akerman's support. That changed as Akerman began to abandon his leadership role after the 1978 election. MacEwan, who considered himself "Jeremy's logical and proper successor,"[28] attempted to step into the void, further exacerbating his relations with the party executive.

To complicate matters, an NDP member from MacEwan's riding who was running for a Cape Breton County Council seat wrote a letter to the party executive in November 1979, accusing MacEwan of attempting to raise money for his own account by falsely invoking the party's name: "As you may be aware," MacEwan's fundraising letter began, "the NDP is sponsoring candidates running for municipal elections...." Two months later, a Halifax company asked the party for a tax receipt for a $500 donation it had made to "Paul MacEwan in Trust," with half of the funds intended to support Alexa McDonough's 1980 federal campaign. Party officials could find no record of receiving such a donation, nor a similar donation from the year before for Alexa's 1979 campaign.[29]

While the party poked into those allegations, MacEwan began firing broadsides at party officials. He accused the executive of being behind what he called a "clever [campaign] to destroy Akerman and myself simultaneously" with the intended end result of "making one of your group...leader of the party." He advised the Halifax-based plotters—whom he claimed included Bob Levy, the party's president; Dennis Theman, its first vice-president; Lloyd Shaw, the treasurer; Serena Renner, the provincial secretary; and Alexa, a member of the provincial council—"to go to Akerman on bended knee, repenting of past errors, making amends and offering to step aside" at the upcoming party annual convention."[30]

He'd then dispatched a letter to the executive accusing Theman of being a Trotskyite. Theman, a legal aid lawyer, had become active in the party in the late seventies after Alexa and Muriel Duckworth showed up at his doorstep campaigning. "That pair," he joked. "There was no stopping them." After helping out in a campaign, Alexa invited Theman to join her constituency association. "Before I knew it, I was the president."

A Trotskyite? In the often-Byzantine world of left-wing politics, a Trotskyite is someone who believes, like the late Russian revolutionary leader Leon Trotsky, that the only path to socialism is an ongoing worldwide revolution led by the working classes. MacEwan's primary evidence against Theman seemed to be that, in the fall 1979 issue of the party's newsletter, *The New Democrat*, Theman had offered a suggested reading list that included a Toronto-based publication called *Forward*, which MacEwan claimed was a Trotskyist publication.

Theman's bemused defence: "I have never even read any works by Trotsky."[31]

The whole affair became less amusing, however, when, after Akerman's resignation, MacEwan suggested darkly to reporters he had resigned because a "communist element" and "advocates of Trotskyism" had infiltrated the party.

At the same time, MacEwan escalated his private attacks on individual members of the executive, sending a letter to the director of Nova Scotia Legal Aid, which employed both Theman and party president Bob Levy, claiming they'd been using legal aid's postage meter and photocopying machine for nefarious NDP activities, and demanding they be disciplined.

Eventually, it all became too much. In a June 4, 1980, letter addressed to "Dear Mr. MacEwan," Levy wrote: "You are hereby notified that charges have been preferred against you on motion of the executive of the Nova Scotia New Democratic Party that you have acted contrary to the principles and constitution of the Nova Scotia New Democratic Party and that your membership is adverse to the best interests of the party." The list of seven particulars ranged from having actively "promoted factionalism" to "financial irregularities."

"This business is an awkward, troublesome nightmare of a situation," Levy admitted to the *Globe and Mail*, "and, yes, we can imagine the consequences of what we're doing."

Two weeks later, the provincial executive held a disciplinary hearing—MacEwan refused to attend—and unanimously expelled him from the party. That decision was upheld by the full provincial council in early July after a ten-hour meeting presided over by former federal leader David Lewis, who had, with what he called "prepidation," accepted Levy's request to chair it. Although she wasn't vocal at the meeting, Alexa McDonough counted herself firmly among the fifty-six of sixty-eight members of provincial council voting to expel MacEwan. But the party's MLAs—including lame-duck leader Akerman and Cape Breton Centre MLA James (Buddy) MacEachern—then voted 2–1 to allow MacEwan to continue as a member of the legislative caucus, thus publicly baring a bitter divide between the party's elected MLAs and its executive.

While what *Globe and Mail* Atlantic region columnist Barbara Yaffe would describe as the NDP's "death rattle"[32] continued, MacEwan announced plans for a tell-all book[33] that would forever put the party's "academic boffins, Halifax radicalogues and pipe puffers, pseudo intellectuals and double PhDs" in their place. Akerman himself briefly emerged from his self-imposed cone of silence. He was not only quoted in MacEwan's book — "I have been treated like a criminal in my own party" — but also penned the foreword in which he described MacEwan's account as "legitimate...an adequate summary of its subject."

For his part, MacEwan declared that "the book may have my name on it but it's really a collaboration between myself and Akerman. He's read and reread every word." MacEwan announced his book would be released less than three weeks before NDP delegates converged on Halifax to choose their new leader.

10

While MacEwan lobbed his rhetorical cannonballs at Theman, Levy, and provincial secretary Serena Renner during the winter and spring of 1980, Alexa herself managed to stay mostly out of his direct firing line. MacEwan seemed to see her, at worst, as a minor player in the larger conspiracies against him.

Having been kicked out of the party, MacEwan was ineligible to run for the leadership. But the two remaining members of the party's legislative caucus could — and did — quickly throw their hats in the ring for the November 1980 leadership convention. Neither inspired much excitement.

Forty-year-old James "Buddy" MacEachern was "decent to everybody and there were no airs about him," as a colleague put it, but the story of why he'd decided to become a politician seemed to say too much about his lack of larger ambitions. "He was from a coal mining community, but he didn't really think he wanted to go down into the mines," Alexa explained many years later. "So, one day he happened to walk past a sign with a posted notice of an NDP nomination meeting in New Waterford and he thought that if he won that he wouldn't have to go underground. And he won it!"[34]

Len Arsenault was a well-liked forty-six-year-old junior high schoolteacher, best known locally as a sports coach and jazz aficionado. In 1978, on his third try, he'd become the first-ever NDP MLA for Cape Breton North, but his workmanlike performance during his first two years in the legislature had not resonated much beyond his own constituency.

The only other potential candidate who could have generated real excitement ruled himself out before the race even began. Although Bob Levy's central role in the MacEwan affair might have made him anathema to some in Cape Breton, he was universally acknowledged as a forceful, stirring orator who would have made a fine leader. Like Alexa, he'd run in two recent federal elections, and had taken on what became the thankless role of party president during the MacEwan debacle. But Levy — MacEwan's suspicions notwithstanding — wasn't interested. "It was not on my radar," Levy told me years later. "I had a family to feed and leading the NDP at that time did not seem like the best meal ticket."

Meanwhile, Alexa came under increasing pressure to run, including by key voices in Cape Breton like Gerald Yetman, the charismatic Cape Breton-born but Halifax-based national representative of the Canadian Union of Public Employees. Ed Murphy, another proud born-and-bred Cape Bretoner who'd run for the party federally, pledged his support. As a Roman Catholic, he was "ambivalent" about Alexa's pro-choice views on abortion, but he admired "her spunk, her tenacity, intelligence and her endless energy."[35] He also understood, as did others in Cape Breton, that the party's best hope to expand past the causeway was to elect a leader who could speak to voters across the province. Muriel Duckworth nudged, and Rosemary Brown telephoned, reminding Alexa of their earlier conversations and promising to speak at the leadership convention if she ran.

Before long, said Dennis Theman, there were Alexa-for-leader committees across the province "with representatives from each electoral district."

And then, too, there was this. Her two rivals for the job came to see her and privately pledged their post-leadership convention support. Although they would both stay in the race to give it legitimacy, they told her: "We know you'll win if you run, and we really want you to be the leader." Most importantly, they believed she could win in Halifax.

Alexa remained unconvinced. "I told them, 'That's ridiculous. We're not going to win a seat in Halifax in our lifetime.'" But they countered that if anyone could, Alexa would. And when she trotted out her by now standard-issue rationales — young mother, busy lawyer-husband — they reminded her, "Aren't you the one who's so big on getting women elected?" And they pledged that when she won — not if — "'We'll both be there to support you and work with you and endorse you, and together we will build the NDP into a province-wide force.'" Given the very messy public splits between Cape

Breton and the mainland, and between the caucus and the party executive, such support would be critical.

On September 25, declaring it was "way beyond time for women to assume a leadership role," Alexa publicly announced her candidacy. Pollyanna-like, she attempted to turn her perceived weaknesses into strengths. "A House leader from the legislative caucus and a party leader representing the broader social commitment," she mused to reporters, "one from Cape Breton, the other from the mainland, the caucus leader a man and myself, a woman, as party leader.... This combination could persuade delegates and the people of Nova Scotia... that some of the historical gaps that plague our community and limit the effectiveness of government could be bridged."[36]

She even offered an olive branch to MacEwan, telling reporters "the ball is now in Paul's court." If he was willing to pledge to abide by party policy and principles, she said she would welcome him back into the party with the hope "he will again take an active part in building the party throughout Nova Scotia."

Less than a week after her announcement, she reached out to Reeves Matheson, a Glace Bay lawyer who was the party's candidate in a December by-election to replace Akerman. MacEwan was Matheson's campaign manager. "Glad to have the opportunity last evening to discuss 'matters of mutual concern' (How's that for a euphemism for the mess we're in!!!),'" she wrote in a typed, single-spaced three-page letter on September 30. She had begun, she explained, "with the intention of dropping you two lines and I've really rattled on."[37]

Pleading with Matheson not to make Paul "*the* issue of either your campaign or the leadership race," Alexa did her best to thread the needle, making the argument it was up to MacEwan to "demonstrate he is indeed committed to the NDP, as you have always maintained," and encouraging Matheson himself to try to convince MacEwan to change his behaviour. "If you can't get some co-operation from him along these lines, who can?"

Despite her own description to Matheson of hers as a "candidacy by default," there was no doubt she'd become the leadership race's front-runner simply by announcing her candidacy. "The so-called MacEwan affair hovers like a dark cloud over the entire party," wrote Brian Butters of Southam News, but "some party insiders say [McDonough] would have to insult every delegate personally to lose."[38]

She didn't, although the three-day convention got off to a rocky start Friday evening, when members of the Cape Breton–based steelworkers and miners' union delegations stormed out. The convention had voted in favour of a resolution proposed by a Halifax delegate squarely aimed at MacEwan: members of the NDP legislative caucus must be members in good standing of the party too. Alexa and Len Arsenault both spoke in favour of the resolution. Luckily, MacEachern and Reeves Matheson, who'd spoken against it, acted as peacemakers, quickly bringing the union members back into the hall.

Everyone, including MacEachern and Arsenault, stressed party unity and downplayed the notion of a split among the faithful. All leadership candidates, Buddy MacEachern declared from the podium, "stand for party unity above all else. I know the Liberals and Tories are watching the convention on television and rubbing their hands with glee, saying, 'They're going to tear themselves apart.' Well, let me tell you there was no blood spilled here."

In truth, the convention was more coronation than competition. Rosemary Brown spoke. Rita MacNeil sang. MacNeil, the acclaimed Cape Breton–born singer-songwriter who'd become a darling among Canadian feminists for songs like "Born a Woman," had contacted Alexa when she was still debating whether to run. "If you'll run," she said, "I'll come and sing at the convention."

The outcome was stunning, if anti-climactic. Alexa won 78 per cent of the 320 votes cast. MacEachern, who'd earned 41 votes, and Arsenault, who'd taken 42, flanked Alexa on stage, raising their collective arms in triumph and declaring the result unanimous.

Harry Flemming, a former Liberal insider turned CBC political commentator, marvelled, the NDP "has become a real political party that wants to win."

"What McDonough's election...does for the party goes beyond her reputation as a hard worker and her undeniable charm and fresh-faced good looks," added Southam's Butters. "She is being counted on to take the party past its traditional reliance on the trade union link and establish it as an alternative for Nova Scotia voters who have bounced back and forth, generation after generation, between the Liberals and Conservatives."[39]

Alexa understood that. "There's been a self-defeating attitude in our own party," she said after her victory, "a feeling of not being totally convinced that we can do it. We have to get away from that and launch the kind of province-wide campaign that we've never had."

But first, there were the small matters of the Cape Breton by-election and, oh yes, Paul MacEwan.

•

Since even before she won the leadership, MacEwan had been doing his best—in his own peculiar way—to wheedle his way into Alexa's good graces. On October 2, for example, he wrote to excuse her vote to expel him back in July. "You did not have the facts," he suggested. He blamed Akerman for being "the instigator" of his fall from grace. After Alexa won the leadership, he wrote again, claiming the party's former leader, and the man he had extolled in his soon-to-be published biography, "found it to his advantage to have me at odds with leading New Democrats," and "insisted on the campaigns against individuals within the party and encouraged me on in anything I did that way."[40]

Alexa, whose own trademark would eventually become her sharply worded Sharpie comments and edits on the work of others, wrote in the margin of his letter: "Unadulterated BS."

"I have now been sitting in the penalty box for three months and surely that is long enough," MacEwan noted in asking for reinstatement. Such a decision would be in Alexa's own best interest, he added, pointing out that, while he'd dismissed her as a "purist" in his book, he would now be able to tell interviewers: "Ah yes, but since then Alexa McDonough has taken a leading role in trying to bring the party back together. Why, she has stated publicly that she would welcome me back into the party with open arms."

She didn't. In December, after Alexa had become party leader, MacEwan sent another rambling four-page letter, this time officially reapplying for party membership. Two days later, Alexa met with MacEachern and Arsenault, after which she announced she and the caucus had unanimously agreed not to allow MacEwan to return. Two days after that, MacEwan replied in a briefer and less conciliatory letter: "It would not be in my best interest to have anything further to do with the outfit you head," he declared.

By the end of the year, he had asked the Speaker of the House to permit him to sit as an Independent Labour MLA and mused publicly about the possibility of establishing a Cape Breton Independent Labour Party. In a year-end interview with the *Cape Breton Post*, he had what should have been — but, unfortunately, wasn't — his final word on the leader of his former party: "She knows full well in her heart that she cannot get elected to the legislature in the next election," he declared. "She is leading the party into oblivion...and will not rest until the party has been eliminated completely from the legislature."[41]

Alexa was not off to an auspicious start. In the course of a tumultuous year, the Nova Scotia NDP had gone from four legislature seats to three with the resignation of its leader in May, and then to two following MacEwan's expulsion. And now, on December 5, 1980 — in the first public test of the NDP under Alexa McDonough's leadership — Reeves Matheson had been defeated in the Cape Breton East by-election.

Alexa McDonough, October 1984

(courtesy of Michael Creagen)

BELLY OF THE BEAST

1

The woman standing at her apartment door on this rainy Monday afternoon was not simply an uncommitted voter. She was in the process of relocating, she told Alexa, so she wasn't sure where—or maybe even if—she would vote in the October 6, 1981, provincial election. Their conversation had been brief. Alexa introduced herself as the local candidate, handed the woman an NDP pamphlet with her picture on it, and asked if she had any questions. The woman hadn't hinted she was considering voting NDP. Still, Alexa insisted on writing down her name and contact information. "Someone from my staff will be in touch with the information you need about voting."

The reporter accompanying Alexa was curious. Don't you worry, he asked later, that you might be inadvertently helping that woman vote for some other party? Alexa shrugged. If her campaign staff didn't help the woman, she explained, "We would lose the woman's vote for sure."[1]

One vote at a time. Never abandon hope.

Alexa had chosen to make what many inside and outside the party believed would be her first and also final quixotic electoral stand as leader of the NDP by deciding to run in Halifax Chebucto, a central Halifax constituency. Few believed it was the right decision. For starters, running in Chebucto meant not running in Halifax Cornwallis, the well-to-do South End riding where Alexa had grown up, now lived, and was well known and liked, even by those who didn't like socialists.

Becoming the party's standard bearer in Chebucto, the neighbouring working and middle-class district, meant running against two mainstream, good-old-boy politicians, each so well known they were referred to by sporty nicknames. The incumbent, Liberal Walter "Googie" Fitzgerald, was the city's former mayor and a former provincial cabinet minister who'd bucked the anti-Liberal tide in 1978 to hold on to this very seat.[2] The Progressive Conservative candidate, Donald C. "Dugger" McNeil, had once been a star defenceman for the Halifax Wolverines senior hockey team, served for seven years during the 1960s as an MLA, and now owned Dugger's, a popular men's clothing store.

Insiders from the other parties were delighted to suggest, anonymously of course, that Alexa's real goal must not even be to get elected. "If she really wanted to have a fighting chance of getting a seat,"[3] one Liberal organizer told the *Globe and Mail*, "she should be down in Cape Breton." A Tory backroom operative was even more blunt—and sexist. "She would much rather get her pretty little face on national television than sit in the provincial legislature."[4]

Alexa justified her choice. "You've got to look at the potential for growth when you choose a seat, and we see real chances here," was the official line she offered skeptical reporters. But her defence appeared, in the words of Southam News, "long on rhetoric and curiously short on statistical probability."[5] In fact, her decision was based on hunch and hope. While she may have lost in both the 1979 and 1980 federal campaigns in Halifax, the reasoning went, she'd done better than any previous NDP candidate here while generating plenty of free name recognition in the process. "We took a reading and said, 'What's the most winnable seat?'" Alexa recalled years later. "We decided that was the most winnable seat." She laughed. "God knows what made me think I could win it."

The most persuasive voice favouring Chebucto came from Cliff Scotton, a veteran federal NDP organizer and friend of Lloyd's who'd travelled to Halifax to help out with the party's campaign and had become, along with his wife, Joyce, a key adviser. Scotton's argument was that voters in a solidly middle and working-class constituency like Chebucto would stay loyal to a good MLA, while Halifax Cornwallis was "full of university types who were among the most fickle and unreliable voters one could find."[6]

But if there'd been internal disagreement about where Alexa should run, and there had, there was universal agreement her future, and her party's, depended on winning the Chebucto seat. That was no sure thing.

•

The party Alexa inherited was a mess. Constituency organizations were "depleted and demoralized" because of never-ending infighting and lack of leadership. The party's policy-making apparatus had become "paralyzed... by inertia." Fundraising had collapsed. At one point, Dennis Theman remembered examining the party's books and realizing revenues for the year totalled just $40,000. "That was the lowest point, as far as I was concerned." And, thanks to all the various Cape Breton/Halifax, worker/intellectual, movement/party, revolutionary/pragmatic divides that had riven the NDP, relations between the party hierarchy and its Cape Breton–centred trade union base were "terrible." The party had become "a profound embarrassment to its own members and a deep mystery to everyone else."[7]

Alexa's official coming out as party leader had been equally inauspicious. On a "very mild, sunny day" in February, as Hansard described it, the provincial legislature formally reopened for what was expected to be its final session before an election. The opening had all the usual pomp and circumstance, including a "fashion parade." It was a quaint, "mid-Victorian" custom in the all-male legislature for the wives of MLAs to dress in their finest and parade into the spectators' gallery. The next day's social pages would be full of photographs and descriptions of who was wearing what. Despite an invitation to join and his threat to wear a baseball cap if he did, Mr. Alexa McDonough chose not to participate in what his wife, the actual political leader, described as an "absolutely humiliating march."[8]

Alexa—still unelected—was limited to observing from the visitor's gallery instead of participating on the floor, but the spring session worked out "very well." MacEachern and Arsenault were as good as their pre-convention word, offering Alexa co-operation and moral support as well as agreeing to split their publicly funded caucus financial resources with the leader. Still, both men were subject to "ridicule" for finding themselves "in the embarrassing situation of having a woman leader." When she finally took her own seat in the legislature after the 1981 election, Alexa explained what had happened, during her maiden speech, suggesting it was "instructive, particularly for the women of Nova Scotia" to know how some politicians regarded the presence of women in leadership positions.

But led by a woman or not, her party clearly wasn't ready for an election when Premier G.I. Smith finally pulled the plug in the middle of the Labour Day weekend. The NDP's recently hired provincial secretary, Mary Morison, who'd previously worked for Stephen Lewis in Ontario, later confided she and those around Alexa "had no grasp of how to mobilize the tremendous interest and potential support Alexa had generated." Dan O'Connor, who would later become chief of staff, explained that in part they simply knew far too little about the party's support and prospects for growth in most constituencies. "They sent Alexa to various points, like Port Hawkesbury, without any consideration of where Alexa's presence might get the NDP closer to winning."

Because Alexa was the party's only marquee attraction, she criss-crossed the province from Yarmouth to Sydney in the campaign's early weeks, speaking at more than thirty nominating meetings. That, of course, left Chebucto open for her rivals, who had no ambitions beyond winning votes in the riding.

During her forays into Cape Breton, Alexa smacked up against the impact of both the legacy of her party's internecine wars and the complications of trying to lead a truly provincial party. While the Liberals and the Tories navigated around commenting on an ongoing strike by four thousand Cape Breton coal miners, Alexa waded into the fray, supporting the miners and calling for the province to order provincial agencies to pay a premium to buy Cape Breton coal. There's no evidence to suggest her support helped the NDP in Cape Breton, but it is likely her position, which would have led to increased power rates across the province, didn't help her cause on the mainland.[9]

Both Buddy MacEachern and Len Arsenault were in trouble in their Cape Breton ridings, while their — and Alexa's — nemesis, Paul MacEwan cruised to victory in Cape Breton Nova and worked to undermine the NDP elsewhere on the island. As she went door to door with MacEachern, Alexa implored constituents to vote for Buddy, "because I don't want to be alone in the House."[10]

But could Alexa even win her own riding? When she could escape provincial obligations, she campaigned door to door in Chebucto. Her technique, noted a Canadian Press reporter, was "low-key, disarming and effective.... Almost everyone is downright friendly to her." One young mother told her she was glad to see a woman running. A young man claimed his father, traditionally a PC supporter, was voting for her this time. But would he really?[11]

•

On election-day morning, Peter encountered Alexa's Liberal rival, Walter Fitzgerald, during a visit to a polling station. Fitzgerald, who'd dismissed Alexa in public as a "socialist millionaire," seemed supremely confident. Alexa didn't have a chance, he told Peter. He was worried about McNeil, he confided. Alexa? "Never."

"Far from the political bravado one might expect from a politician at the end of a campaign," noted the *Globe and Mail*'s Michael Harris, "Mr. Fitzgerald's pronouncement represented the general assessment of Mrs. McDonough's chances."[12]

As Alexa continued her door-to-door election-day scramble for every last vote, she was attacked by a German shepherd whose bite broke the skin on her leg. After a quick trip to the emergency room and a tetanus shot, she was back knocking at the next door in the hours before the polls closed.

It paid off. Alexa polled 3,898 votes — 40 per cent of the total versus the NDP's fourteen in 1978 — 500 more than McNeil and nearly 1,500 more than Fitzgerald. "So, when Mr. Fitzgerald paid a visit to Mrs. McDonough's headquarters to congratulate her," noted Harris in the same *Globe and Mail* article, "his surprise at the results was as real as that of several other politicians and a flock of red-faced political commentators." About the only one unsurprised was Alexa herself. "You don't get into these things by listening to other people tell you how poor your chances are," she mused. "I was told I couldn't win the party leadership last November because I didn't have any support in Cape Breton. When I was being told that, I already knew I had the thing won."

Although MacEachern and Arsenault both lost their seats and, in fact, no New Democrat won anywhere except Alexa, the news from around the province was not all bad. Since 1978, the party had increased its overall vote totals by more than 12,000, and those votes were more evenly spread across the province. Significantly, the NDP had been in a real race for second place with the Liberals in seat-rich Halifax-Dartmouth, giving the party a more solid base on which to elect more mainland members next time.

Although the NDP's election of just one MLA meant it didn't technically reach the two-seat threshold to qualify for official party status, and the staff and public resources that came with that designation, the more significant fact from Alexa's point of view was that the party's share of the popular vote had now reached 18.4 per cent. That was 4 per cent higher than it had been in 1978, when the party did get official status. "I've done some research on how official party status has been treated here and in other jurisdictions," a hopeful Alexa told reporters, "and I'll be seeing Premier Buchanan as soon as I can arrange a meeting."

Her hopes were dashed. One of the government's first orders of business was to direct the Speaker "to begin dismantling the NDP's legislative office. The party's four staff members were told their services would no longer be required after December 15."[13] The decision cost the party about $100,000 in publicly financed research salaries and office spaces. "If there's one thing that scares the hell out of me," Alexa confided at the time, "it's the thought of trying to represent Chebucto as well as the other fifty-two constituencies without a staff or a proper legislative office."

Buchanan did eventually relent, if ever so slightly. He allowed the NDP to keep half its office space and some of its support staff, but he refused to grant it official status. Worse, Buchanan offered MacEwan, the now independent MLA, unspecified "aid in lieu of staff."

"As the only giant-killer on the political block," Michael Harris wrote in the *Globe and Mail* on October 20, "Alexa McDonough may find that the coldest spot in Nova Scotia this winter will be the provincial legislature."

He didn't know the half of it.

2

Alexa McDonough's career as an elected politician began badly, and quickly worsened.

No matter that Alexa was the leader of a New Democratic Party that could now claim the support of close to one in five Nova Scotians, or that she was the history-making first woman leader of any major political party in Canada actually elected to office, or that she was only the third female in Nova Scotia history to become a member of the legislative assembly.... When she officially took her seat for the first session of the Fifty-Third General Assembly on February 18, 1982, she was, as the writer Harry Bruce put it in a profile in *Atlantic Insight* magazine, "utterly alone among fifty-one political enemies, all men. Their attitude toward her ranged from bemused tolerance for 'an intelligent gal' to the undisguised hatred of Paul MacEwan."[14]

Arthur Donahoe, the Tory speaker of the legislature, "reneged on commitments to me," Alexa would later claim. "I was duped." Because the NDP didn't have official party status, Alexa had no right to speak on matters of public moment as a recognized leader inside the House and had to wait in the backbench queue for the occasional chance to even ask a question in Question Period.

Because she was not a lawyer or experienced in "the legalistic maneuverings and the procedural wrangles" of the legislature—and had no veteran NDP MLA to school her in the ways of that arcane world—she made occasional missteps, which the Speaker and other MLAs seemed to delight in amplifying. "Order, please," the Speaker admonished her on one typical occasion. "It is the third time in her remarks that the honourable member has referred to the member for Cape Breton Nova [Paul MacEwan] by his name and I should advise her that that is contrary to the rules and practices of the House."[15]

Alexa was not without secret support, however, inside and around the chamber. "I had angels who looked after me," she marvelled. One was Shirley Elliott, the veteran legislative librarian who'd attended Acadia with Lloyd Shaw and "identified with me as a woman. I'd be on my feet in the middle of a debate and didn't know what I was talking about when, to my absolute amazement and eternal gratitude, she would send some very helpful reference in from the library that she thought 'you might find useful.'" Henry Muggah, the clerk of the legislature, was her best friend Betty's father-in-law. Often, when the government was doing its utmost to prevent her from making a point or introducing a bill or motion, she would receive a note from Muggah. "'You might want to know there is no rule that disallows you to do the following,'...which was as close as he could get to giving me freebees and coaching." Both Elliott and Muggah, she recalled years later, "felt it was in the public interest for me not to implode or totally collapse."

But Alexa also quickly came to see for herself how politics actually played out from the House of Assembly floor and found it, along with many of her fellow MLAs, wanting. She said so. She skewered many of them for appearing to consider their days inside the chamber as a "lark" and being "inattentive and rude" when they were supposed to be seriously considering serious matters. She compared the theatrical goings-on in Question Period to "watching fake wrestling" and even suggested, more darkly, that some MLAs "do not really believe in the democratic process."

None of which, of course, endeared her to them.

Some MLAs were quietly supportive. Bruce Cochran, for example, a genial public relations man who was the Tory MLA for Lunenburg Centre, would often return home after legislative sessions and confide to his wife just how badly Alexa had been treated. As a result, Alexa remembered, Maxine Cochran "found ways to see me."[16] Guy Brown, a Liberal MLA, would occasionally let Alexa know he planned to raise a particular issue she was also concerned about, and invited her to tag-team with him to bring the issue more public attention. Roland Thornhill, the Tory deputy premier who'd survived a personal financial scandal in the lead-up to the 1981 election and whom Alexa had expected to be a "jerk," would sometimes call her at home to warn her of potential pitfalls she might not have been aware of.

More often than not, however, Alexa was confronted daily not only with open hostility from many of her fellow MLAs but also with incontrovertible evidence the Buchanan government didn't believe women belonged in politics. Start with the House of Assembly's official message pad, which MLAs used to communicate with one another and those in the galleries. The pad "has provision for a message to an honourable, to a doctor, and to a Mister," Alexa chided in her maiden speech, "but there is absolutely no provision for any message to be sent to a Miss, Ms. or Mrs."[17]

Many of the messages delivered to Alexa's desk by the legislative pages weren't written on official message pads. Often the messages were juvenile — "I did not call you a witch. (Signed) Count Dracula" — or worse, sexist and filled with sexual innuendo. In the middle of one evening session during debate on the throne speech, for example, Alexa opened up a folded note that read: "If you belonged to me, I'd want you home this evening. (You look smashing!)" It was unsigned, of course.[18]

The Buchanan government's attitude to women and women's issues was perhaps best exemplified by its mid-session announcement that G.H. "Paddy" Fitzgerald had been appointed to study proposed changes to the province's liquor control act. Fitzgerald had been a well-known Halifax trial lawyer who'd served as a Tory MLA and Speaker of the House, and he had been handed the competition-free, five-month $15,000 contract, according to the government, because of his "long experience in the law." It was all political patronage business as usual, except... Fitzgerald also happened to be a convicted rapist who'd only recently been paroled from prison after serving time for raping a divorced client in his office. In addition, he'd been convicted of tax evasion and been disbarred for "misappropriating" a client's trust fund.[19]

While Liberal leader A.M "Sandy" Cameron simply demanded to know the financial details about Fitzgerald's "political plum" contract, Alexa captured the broader sense of public outrage about what she described as the widening gap between the "dignity and decency" of Nova Scotians and the insensitive "male culture" of the legislature.[20] She compared the government's contract gift to an acknowledged tax cheat with the "harshest and most punitive measures" the government imposed on social assistance recipients for even accidentally misrepresenting their incomes. And, more significantly, she highlighted for her male colleagues the province's growing and "very serious problem with domestic violence and with violence directed against women. The implicit message" of the appointment," she said, "is that this is a matter that is not taken very seriously by this government. One is left feeling that it is not the victims of rape who are seen as the victims but, in fact, it is the man who happens to be caught that ends up being viewed as the victim and for whom the government should make special provisions."[21]

As if to amplify her argument, Premier Buchanan stood up in the legislature to complain about those, like Alexa, who would "hit a guy when he was down."[22] In the end, Fitzgerald resigned, telling reporters the "public reaction to his appointment had caused hardship for his family."[23]

Blatant sexism ran like a raging river through Alexa's years in the legislature. In 1983, for example, she asked for the unanimous consent of the House for a resolution condemning the views of a one-time Tory MLA turned *Chronicle-Herald* columnist who had lamented in his column that husbands could no longer beat their wives, "even when their wives deserve it." Hansard noted several MLAs declaring "No" to her request.[24]

Adding to the unwelcoming environment of the legislature during her first session was the fact no women's washroom had been built in the MLAs-only section of the chamber to accommodate the fact there was now a woman in the House. While male MLAs could just step past the curtains to find the entrance to a men's, "I had to come out of the 'leg' chamber, go through the coatroom and out into the foyer and go through the crowds of people who were lined up waiting to go into the galleries and the other people who were lined up to go into the washroom. And that wasn't very convenient," she joked, "given that I'd been drinking coffee all day."

While others, including many of her supporters, were eager to (and did) make an issue of the lack of an MLA's women's facilities, Alexa herself was careful, as she usually was with such gender issues, to acknowledge just how privileged she was in her own workplace compared to other women and then to flip the negative into a Pollyanna-positive. Because she had to line up with other women who'd come to the legislature to sit in the gallery — members of women's organizations, women's auxiliaries, church groups, civic action groups — "I always came away with great information." Women would see her and say, "'Oh, aren't you Alexa McDonough?' And then they wanted to tell me about some scandal or some research effort that could prove to be worthwhile on a policy we were trying to champion. People would give me their phone number and say, 'Call me if you want to know more about this....' If there had been a women's washroom for women legislators, I would have missed out on all that information I gleaned in the lineup. And that was an advantage that the fifty-one male members of the leg didn't share."

But standing in the lineup for the loo would turn out to have been one of Alexa's very few "advantages" over her male colleagues. Certainly, none of them had to face vicious daily personal onslaughts from a fellow legislator who "behaved in the legislature as though he believed his highest duty was to vilify her family 'til she wept in public."[25]

3

Paul MacEwan now openly mocked Alexa as the "member from Shawbucto" and the party she led as the "New Plutocratic Party," whose motto should have been "ALL POWER TO THE $HAHS." MacEwan had even imaginatively reimagined the origin story behind his expulsion from the party. He hadn't been kicked out because he'd publicly and falsely accused members of the executive of Trotskyist tendencies or personally engaged in financial irregularities or even as a backdoor way to thwart his own rightful claim to the party leadership. Instead, he now claimed he'd been booted out of the party because he'd uncovered a massive land sale scandal involving Shaw-connected companies and the then Liberal government. "That is why they kicked me out of the NDP because I was on to this," he declared in the legislature. "I have suffered great persecution for my desire to protect the taxpayers of this province."[26]

MacEwan had spent much of the time since he'd been expelled from the NDP consumed by a desire for revenge, amassing banker's boxes full of material — a blizzard full of deeds, housing commission minutes, newspaper clippings, etc. — he claimed proved his case. MacEwan's case, put simply, was that, in 1975, the then Liberal government had acquired more than four hundred acres of land in an area of Sackville known as the Millwood subdivision from Clayton Developments Ltd., a company owned by L.E. Shaw Limited. That company acquired the properties for approximately $250,000 and sold them three years later "to a favourable Liberal Government for $1,633,932." Alexa's brother, Robbie, MacEwan pointed out, had been the president of Clayton at the time of the sale but soon after became principal secretary to Premier Gerald Regan. He had used his political influence to inveigle the government to buy the land, MacEwan claimed, and Robbie and Alexa, among other Shaws, profited from the sale, which he said had earned the company a $1.5 million profit.

"During the session, Mr. Speaker," he added ominously, "we are going to show you where this [scandal] has been going on. We have got all the proof. I have got three boxes of it and we are going to be bringing it in here one day after another."

And he did. Day after day after day. There were lengthy harangues, resolutions demanding the Attorney General investigate the Shaws and their companies, house orders requiring government departments turn over information about them. When he wasn't re-fighting his old ideological battles with the NDP, claiming in one resolution, for example, that Alexa had "urged compassion" for people who were "foreign subversive elements dangerous to the national security of Canada," he was issuing endless notices of motion

requesting information about the public service records of members of the
family and all contracts any Shaw-connected company had ever received
from any government department or agency.

Alexa claimed MacEwan knew — as did the other MLAs — his requests
were spurious, "for the sole and express purpose of trying to mislead this
House, mislead the press, and mislead the public into believing claims, which
would, without question, undermine the confidence of my constituents in
my integrity."[27]

But MacEwan's notices of motion got action. At one point during the
session, the Buchanan government had approved twenty-six house orders for
information from MacEwan compared to just six from Alexa.

Why the discrepancy? John Buchanan's Tory government was enjoying
the show. "The sleaziest aspect of the affair," Harry Bruce noted in *Atlantic
Insight*, "was Tory complicity in MacEwan's verbal mugging. The longer he
lashed Shaws, the more likely he'd embarrass Liberals, and the less likely
anyone would get floor time to attack the government on grounds the
province's credit rating had dropped."[28]

Some government members, including Thornhill, attempted to whitewash
MacEwan's daily drumbeat of personal invective and family attacks as mere
"differences of opinion and wrangling between the honourable member for
Halifax Chebucto and the honourable member for Cape Breton Nova." His
government colleagues applauded. "I want to say to those two particular
members that if they insist, and persist, in fighting like a couple of cats,
would they do it on the street, and not in this Chamber?" More applause.[29]

Privately — but only privately — some Tory MLAs offered sympathy.
David Nantes, the member from Cole Harbour, wrote a note to Alexa,
calling MacEwan's attacks, "distressing to me. It appears to me to be a misuse
of the legislature." Buchanan's labour minister, John A. "Jack" MacIsaac, sent
Alexa a "strictly personal" note: "I can assure you, for whatever it is worth,
that Paul MacEwan had never received any legitimate support from me in
any of his efforts."[30]

The simple truth was no one on the Conservative or Liberal benches
wanted to publicly confront the allegations of the increasingly obsessed
MacEwan. When Alexa claimed MacEwan's attacks had violated her
privilege as an MLA, Speaker Donahoe first reserved decision and then
refused to render a meaningful one. After MacEwan offered an unapologetic

"withdrawal" of his attacks without promising not to renew them, and after Alexa replied that that wasn't good enough, Donahoe simply ruled the matter "concluded."[31]

But Paul MacEwan was far from concluded. He eventually won a showdown-at-high-noon public hearing by the province's public accounts committee.[32] The Conservative-dominated committee called nine witnesses, including Lloyd, Robbie, Alexa's cousin Allan, the current president of L.E. Shaw Ltd., and Rae Austin, the executive director of the Nova Scotia Housing Commission at the time the land was sold. Peter McDonough acted as the Shaws' lawyer for the hearings.

The concrete facts turned out to be far different from MacEwan's patchwork of allegation and assumption. According to Allan Shaw, Clayton Developments bought four different Millwood properties between 1973 and early 1974 to create a 434-acre land assembly in Sackville. The intention "was to develop a planned residential community." But by 1975, a "rapidly changing housing market" convinced the company to rethink its plans, focus on increasing investment in some of its other properties and sell Millwood. Robbie, then Clayton's president, negotiated the deal with Austin and, on December 15, 1975, the housing commission purchased the development-ready land for $1,505,772. After the company's investment in preparing the properties for development, Allan Shaw said the company's actual profit was just $196,530, "*before* taxes and without any assignment of overhead," a tenth of what MacEwan claimed. Robbie, who left the company to become Regan's principal secretary soon after the sale, testified there'd been no political pressure brought to bear in the negotiation or sale. Lloyd Shaw testified he was still the CEO of L.E. Shaw Ltd. at the time and there'd been "no overlap" between negotiations over the land sale and Robbie's negotiations with the premier's office. Both Lloyd and Robbie challenged MacEwan to repeat his charges outside the legislature so he could be sued. He didn't.

In fact, outside the hearings, MacEwan admitted to reporters he was "carrying on a campaign to discredit Alexa McDonough, but said it was only in retaliation for his treatment at the hands of the NDP when he was kicked out of the party two years ago...."[33] "It stands to reason that, after what they did to me, I would not stand idly by."[34]

After a series of highly charged, often obstreperous hearings that produced nothing of substance, Fraser Mooney, a Liberal member of the committee, finally introduced a motion to bring it to an end by thanking the witnesses and concluding that "based upon the evidence, the committee could find no fault in this particular matter." But Tory committee member Ron Russell tacked on an amendment to delete the section of the motion finding no fault and simply thank the witnesses. The four Conservative members of the committee, along with MacEwan, then voted in favour of the amended motion while the two Liberals voted against.

Paul MacEwan was free to continue his vendetta. And he did.

But if MacEwan expected his daily vilifications would bring Alexa, weeping, to her knees, he had clearly misunderstood her. As had any Tories who imagined she might be diverted from calling them to account. Harry Bruce catalogued some of the many issues Alexa raised during her first session as an MLA:

> First, she...flew into Premier John Buchanan not only for
> uttering "double-talk" that was undermining the Sydney steel
> plant but also for his "unholy engagement of convenience" with
> Trudeau on "the ruinous restraint program." She lambasted
> Labour Minister Jack MacIsaac for "his hypocritical and
> patronizing [Labour Day] message to working people," tens of
> thousands of whom could not find work. She ripped Attorney
> General Harry How for "cutting out the heart of the legal aid
> system." When Lands and Forests Minister George Henley
> smeared environmentalists who opposed herbicide spraying
> as "subversive elements," she denounced his "intemperate,
> ill-considered and idiotic" comments. She was no kinder to
> Liberals. Choosing between Grits and Tories was choosing
> between "yellow fever and smallpox."[35]

That was her public persona. In private, of course, it took its toll. "Literally, it made me sick to my stomach to talk to the member for Cape Breton Nova," Alexa would recall years later, this time using the parliamentary proper reference for her nemesis. "During that first legislature session, I would come home, beside myself." She paused, thought for a while. "But I never once considered walking away. And I would never cry. I would not give him the satisfaction."

Her only sort-of escape that winter and spring came with occasional between-sittings dinners with Peter. While their housekeeper fed the boys, Peter would walk from his downtown law office to the legislature to meet Alexa. They'd cross the street to the Carleton Hotel, find a quiet table in the back of the restaurant and have dinner together. They tried to focus on happier topics, but rarely could. Most of the time, Alexa vented. Peter listened and commiserated. And then walked her back for the evening session in the legislative lion's den before returning home to be with their boys.

"I'd get totally annoyed, angry," Peter would remember. "I didn't think they had any cause to treat her the way they did." But there also seemed little he could do or say except be there to listen. His own law firm was "not exactly a hotbed of NDPism," he joked at the time, so he had to appear at least "somewhat apolitical." And, though his own political views still tended Liberal and he wasn't personally close with any of Alexa's NDP co-workers and friends, "I've learned to admire what I've been exposed to in the NDP," he told the writer Harry Bruce. "They're in it because they believe in it, not because they expect something out of it. After all, there aren't too many NDP senators, are there?"

By the time the legislature's spring session sputtered to a close on a Saturday morning in late June 1982, eighty-six gruelling sitting days later, Alexa McDonough was no longer a legislative neophyte. She was a weathered veteran of Nova Scotia's political wars. And she was ready for more.[36]

Given her belief in her own and her party's future, a trait she'd clearly inherited from her father, it is possible to imagine Alexa reading the last lines of Harry Bruce's glowing profile of her in *Atlantic Insight* and smiling in agreement. "It is possible to believe," Bruce wrote, "that the cause of her misery in the legislature stemmed from a recognition among Grits and Tories that this unsettling woman, with her strong, even features and blue eyes that glitter with force and intelligence, was potentially dangerous."

4

"You know my father," the woman at the other end of the telephone explained to Brenda Taylor. "My father told me he thinks you're one of us." The woman asked if they could meet. The woman doing the calling was Alexa McDonough.

Alexa's father had been wrong about one thing. Plain-spoken Brenda Taylor was not a New Democrat—not yet. In fact, she was no fan of politicians of any stripe, whom she had long ago concluded spoke a language called "doublespeak" and inevitably were more interested in their "own ego brand recognition" than in doing good for people. That said, Taylor did know and like Alexa's father, Lloyd. Lloyd was on the board of the local branch of the Council of Christians and Jews (CCJ), originally a British-based volunteer group set up during the Second World War to counter anti-Semitism and other forms of intolerance. Taylor was the council's Atlantic region executive director.

A few weeks before, Peter Herschorn, a local hotelier also on the CCJ board, invited Taylor to lunch at his Lord Nelson Hotel. Lloyd Shaw was his other guest. They'd chatted about matters of current public interest, including the case of a young Indigenous man named Donald Marshall Jr., who'd been imprisoned for eleven years for a murder he claimed he didn't commit.

Taylor knew far more about the case than most Nova Scotians. Her partner, Jack Stewart, was the "streetwise" superintendent of Carleton House, the Halifax halfway house where Marshall, finally on parole, was a resident while the justice system decided his legal fate. Stewart had developed close relationships with Marshall and Stephen Aronson, the young Halifax lawyer working to win Marshall's vindication. Although Taylor couldn't say much about the evidence she'd seen and heard, she said enough that Lloyd, still one of Alexa's closest advisors, alerted his daughter that Brenda Taylor was someone she should seek out.

The still unfolding and mostly unknown story of how a racist, law-for-the-rich, law-for-the-rest Nova Scotia justice system had failed Donald Marshall was one among many controversial cases and causes then piling up on Alexa's NDP desk. There was also, for example, the case of the twenty-three school bus drivers in Digby in southwestern Nova Scotia who'd been on strike against their local school board since before Alexa made her first failed bid for Parliament in 1979. The strikers had little support even among their neighbours in anti-union Digby. "It makes us sad to say it, but no, the town hasn't really been split over this thing," the local union president told the *Globe and Mail*. "Almost from the beginning, most people have been for the school board.... They still think unions are communist-backed."[37]

By the time Alexa took her seat in the legislature in 1982, the bitter wage dispute — the Digby drivers earned one-third less than drivers in a neighbouring county — had the distinction of being the longest strike in Nova Scotia history.

Two months after the walkout began, the Nova Scotia labour relations board found the school board guilty of unfair labour practices and ordered it back to the negotiating table. The school board ignored that order, along with subsequent recommendations of a provincial judicial inquiry, another labour relations board ruling that the board had acted in bad faith, and even contempt citations against two school board members. Instead, the school board hired replacement drivers and began an expensive legal campaign to avoid dealing with the Canadian Union of Public Employees.

Because the provincial government not only appointed three members to the Digby school board but also footed 83 per cent of its annual budget, including its lawyers' fees, Alexa introduced a bill to legislate an end to the strike and amend the trade union act to make sure school boards couldn't flout rulings by provincial tribunals in future. The government easily defeated her motion.[38]

Then, too, there was the case of Bruce Curtis, a Nova Scotia teenager convicted of murder in New Jersey. In late June 1982, Bruce had travelled to New Jersey to visit Scott Franz, a schoolmate from King's-Edgehill, the Nova Scotia private school they both attended. On the morning of July 5, Scott got into an argument with his stepfather — who had previously fired a gun at Scott — and the young man shot and killed his stepfather. "Hearing the shot, Curtis, carrying a rifle, ran down a narrow hallway toward the door where he ran into Rosemary Podgis, Franz' mother," the trial heard. "Curtis's lawyers said he accidentally shot her. The prosecutor said the shooting was intentional."[39]

Scott Franz, who pleaded guilty to first-degree murder, received the minimum twenty-year sentence. Bruce, who had no criminal record as well as "outstanding character references," was sentenced to the *maximum* twenty years in prison on the lesser charge of aggravated manslaughter. According to Bruce's lawyer, who described the outcome as a "legal lynching," Scott had made a deal for a lesser sentence by offering to lie about Bruce's role in the murders at his trial.

The case touched off a media firestorm in Canada where Bruce's parents launched a national appeal to have his sentence reduced, or a new trial ordered.[40] Support committees sprang up across the county. Jennifer Wade, a British Columbia human rights advocate who helped coordinate the effort, wrote scores of letters to politicians across the country. "She received only one immediate and personal reply." That came from Alexa McDonough, who telephoned to invite Wade to meet with her at her office in Halifax.

The case had left Alexa "with two impressions." She was the mother of two now teenaged sons who "had been raised in a protective, supportive family environment far removed from domestic strife, and they were often billeted in homes in Canada and the United States while attending tennis tournaments. Her heart had stopped . . . when she considered how easily either of her sons could have found themselves in a similar predicament." At the same time, she understood she'd have difficulty getting the Buchanan government to make a stand. They "could easily blunt a frontal assault by asking, correctly, what on earth a provincial government could do about a foreign affairs dilemma." Still, she agreed to Wade's request to raise the issue in the legislature and to write a letter to Bruce's parents "to let them know one of the province's political leaders cared about their son."[41]

But then, to Wade's surprise and delight, she offered to do more. Because Wade worried Bruce's original New Jersey lawyer was a "nice guy but a wimpy guy," Alexa picked up the telephone and called her cousin, Eric Shaw, Pop Shaw's son, now a corporate lawyer in New York, to ask his advice. Shaw contacted a friend from Harvard, a high-powered and expensive criminal lawyer in Manhattan, who agreed to take on Bruce's case for the same fee his current lawyer was charging.[42]

But the most controversial, and ultimately historic, case on Alexa's personal docket of lost causes was the Donald Marshall Jr. wrongful conviction case. When Alexa called Brenda Taylor in the spring of 1982, the specifics of what really happened and why were still murky and muddied by controversy.

This much was known.[43] In 1971, Marshall, then only seventeen, had been convicted of murdering a young Black friend named Sandy Seale in a Sydney park and sentenced to life in prison. Because he insisted on his innocence, Marshall was never granted parole and so had rotted in prison for eleven years. Finally, in early 1982, the RCMP agreed to reinvestigate. They quickly realized key prosecution witnesses had lied. Some claimed Sydney police coerced them to make up stories to convict Marshall. Investigators discovered another man, Roy Ebsary, had confessed to acquaintances he was the murderer, and they had even found the knife used to kill Seale in Ebsary's former apartment.

With that new evidence in hand, Marshall's lawyer convinced the parole board to release him to the halfway house while the courts reconsidered his conviction. On May 1, 1983, the Supreme Court of Nova Scotia officially acquitted Marshall of the murder but also absolved the Sydney police and Crown prosecutors of any blame. Instead, they claimed, without citing any credible evidence, Marshall had been planning to rob Ebsary so "any miscarriage of justice is more apparent than real." That, of course, touched off even more controversy as Ottawa and Nova Scotia sparred over whether Marshall actually deserved compensation, how much, and who should pay.

While all this was going on, Alexa had been quietly working behind the scenes with Jack Stewart and Marshall's new lawyer, Felix Cacchione,[44] to pressure the Buchanan government to deal fairly with Marshall and to appoint a royal commission to investigate the miscarriage of justice. She also reached out to Marshall in a personal, handwritten letter. "I have been very concerned about the horror, *for you*, of the continuing public spectacle of politicians trying to score political points at your expense on the one hand, and doing so little to help you get on with your own life on the other hand," she wrote. "The very last thing I would ever want to do would be to participate in that public spectacle for political gain. And yet I have also recognized the urgency of putting political pressure on the government once it became clear they weren't going to move without it.... If I were you," she added, "I'm sure I would want everyone to leave me alone and let me live in peace." She promised to respect his wishes, whatever they were, but added that he could give her a call "at home or at the office at any time if you'd like to get together."

He did. Alexa soon became, as she so often did in such circumstances, a friend as well as an advocate.

When the *Royal Commission on the Donald Marshall, Jr., Prosecution* published its final report in 1989, Nova Scotia's political and judicial systems had been undressed in public. The commission concluded the system "failed Donald Marshall, Jr., at virtually every turn from his arrest and conviction for murder in 1971 up to, and beyond, his acquittal by the Court of Appeal in 1983." Worse, the commission concluded there were two systems of justice in Nova Scotia—one for minorities and the poor, people like Marshall, and another for the well-to-do and well-connected people like Alexa's fellow MLAs. The report cited the cases of Roland Thornhill, who'd been publicly cleared by the Attorney General in connection with a sweet deal he'd received to settle his debts with four banks, even though the RCMP recommended he be charged, and Billy Joe MacLean, whose forged MLA expense claims senior justice department officials excused as "accounting irregularities."[45]

All that was still far in the future when Alexa first contacted Brenda Taylor. Taylor's initial meeting with Alexa became the first of many—"We'd get together three or four times a month"—and the conversations quickly expanded to include Mary Morison, Alexa's chief of staff, and Pamela Whelan, a Newfoundlander who'd recently been hired as Alexa's administrative assistant. There was no hierarchy and no distinction between Alexa and her staff, or guests. "It was just, 'What do you think of this?'" Taylor remembered. "I loved being part of all these discussions with such intelligent, passionate people. It was so pleasant, knowing she cared about all these issues. And she'd always tell me how gracious I was being with *my* time."

Taylor changed her mind, too, about politicians. Or at least one of them. "Alexa was different," she said many years later. "She was a genuinely ethical human being, the only politician I ever met in whom I had complete faith."

And, oh yes, like many others who found themselves in her orbit, Taylor, too, became a supporter of the New Democratic Party.

5

"The honourable member for Halifax Chebucto," intoned the Speaker.

It was the afternoon of Wednesday, March 30, 1983, and opposition MLAs were in the midst of introducing a series of notices of motions of resolutions and house orders. Most of the time, the resolutions were tabled. A few might eventually be debated; most just disappeared into the pages of Hansard, never to be spoken of again.

Resolution 120 was to be very different. "Mr. Speaker," Alexa began, "I hereby give notice that on a future day I shall move adoption of the following resolution:

Whereas members of this House are paid in advance for sitting on committees; and whereas none of the Liberal members of the Human Resources Committee were present at today's meeting.... Therefore, be it resolved that all members of this House take seriously their committee responsibilities rather than appearing to be indifferent to the committee system."

Cape Breton Liberal Vince MacLean jumped to his feet, declaring his party "would only be too pleased to waive notice and [immediately] debate that resolution." The request required unanimous consent. Consent given.

The fact was Alexa's fellow legislators had been spoiling for this fight since before the House opened. During her first legislative session the year before, Alexa had discovered the politicians' dirty little secret: for years, MLAs had quietly topped up their official $28,000 salaries with committee fees that added an average of $9,000 more to their pay packets. Under the system, "unique in Canada [and] devoid of logic," as Parker Donham noted in a column, members received extra pay—from $1,500 to $3,000—for each committee they sat on, whether they attended the meetings, whether the committee even met. There were twenty-four such committees, most with ten or more members.

When Alexa, who earned $8,700 for her committee assignments, understood exactly how the system worked, "or, I might say more accurately, malfunctioned," she privately took her concerns to an "independent" commission, whose members included a former Liberal cabinet minister who was now a judge. The commission had been set up to make "binding" recommendations on MLA pay. But when Alexa discovered the commission "chose not to deal" with her concerns," she began looking for other ways to raise them, both privately and publicly.

Earlier that day, she'd written to the chair of the human resources committee to complain about the failure of other members to show up for its meeting. She had been "appalled," she said, to learn the committee had to cancel four meetings the previous session because of the lack of a quorum. During the entire legislature session, there had been only one nineteen-minute committee meeting, which had cost taxpayers $15,000 in committee fees. "It seems to me, Mr. Speaker, that it has to be recognized that the present system is wide open to this kind of inefficiency and wide open to abuse."

Her fellow MLAs were not amused. "For two-and-a-half uninterrupted hours," provincially syndicated columnist Parker Donham reported in the *Kentville Advertiser*, "the fifty-one male members of the legislature—Liberals, Tories and Labour—heaped scorn on McDonough with an air of personal rancor rare even in this acrimonious forum."[46]

They claimed she was playing to the press. The CBC TV program *Inquiry*, they noted, had scheduled a segment on the committee system for later that night. It included an interview with Alexa. They argued they were underpaid and that committee fees were simply a reasonable way to bring their incomes closer to elected officials in other provinces, without explaining, of course, why those fees needed to be kept secret. And they accused Alexa of attacking them personally—while attacking her personally for having been born with "a silver spoon in her mouth." As McDonough herself put it, "they thought only a little rich kid could be a spoilsport like that."[47]

"Not only am I hurt, but I am angered," declared Tory MLA Malcolm MacKay. "But I do not really get emotionally angered when it is somebody from the opposite sex that is chastising me.... I better be careful what I say now because I consider myself to be a gentleman." Looking at Alexa, he added, to laughter from his colleagues, "I would not feel comfortable holding you up by the scruff of the neck."[48]

Alexa's nemesis, Paul MacEwan, was delighted. "This afternoon's discussion, Mr. Speaker, comes as close as I have seen, in my thirteen years in this House, to the censure of a member of the House, without the act of censure being specifically so stated."

The reason for the vituperation seemed obvious. "McDonough had broken the code of silence that shrouds the perks of legislative life," Donham wrote. "She violated the rules of the old boys' club, and so she was punished.... The anger McDonough aroused with this issue proves only that she touched a raw nerve. MLAs have been caught at a sleazy bit of deception, and they know it."

It had been another good week, not to mention a much better legislative session for Alexa, who'd begun to master the ways and wiles of the House of Assembly. She'd learned from her first session as an MLA when, as she admitted to Canadian Press reporter Elaine McCluskey, she'd sometimes come off as "sanctimonious and holier-than-thou. I worked so hard at distancing myself from the old boys' club that I made it hard for anyone to be even slightly friendly."[49]

Years later, in a conversation with journalist Sharon Fraser, she tried to put her approach in context. "I was really driven by the notion that I had to be strong, that I couldn't appear to be weak in the face of these fifty-one male adversaries," she explained, adding, "I think it wouldn't have taken such a toll on me if I had learned to...depend upon more people for emotional support.... But when people say, 'Oh come on now, lighten up,' they don't understand the passion that I feel about the issues, the passion that fuels my involvement."

That passion, leavened at least slightly by what she'd absorbed in her first session as MLA, helped her in her second session, she told McCluskey. "I sort of feel that I have my feet on the ground and some little bit of confidence about being able to stand on my own."

The key now was to keep pushing, keep the pressure on the government and the opposition. Which was what brought her back to the NDP's downtown office on Saturday, April 2, 1983, to plan strategy for the next week in the House.

One moment, Alexa would remember years later, she was standing in her office talking to a member of her staff. The next moment, "I passed out cold."

•

At first, doctors at the Victoria General Hospital believed she was suffering from a simple sinus infection. They examined and then discharged her, advising her to take it easy for a few days. Easier said than done, of course, for a one-person political party in the middle of a hectic legislature session. A week later, she was back at the hospital, complaining now of horrific headaches, and it soon became clear this was not just a simple sinus infection. But what was it? She was admitted.

During her first days in the hospital, Alexa would dictate daily news releases and open letters to government officials from her bed. In one letter that attracted national attention, she called on Premier Buchanan to demand curmudgeonly Attorney General Harry How's resignation for having written a dismissive letter to the Indo-Canadian Association of Nova Scotia. How defended Acadia University's decision not to hire Dr. M.K. Jain as the college librarian. "Many of those kind of people," he complained, "frequently write a letter to politicians complaining of discrimination when they're passed over for a job. . . . Other things being equal," he added, "we ought to give native Canadians a preference" in hiring at publicly funded universities. But Jain was, in fact, a Canadian. Buchanan attempted to argue the letter—on government stationery—was just How's personal opinion. But the point had been scored.

But as Alexa's condition worsened and her concentration waned, the party began designating surrogates to speak on specific issues. It rarely worked. Ray Larkin, a lawyer and the NDP spokesperson on labour and economics issues, understood the problem. "We're not quite as glamorous," he told the *Globe and Mail*.[50]

Meanwhile, there were tests and more tests. Alexa's hospital days turned into weeks, the weeks approached a month. Alexa lost weight, became eerily silent, and seemed "totally traumatized," recalled her brother Robbie, who visited her every day. "There were no tears, no 'woe is me.' But I knew she was in really bad shape. She looked, spoke, and acted as if she might die. . . . I *thought* she was going to die."

Finally, Dr. T.J. "Jock" Murray, the chief neurologist at Halifax's Victoria General Hospital, took charge. After examining her, he contacted colleagues at University Hospital in London, Ontario, where more sophisticated testing was available to confirm his suspicions.

While that was being organized, Alexa, eager to make clear she was still functioning, organized a hospital-bed news conference for the afternoon of May 8, 1983. Instead, her condition worsened that morning, the news conference was abruptly cancelled, Peter and the boys were called, and Alexa found herself being bundled into an air ambulance for an emergency flight to London with Peter at her side. "I remember saying goodbye to my kids and not knowing if I would see them again," Alexa said years later. "It was really scary, not knowing what it was."

Rumours that Alexa might actually die sparked a variety of heartfelt responses across the province. In Cape Breton, John Arthur Murphy and his wife, Dr. Lindsay Myers, long-time NDP supporters, named their newborn daughter Lindsay Alexa after the NDP leader. A union made plans to plant a magnolia tree in her honour at Conrose Field near the McDonough house. In the provincial legislature, members pressed pause on their usual partisan rancour long enough to unanimously approve a get-well resolution. "Whereas while members of this House may disagree, even profoundly, on political matters," it began, "when it comes to health, surely none of us would wish ill to one another. Resolved that this House asks Mr. Speaker to convey to the member for Halifax Chebucto all of our sincere wishes for a speedy and successful recovery." The resolution had been introduced by none other than Paul MacEwan.

Luckily, it didn't take doctors in London long to diagnose—and begin to treat—what ailed Alexa McDonough. She had an intra-cranial infection, a brain infection probably brought on by sinusitis that had caused her brain to swell. It could easily have been fatal. That diagnosis notwithstanding, it was hard not to acknowledge there might also be truth in Alexa's own later assessment. "I just literally burned myself out, physically, mentally, and emotionally, and I was unable to fight back when I got sick."[51]

She returned home a week later, on May 16, to rest and recuperate, returning to work, in the words of a party press release, "as her health permits." But, just two weeks later—having missed seven weeks of the spring session—she was back in her seat in the legislature. She rose "reluctantly," as she put it, "trying to obey doctor's orders and make a slow re-entry," in order to participate in a debate on the government's new Canada-Nova Scotia Oil and Gas Agreement Act, which she complained was "virtually substance-less" and "will confirm the worst fears of Nova Scotians about the whole way in which this government has been approaching the handling of offshore development matters."

Alexa McDonough was back in the business of making life uncomfortable for John Buchanan's government.

6

It was 4:23 on Monday morning, December 5, 1983, and an angry Alexa McDonough was in the middle of composing a scorching single-spaced, two-and-a-half-page missile of a rebuke aimed directly at Rod Dickinson, the

NDP's provincial secretary. "I'm frustrated, aggravated and frankly puzzled about what appears to be a total lack of follow through on your part," she declared.

The issue was a plan to recover NDP support in industrial Cape Breton in the lead-up to the next provincial election by taking "a more aggressive and more effective approach" to mobilize key supporters there. Waving off Alexa's offer to help, Dickinson had not only winnowed the number of key players to contact down to one — the party's Cape Breton vice-president Helen MacDonald — but he also insisted he be the one to contact her because, as Alexa summarized, "it was appropriate to your role as provincial secretary and because this would convey the important nature of the exercise." Instead, Alexa wrote, Dickinson had reported back to a table officers' meeting that Sunday that he "phoned Helen once and, when her line was busy, you just forgot about it. . . . I'm in a state of utter dismay to try to understand your casual explanation."

Despite her Pollyanna public image, which was a genuine reflection of how she related to most people most of the time, Alexa McDonough could also be a hard-nosed and demanding boss. Her saving grace, and one of the reasons she inspired heartfelt and usually lifetime loyalty, was that she was even more demanding of herself. She began most days at 7:30 a.m., "slowly getting up," as she put it, and then headed off to the party's downtown office for a day filled with meetings, telephone calls, speech writing, researching, meetings, and more meetings. During legislature sessions, of course, she spent most afternoons and some nights in the House of Assembly. Although she tried her best to be home for dinner with Peter and the boys, she usually spent at least a couple of nights a week on the road. While the family used to spend summer weeks hanging out at their log cabin in Chester, she conceded to *Chatelaine* they'd "stayed there only three nights" in the summer of 1983. Her daily goal was to be home in bed by 12:30 or 1:00 a.m., but there were often nights, like this one in December, when she was unable to banish work from her mind long enough to fall asleep.[52]

All the mountains she had set out to scale were Everests. Her day (and night) job as the member of the legislature representing and responding to the usual-to-urgent concerns of residents of her Halifax Chebucto riding could, by itself, have occupied more than anyone's full time. But since she was the NDP's only member in the provincial legislature, she also had to be its singular voice for the concerns of the rest of the 18 per cent of Nova Scotians who had voted for her party. As a caucus of one, she had to make herself expert and critic on the doings of every provincial government department from finance to fishery, not to forget keeping tabs on an alphabet soup of provincial boards and agencies, all of which made decisions, often behind doors they preferred to keep closed.

Then, too, as the leader and public face of a provincial political party whose outsized ambition was to form a government one day, Alexa had to spend inordinate hours on the road, often driving herself across the province just to speak to some group or other whose members might someday, or never, support the NDP. "Our guest speaker this week was Mrs. Alexa McDonough," reported the Truro Rotary Club's *Weekly Spokesman* on February 16, 1982. Describing the leader of a provincial political party as a "charming and capable young lady," the newsletter then noted, without explanation, that "a lively question-and-answer period" had followed Alexa's talk, zeroing in on such NDP-unfriendly topics as the "right to strike in essential services . . . and the strong lobby to remove rent review legislation."

Alexa had already become more than just another provincial politician. She was such a popular public figure her presence was now considered *de rigueur* at feminist events across the country. During the 1984 federal election campaign, for example, she travelled across the country, popping in on a gathering of single mothers in Toronto's Regent Park, and then flying to Vancouver to serve as the star attraction at a mainstreeting event for three female NDP candidates.

She attempted to do all this with a bare-bones, over-worked staff who did double duty supporting both the provincial party and also its legislative caucus of one.

Dickinson — the object of Alexa's middle-of-the-night ire — was a former special assistant to Saskatchewan premier Allan Blakeney. He'd been brought in to run the Nova Scotia party and build its organizational strength for the next provincial campaign. Alexa's criticism notwithstanding, Dickinson was a go-to campaign manager/fundraiser for New Democratic provincial parties fighting elections all over Canada.[53]

Mary Morison, who'd recently moved to Halifax, where her husband was doing his surgery residency, had become Alexa's de facto caucus office — chief of staff, primary policy adviser, researcher, and friend. Serena Renner, the party's former provincial secretary who'd quit in frustration over the MacEwan mess, had returned to take control of Alexa's constituency caseload. Pam Whelan, who'd just moved to Halifax with her young family, was hired as an administrative assistant for the duration of a maternity leave but made herself indispensable. So too did Mary Jane White, a Maritime School of Social Work student who began as an intern — students eagerly competed to intern for a progressive woman in an office made up mostly of women — and soon became another key figure.

But Alexa, recalled Morison, was always, inevitably, at the centre of it all. "She would write back to every single person who wrote to her." When a group of high school students, members of an anti-abortion group, wrote her letters criticizing her position on the issue, she replied to each one individually. "She insisted." Staff tried to convince her to use form letters to reply to at least the routine correspondence. "Nothing doing." She would endlessly revise and rewrite every speech anyone had prepared for her, liberally scrawling notes and corrections on every page. And, of course, added Morison, "She would see and talk to everyone who asked to see her. She was tireless. She wore us all out."

And she was not without successes, even within the unfriendly confines of the legislature. "The NDP pushed to effectively ban extra-billing by Nova Scotia doctors, to retain rent review, to strengthen tenants' rights and to put teeth in the provincial labor relations board," noted the *Globe and Mail*. "'It astounds me,'" Alexa told Michael Harris, "'what we've been able to accomplish just by virtue of having one crummy little member in the provincial Legislature.'"[54]

And she was eager to accomplish even more — by getting more New Democrats into the legislature, including, she hoped, by winning back traditional supporters in Cape Breton. That was the real reason for her pre-dawn outburst that December morning. Many NDPers, "myself included," had come to believe Cape Breton "does not occupy any priority claim on your time and the party's resources," she wrote. "That would be a disaster for both our long-term and short-term prospects in this province. Please, please, please. Can we try to come to terms with these concerns?"

7

There was no good reason for John Buchanan to call an election in the fall of 1984. His PC government was barely three years into its second electoral mandate. The Tories held thirty-eight of the legislature's fifty-two seats and could be assured of passing whatever legislation they put forward. There were no new pressing issues that required them to seek a fresh mandate. There was, instead, opportunity. The Liberals, under lacklustre leader Sandy Cameron, were in disarray. Paul MacEwan planned to run a full slate of his fledgling Cape Breton Labour Party candidates on the island, making it unlikely the NDP could wrest back any of its former seats, even perhaps creating an opportunity for Tory candidates to squeeze their way to victory in four-way races. Some Tory strategists even hoped that, with the right female candidate of their own and a parade of cabinet ministers and outside Tory stars showing up in Chebucto, they could also write an end to the political career of Alexa McDonough.

And so, less than four weeks after Brian Mulroney's Progressive Conservatives swept into power in Ottawa with a landslide victory, Buchanan announced Nova Scotians would head to the polls on November 6, 1984.

"I don't believe elections should be fought on issues," an upbeat Buchanan told reporters. "Elections should be fought on the basis of asking for a new mandate to carry out the policies of a government." If there was substance to the "thin political soup" of his election plan, suggested the *Globe and Mail*, "it is the promise of renewed prosperity, based on federal and provincial Tory governments scratching each other's back to the benefit of all." His campaign would be "based on Mr. Buchanan's tried and true political style—a good-times, promise-free approach that shrinks from debate of issues and offers instead a substantial slice of pie in the sky to potential supporters."[55]

There were issues to discuss. Since Buchanan became premier in 1978, Nova Scotia's net direct debt had more than quadrupled to $2.3 billion while its credit rating had slipped. Recession hit with a vengeance.[56] In the year leading up to the election, the government increased electricity rates by 35 per cent. The promise of offshore oil and gas, which had been the pot of gold at the end of the political rainbow since Gerald Regan's first term more than a decade earlier, remained as elusive as ever.

There were issues the NDP, in particular, should have been able to exploit: the reality that 50,000 Nova Scotians were unemployed; the fact the government had waited until the day after the legislature stopped sitting to quietly hand out permits to multinational companies to spray provincial woodlands with controversial herbicides; and the truth a public inquiry into uranium mining the Buchanan government had been forced to appoint that had disappeared so far underground "it would take a Geiger counter to find."

And yet... none of the premier's political opponents, including Alexa McDonough, seemed able to even muss his hair. *Globe and Mail* columnist George Bain marvelled, "John Buchanan has been able to get away with campaigning as if his highest purpose was to demonstrate that butter wouldn't melt in his mouth."[57]

Alexa wanted to run a real province-wide campaign in 1984, Pam Whelan recalled, but everyone understood prospects were "pretty bleak, especially in Cape Breton." It was a "shoestring campaign." Instead of renting a van or even a car for the leader's tour, volunteers drove Alexa's car. Instead of booking rooms in hotels for the end of the day, she "slept around," joked Whelan. "It was a sofa-surfing campaign."

Alexa herself was even publicly pessimistic, or at least realistic. "As skeptical as people are about the Tories, I don't think there's any headlong rush to sweep in slumbering Sandy [Cameron, the Liberal leader] and the docile dozen," she told the *Globe and Mail*. "I think, frankly, and I know I've been criticized for my ineptness in saying it, we in the NDP are not in what you'd call a winning position either. The fact is that, barring a miracle, John Buchanan will blue-sky his way through yet another provincial election and remain Premier after November 6."[58]

Behind the scenes, however, the party had quietly identified half a dozen seats — based on the results of the 1981 election and the quality of their own local candidates — where they thought they had a chance of winning. Polling narrowed that to just four: King's South, where legal aid lawyer Bob Levy had come second the last time around; Halifax Citadel, where a dynamic schoolteacher named Eileen O'Connell had agreed to run; Sackville, where John Holm, another schoolteacher and community activist, was making his second run for the party; and, of course, Chebucto, where Alexa was in a tougher race than expected.

While Alexa spent as much time as possible campaigning in those other possibly winnable seats, Buchanan, hoping to capitalize on the recent federal Tory wave, "personally [led] a celebrity blitz in the NDP leader's home riding, in an effort to win the seat for another woman, Conservative Helen Gillis," noted the *Globe and Mail's* Michael Harris.

"Buchanan has me running scared, you know," Alexa confided. "Every time I turn around, there's either a Tory cabinet minister from Ottawa or Nova Scotia in the riding, and I guess I see it as important for me to have as much contact with the voters as possible." But that, of course, only made it more difficult for her to campaign—and for her to be seen campaigning—provincially. "Frankly, one of the things that unnerves me a little bit is that we did make fairly dramatic gains in the last election in the face of pretty overwhelming odds and some pretty awful setbacks in industrial Cape Breton," she explained. "So, you know, I worry about how much energy, beyond hanging on to those gains, we've got to give it to make additional gains."[59]

By keeping expectations low, Alexa could minimize day-after disappointment.

8

Even though the NDP again finished third in a three-party race, Julian Beltrame of Southam News reported many observers considered them the election's "unofficial winner.... The hybrid creation known as the Alexa McDonough Party has yet to stop celebrating its 'victory,'" he wrote. "Days after the province's New Democratic Party produced its best electoral showing in years, flowers were still being delivered to the fourth-floor office of its bright, dynamic leader."[60]

The New Democrats had tripled their seat count, from just one to three, painting NDP orange on King's South (Bob Levy) and Sackville (John Holm). The numbers alone might not have seemed significant but, for Alexa, "the difference between one and three is the difference between heaven and hell."[61] Meanwhile, the Liberals, under Sandy Cameron, had seen their numbers cut in half, from a dozen seats to six. The NDP had also run second in almost every key metropolitan Halifax seat it hadn't won, but the province-wide reality was that its percentage of the overall popular vote had dropped by 2 per cent from the 1981 election. Paul MacEwan's freshly minted Cape Breton Labour Party (CBLP) had run in all island seats, and siphoned votes from NDP candidates. Despite this, MacEwan had been the only CBLP member elected and his so-called party managed to attract an anemic 2 per cent of the popular vote. But the larger, inescapable reality was that John Buchanan's Progressive Conservatives were still firmly in power, having won a 14 per cent increase in voter support and, for the next four years, a choke-hold majority of forty-two seats in the fifty-two-MLA legislature.

Alexa McDonough imagined her glass half-full and getting fuller. And there was something to that view. She had begun to reshape the party in her own image, attracting a new generation of young urban professional voters who had never before considered voting NDP.

Nancy Bowes, a come-from-away recently arrived with her husband from the West Coast, was one. She signed up for NDP membership partly because she was "intrigued" by the fact the party had a woman leader and partly because the person who called to invite her to join showed up at her door ten minutes later with her card. During her South End Halifax constituency's next annual general meeting, she volunteered to be the "women's rights rep." Soon after, Alexa invited Bowes and the other local women's rights representatives to a weekend at Shaw Island to "meet each other." Alexa, "was charming and energetic and friendly. It felt like there was no distinction between her and us." When it was over, Alexa drove Nancy back to Halifax.

"I was always impressed by how smart and articulate Alexa was," added Michael Kirby, a Liberal pollster and later federal senator. "She was an NDPer but not what a lot of people, especially in Nova Scotia, thought of as an extreme NDPer. In Nova Scotia, the 'alternative' to the Liberals had always been the Tories, and vice versa. She began to change that." Although the NDP label would continue to act as an anchor on her personal popularity, Kirby's polling in the mid-1980s showed that if she'd been leading a different party, "she would be way ahead—like way ahead—of any of her rivals. She could have been premier."

Alexa needed to broaden her party's tent. She did that, in part, by focusing on policy—and the ways in which policy gets made. Her own hard-won experience inside the House of Assembly convinced her it was "not a game worth playing." What was worth the effort was getting more people involved in making policy. "The more people who get involved, the faster we'll get on with the job."[62]

She blessed an economic policy development scheme concocted by Ray Larkin, a young Halifax lawyer with deep connections in the labour movement, and Rick Williams, a left-leaning economist who'd recently returned to Nova Scotia to take over Alexa's former job at the Maritime School of Social Work. Although both men were to the left of McDonough, they made the case to her that the party, as Larkin put it, "would never be taken seriously until we could figure out a way to deal with jobs and the economy. Otherwise, we'll always just be this small party fighting for social justice."

McDonough listened. "Economics was never Alexa's area of comfort," Williams acknowledged. But she also knew the party's potential to grow would be hobbled if voters didn't believe her party could be credible on the issues of creating jobs and building the economy.

What particularly appealed to McDonough about the Larkin-Williams' proposal was the way in which they wanted to go about developing policy. "The idea," explained Williams, "is that you don't get two or three experts who come up with policy you then present to the group, but that everyone becomes part of a process of discovery. She was hugely supportive in the background. She was respectful of the process and made no attempt to control it. She let us go and let it happen."

In the end, it consumed more than two years of issue papers, ongoing discussion, and vigorous debate involving close to four hundred Nova Scotians. The participants came from all over the province and, essential for a party trying to grow its base, included more than traditional New Democrats. "We went out of our way to make sure we were bringing in people who may not have been party activists but who were interested in the issues," Williams explained.

After a large-group conference to lay out the various issues and options, participants broke into smaller regional study groups to hammer out specific proposals before reporting back to another plenary, an August 1985 conference at Mount Saint Vincent University, where the delegates finally agreed on a "set of principles" for economic development.

The result wasn't what Larkin or Williams expected. "Ray and I used to refer to each other as the Stalinists," Williams joked. They assumed the process would lead to support for large-scale development projects and greater public ownership of industry, "but the outcome was exactly the opposite." Perhaps because Nova Scotians had been burned by decades of failed mega projects and government involvement and ownership of failing and failed ventures in steel and coal, there was a "strong anti-development zeitgeist." The mantra that emerged from the Mount Saint Vincent conference was that "small is beautiful."[63]

Not that such support was unanimous. One delegate tore up his party membership card in front of the TV cameras to protest a newly approved policy that allowed the party to raise funds from small business owners and companies whose shares were not traded publicly. Not coincidentally, the new policy had been championed by Alexa's father.

"Alexa was thrilled with the process and its outcome," said Dan O'Connor, who became McDonough's chief of staff soon after.[64] "At the first opportunity she had me write a speech for the legislature conveying the main points. She delivered it in March 1986." While O'Connor said he "poured some cold water by expressing regret that the speech came at the worst point in the election cycle and was likely to be old news come the next election, [Alexa] saw it as a crowning achievement of her leadership."

●

Dan O'Connor's arrival in January 1986 was a result of both the NDP's post-1984 status as an official party (which allowed McDonough to hire additional staff, move to better offices, and get more opportunities to speak in Question Period), and also of the Shaw family and its powers of persuasion.

Though Ontario-raised, O'Connor's mother was a Cape Bretoner, and O'Connor himself attended St. Francis Xavier University in Antigonish and Dalhousie Law School in Halifax. A student activist, he landed a job in 1978 as a research assistant to Winnipeg NDP MP David Orlikow in Ottawa. Two years later, Orlikow recommended him to Howard Pawley, Manitoba's soon-to-be NDP premier, who hired him as chief of staff. By the time he was thirty, O'Connor had become one of the Manitoba government's three most senior officials.

Lloyd Shaw, still an NDP federal icon, and his daughter, the Nova Scotia NDP leader, made it a point "to map anyone in the party with any connection to Nova Scotia," O'Connor explained. During a party event in

Winnipeg, they invited O'Connor to breakfast where they told him it was "important" for him to "come home" to Nova Scotia. Joked O'Connor: "I think their idea was that if enough of us moved back to Nova Scotia, we could form the government."

O'Connor did move back to Nova Scotia to become Alexa McDonough's chief of staff. Government? Well, that was still more than two decades into the future.

9

Alexa McDonough's goal in the summer of 1986 was to develop a provincial NDP policy around the issue of a woman's right to choose, an effort she understood could derail any short-term hope for electoral success.

In the nearly twenty years since Pierre Trudeau's groundbreaking legislation permitting Canadian hospitals to perform therapeutic abortions if a committee of doctors agreed continuing a pregnancy would endanger a mother's life or health, debates over abortion had raged. Dr. Henry Morgentaler, a Montréal physician and abortion rights activist, had challenged the law's limitations by opening his first abortion clinic in Montréal in 1969. Routinely charged with performing illegal abortions, he routinely argued the defence of "necessity," and juries routinely acquitted him. Finally, in 1976, the new Parti Québécois government — recognizing the pointlessness of trying to enforce the law if juries wouldn't convict — threw up its hands and stopped charging him.

In 1983, after Ottawa passed the Canadian Charter of Rights and Freedoms, Morgentaler decided to take the fight to other provinces. Ontario police charged Morgentaler and two colleagues with performing "illegal miscarriages" at his first clinic in Toronto. In late 1984, after a jury there had once again refused to convict him, a jubilant Morgentaler told reporters he'd been receiving calls of support and encouragement from across the country, including from Nova Scotians, asking him to open a clinic there.

Premier John Buchanan, who was religiously and rigorously anti-abortion, pledged to prosecute Morgentaler if he tried, and he also threatened to fire any cabinet minister who dared disagree with his decision. New Liberal leader Vince MacLean, while personally opposed to abortion, preferred the government look the other way. As with homosexuality, he explained, "People are prepared to tolerate practices they might not agree with as long as they're not being done in a confrontational way."[65]

Alexa McDonough's position was unequivocal and long-standing. But was she merely speaking for herself, or for her party? Politicians, she allowed, had traditionally avoided asking such questions. "So many community leaders have hidden out from [abortion]," she noted, "that the polar views have been allowed to prevail instead of there being attempts to build a consensus."[66]

Although "nervous" about what the outcome might be, Alexa was eager to try to build that consensus. Borrowing from the successful bottom-up approach the party had employed to craft its economic policy statement, she tasked the rank and file to come up with a draft reproductive rights policy members could vote on at the next provincial convention.

It was a risky gambit. Many of those who most vehemently opposed easier access to abortion were the Roman Catholic voters in industrial Cape Breton Alexa was trying to win back to the party, as well as folks in traditionally conservative rural ridings she hoped to attract.

In the year leading up to the August 1986 convention, a dozen study committees operating at the constituency and provincial levels met to try to hammer out a consensus. "It has become evident that there are basic disagreements among New Democrats on the abortion issue," reported the authors of the party's *Reproductive Rights in Nova Scotia* policy paper. Those views were "strongly held and involve our most deeply held moral and social values." Still, the participants struggled their way to an uneasy compromise they hoped the party, and its leader, could agree to. The two-pronged approach combined a range of proactive initiatives — mandatory sex education for young people beginning in the first years of schooling, free birth control, anti-poverty programs — all designed to reduce the need for women to choose abortion in the first place, but coupled with a fundamental recognition that the final decision on abortion must belong to the mother. To assuage concerns and ensure support, there were guidelines. During the first sixteen weeks, the woman and her doctor could decide to terminate the pregnancy on their own. After that, they would need to consult with a three-person committee, including two doctors and a "qualified counsellor." Local hospitals would retain the right to choose not to perform abortions, and private clinics like Morgentaler's would not be allowed to operate.

It was far from perfect, and it was not as all-encompassing as Alexa might have wanted. Still, as the *Herald* editorialized, the NDP had come up with "a thoughtful and politically courageous policy [that] could produce some intelligent fresh discussion of a difficult and vital issue."[67] More to the electoral point, however, Bruce MacKinnon's editorial cartoon showed McDonough as a smiling hen sitting on top of what looked like a large egg labelled "Brand New NDP Pro-choice Policy." But the egg, it turned out, was really a bomb attached to a lit fuse.

The Tories did their best to detonate that bomb two years later, when the Supreme Court of Canada struck down Canada's abortion law as unconstitutional because it "clearly interferes with a woman's physical and bodily integrity." Morgentaler announced plans to open a clinic in Nova Scotia; Health Minister Joel Matheson countered the provincial government "won't pay the bills."

When Alexa made the point during a legislature debate that Morgentaler "would not have come to town in the first place if the provincial government were addressing, in a realistic way, the need to both prevent unnecessary abortions and unwanted pregnancies," Matheson "turned nasty," according to the *Daily News*. "Is she, or is she not, in favour of [abortion] clinics being put throughout the province in rural areas at public purse?" he demanded as Tory cabinet ministers and backbenchers "taunted" McDonough, suggesting she wanted an abortion clinic "franchise." "Stand up in the House and answer the question," Matheson repeated.[68]

•

The 1986 convention was significant in other ways too. Convention delegates overwhelmingly approved — by a 10–1 margin — a constitutional amendment requiring gender parity in all future party executive positions. A similar motion had been defeated the year before.

As important, the party's annual summer convention, which rarely attracted much media attention, received a full page of unusually positive reporting in the Halifax *Chronicle-Herald*. Although that reflected the reality the convention had been "unusually large and optimistic," O'Connor recalled the paper's legislature reporter, Alan Jeffers, confiding he'd been "subjected to a grilling by *Herald* editors to determine whether he was revealing some pro-NDP or pro-Alexa sympathies. The stories ran with the positive colour commentary after he convinced them it was an objective report of how the Nova Scotia NDP seemed to be doing at that point."

10

The mid-1980s seemed an auspicious time to be a New Democrat. The federal party, under Ed Broadbent, had won thirty seats in the 1984 election, just ten fewer than the Liberals, and polling afterward showed the federal NDP in first place for the first time ever. If anything, the portents in Nova Scotia seemed even more promising. Despite their resounding victory at the polls, John Buchanan's Tories couldn't get out of their own stumbling way when it came to scandals.

Consider: a 1984 Auditor General's report had singled out flamboyant cabinet minister Billy Joe MacLean and backbencher Malcolm MacKay for flagrant misuse of MLA expense accounts. MacKay, who admitted to improperly pocketing more than $34,000, was never charged and never paid back a penny. In response, new NDP justice critic Bob Levy introduced a motion in the legislature demanding the government "vigorously pursue and collect" overpayments to MLAs the way it did with welfare recipients. "This inconsistency and hypocrisy," Levy railed, "is intolerable in principle and practice."[69]

After MacLean pleaded guilty to submitting false expense claims and was fined $6,000, a tearful Premier John Buchanan recalled the legislature for a special session to expel his friend and ban him from public office for five years, but without giving him the legal right to appeal.

Alexa, who'd been on a speaking tour in northern Nova Scotia, returned to Halifax for the hastily called session suffering from laryngitis and barely able to make herself heard. While she supported the decision to kick MacLean out, she said, she was appalled by the lack of due process. "I don't know what better illustration we could have had that weak leadership yields bleak results than what has been allowed to go on here today and the events that have led up to it," she said.[70]

Dan O'Connor, who rarely attended legislative debates, recalled being present for this historic session, and impressed by his boss's performance. "She spoke from a unique position, due to her campaigns against various forms of patronage and abuse of the public trust and rose to the occasion despite the stage whisper that was the best she could manage."

Some things, of course, never changed. Even as McDonough chastised the government for its poorly crafted legislation, the Tory government's house leader jumped in with an aside Hansard did not record. McDonough helpfully filled in the blanks. "The Government House Leader says, 'why don't you speak to your husband when you get home tonight?' I don't think, Mr. Speaker, I am going to have any voice left to speak with him for a start, but I don't think that that is the way the Nova Scotia House of Assembly ought to go about passing its laws. If no member of this government has been able to stand up and address the legitimate [legal] concerns...and the only answer they have...is to suggest that a member go home and talk to their lawyer spouse, then we have reached a very, very all-time low in the life of this legislature."[71]

But not as low as events would go. A little over a year later, in April 1988, another Tory backbench MLA Greg MacIsaac, was sentenced to a year in jail for forging his landlady's signature on $7,000 worth of receipts.[72] That same month, the *Toronto Star* reported the RCMP wanted to charge Deputy Premier Roland Thornhill with conflict of interest because of his deal with four banks to write off $100,000 worth of personal loans. The province's Attorney General refused to prosecute. After the information became public, Thornhill was forced to resign.[73]

Alexa urged the Thornhill issue be turned over to the royal commission then investigating the wrongful conviction of Donald Marshall Jr. The commissioners not only agreed, they decided to compare the Thornhill and MacLean cases with the Marshall case to determine if there was a two-tier justice system operating in the province. So many prominent Nova Scotians eventually ended up being hauled before the commission to testify that popular local comedian Dave Harley won a laugh at a Neptune Theatre fundraiser, attended by many of the city's finest, simply by asking: "Is there anybody here who has not testified before the Marshall Inquiry?"[74]

There were also plenty of other, non-financial scandals nipping at the heels of the Buchanan government, many of which seemed like delicious softballs tossed into the NDP strike zone. In the spring of 1987, Brenda Thompson, a single mother, complained in an op-ed for the Halifax *Daily News* she could not pay her rent because of a mix-up by the provincial social services department, which she said was "run under the principle of frustration and stupidity." She accused the minister, Edmund Morris, of not caring enough about the poor. Morris, a former Halifax mayor who liked to pontificate, was quick to label Thompson's article a "vicious and venomous" attack on his "persona," and claimed, without citing evidence, her article had been "ghost-written by the NDP." The reason Thompson's welfare payments had been delayed, Morris told reporters, quoting from Thompson's file, was because she twice refused to name her child's "real" father.[75] When Morris refused to apologize or resign for releasing confidential information, Thompson, with fundraising help from a group of local activists, hired feminist lawyer Anne Derrick to prosecute Morris. Morris was convicted and fined $100.

And then there was Attorney General Ron Giffin, who threatened to opt out of Canada's new Charter of Rights and Freedoms to prevent gays and lesbians from becoming police officers. Giffin even threatened to introduce new provincial legislation to allow for the firing of any officers discovered to be homosexual.

In response, Alexa did what O'Connor noted with awe, "only she could do. She got on the phone," put together a coalition of religious and social justice groups, to build momentum to change human rights legislation to make discrimination on the basis of sexual orientation illegal. Her modus operandi, O'Connor remembered, was to "get a whole bunch of people together in a room and see what happened.... She didn't do it for any NDP political gain," he added. There was no election on the horizon, and Alexa had already learned from bitter experience how difficult it was to convert public support around a particular issue into NDP votes at the next election. "But that would never cause her to hesitate for one second to jump in on something where she saw it had to be done."[76]

Still, by 1988, there were signs that Alexa's tireless political seed-planting was actually, finally, generating a few shoots in long-fallow NDP ground. At around the time Ed Broadbent's NDP was briefly topping national polls, the provincial party contracted pollster Peter Hebb, the husband of NDP activist Tessa Hebb, to take the temperature of voters in rural Hants West. O'Connor remembered the party could afford to poll only one riding and they chose Hants West because Hebb said it was the "constituency that most mirrored provincial voting trends — not outcomes, but trends." The NDP, in fact, had finished a dismal third in the riding in 1984, taking just over 10 per cent of all votes cast. But Hebb's poll results showed NDP support in Hants West was now at a stunning 34 per cent, well within the range of a realistic victory in a three-party race, in a riding where the NDP had never done well.

NDP operatives weren't the only ones paying attention. "Focusing their minds on how to take us out of the game," Buchanan's Tories "moderated or changed" some of their positions on social policy issues to cleave away NDP support in metro Halifax where the party finished second in 1984. During the spring legislature session, for example, Buchanan grandiosely announced plans to introduce pay equity in both the public and private sectors in a three-phase, six-year project. He called it a "historic and auspicious day in the life of Nova Scotians, certainly in the life of women in Nova Scotia." While Alexa welcomed the government's belated recognition that women in Nova Scotia earned just 60 per cent of what men did, she also noted pointedly the government had refused to include an implementation timetable as part of its legislation.[77]

But the fact the Tories would soon be returning to the polls was lost on no one. "We saw a strong mood for change in the spring of 1988," said Ray Larkin, the chair of the NDP's election planning committee. "The Buchanan government had lost popularity and we seemed to be gaining. We knew we wouldn't form the government," he continued, "but it felt like this election could be an important stepping stone on that road."

And then John Buchanan did what he did so well.

11

"Alexa?" The voice at the other end of the phone was tentative. Bob Levy, the NDP's other star MLA, was calling. It was the morning of Thursday, July 29, 1988, and Nova Scotia was mere days from the launch of a provincial general election campaign.

"I'm afraid I'm calling with some bad news," Levy began. He paused.

Was he sick, she wondered? "Bob, are you OK?"

"I'm not running." He said it quickly, blurted it almost, then stopped, waited.

Not running? What was he saying? *Not running!* "Bob you can't... Not on such short notice. The election's about to be called, and—"

He cut her off. "Wait, Alexa. You'd better hear the rest because you're not going to be happy when I tell you what I'm doing. . . . I've accepted a judgeship."

Stunned silence. "Bob, you can't!"

"I already did."

She didn't cry, she would remember later, "but I felt like it." Instead, she argued, she cajoled, she begged. "Forget me, forget John Holm," she told him. "We can recover one way or the other, and it's not your responsibility to worry about us. But can't you just think about all those people who bled for you, who worked their guts out to get you elected, who gave you money they couldn't afford, who pounded on doors for you, who pounded the pavement, broke ranks with their traditional Tory and Liberal roots to support you? They're going to be devastated. You can't be..." She stopped, waited. There was another strained, awkward silence from Levy's end of the line, incredulity and mounting anger from hers. "You can't be serious," she continued finally. "I mean you have to wait, at least until after the election—"

"It's done," he said flatly. "The deal's only on offer if I'm willing to..." His voice trailed off. "The announcement is going to be made tomorrow and they're going to call the election Saturday."

Finally, Alexa McDonough, whose relentlessness and persuasiveness in discussions had become legendary, faced reality. "It's a done deal," she thought to herself. "There's no point. It's over. It's just gonna be a hell of an election."

They hung up with the most perfunctory of goodbyes.

Thirty years later, the wounds were still raw. "Once in a while," Alexa said, "someone will ask me, 'What's the worst thing that ever happened in all your years of politics?'" Her unequivocal answer: the personal and political "devastation" of Bob Levy's phone call that morning. Alexa still saw it as a betrayal of everything they'd stood together for, fought against, schemed and dreamed about, even imagined would one day could happen.

After their conversation ended that morning, the two former political soulmates would not speak to one another for more than twenty-five years. And, even then, their conversation would be perfunctory, elliptical, never quite getting to the questions both of them so desperately wanted answered.[78]

•

If you're going to understand the importance of that pivotal phone call to each of them, to their party, and to politics in Nova Scotia, you need to rewind, understand what went before.

They'd worked together in the NDP trenches for more than a decade. As with Alexa, politics coursed through Bob Levy's veins. His father, Clifford, had been a Tory MLA and cabinet minister in the Stanfield era. Growing up, Bob learned the peculiar ways of Nova Scotia's electoral politics on gravel backroads, handing out pints of rum from the trunk of his father's car on election day to those who promised to vote the right way. In 1970, while still in law school, he ran as a Progressive Conservative candidate in Lunenburg West, but was swept into the electoral sea by the Liberal tide that brought Gerald Regan to power.

It was a law school summer job the next year, as a counsellor at the Shelburne School for Boys, a youth detention centre, that he said, "knocked me off my Conservative pins. Those kids had so many strikes against them." He began to see the province's ubiquitous patronage system as part of the problem. By the time he graduated, Levy had given up on electoral politics. At about the time Alexa was abandoning her brief flirtation with the Liberals, Levy had moved to Nova Scotia's Annapolis Valley and gone to work for Nova Scotia Legal Aid, soon realizing that his own political thinking most closely aligned with the New Democratic Party. He began attending local meetings. People could see he was smart, articulate, and witty. By 1978, he'd been elected provincial president, and while Alexa was busy winning their party's leadership, Levy had helped guide the membership through the divisive Paul MacEwan debacle and laid the ground for the party's slow rebuilding.

Levy had put himself on the electoral line too. Like Alexa, he'd run in the 1979 and 1980 federal elections, coming third both times. In the 1981 provincial election in which Alexa finally won her seat, Levy placed second in Kings North. He'd run again in the neighbouring Kings South riding in a 1984 by-election, finishing second once more before finally winning a seat in the 1984 general election, "squeaking out a huge majority" of eighteen votes.

With Alexa's re-election in Halifax and the comfortable victory of John Holm in Sackville, a middle-class Halifax suburb, the NDP finally had a mainland legislative beachhead, and official status as a party, on which to build.

•

Bob Levy would remember his whirlwind four years as an MLA as "wonder-ful. I thoroughly enjoyed the whole experience, working with Alexa and John." The three weren't personally close outside the legislature, "but we worked well together. Alexa led, but not with a heavy hand. If I wanted to go off on a tangent, I was free to do that. We trusted one another."

The issue of Nova Scotia's entrenched, intractable political patronage system was a fundamental tenet for both of them. Levy made a point of telling reporters it had been one of the main reasons he'd left the Conservatives. "I think it's contemptible, I think it's corrupt. I think it's base one hundred different ways."

"He could be so good in flights of rhetoric and on such a high, really charged up and enthusiastic and energizing for other people," Alexa would reflect years later. "He was very effective, and a much better speaker than I was. In particular," she added, "he was a very well-informed, articulate spokesperson and devastating critic of patronage appointments and in particular, patronage appointments of judges."

Opposition to patronage was only one of the key ways in which Levy had established and defined his politics. He, McDonough, and Holm each had to cover half a dozen different critic's assignments, with Levy trying to keep up with the goings-on in such disparate portfolios as fisheries, the justice department, and lands and forests. When they weren't in the House, they were on the road, speaking to small crowds of party supporters in far-flung constituencies, touting their legislature good fights, pressing the flesh, stirring the partisan pot for next time.

Bob Levy fully assumed he would be part of that next time. But then it all came tumbling down.

The year before he'd won his seat in the legislature, Levy had quit his Nova Scotia Legal Aid job to launch a modest one-person practice, hoping to make a better living while continuing to do good. "It was a struggle to get it off the ground," he recalled, made only more difficult because he continued representing many of his legal aid clients pro bono. "That wasn't a help." Once he became an MLA, he had even less time to devote to finding a paying clientele. "I was juggling the last of my mother's inheritance just to keep it solvent."

And then, his marriage to Barb Levy, another prominent NDP activist, fell apart. The breakdown had been coming for some time, Levy admitted, though he had missed the signs. "I wasn't willfully blind," he said later. "I was stupidly blind." They had three sons, two still at home, "and I was not a good father for them. I'd left everything to my wife while I travelled all over the province." He and his wife had already split once in 1987 but they got back together, vowing to try one more time. In April 1988, she told him their marriage was finished.

"I was devastated. I was just a wreck, just stumbling along," he remembered of the days that followed. He sought professional help. His counsellor said to him: "You're forty-one years old. If I was to meet you in ten years when you're fifty-one, what would you want to be able to say to me? That 'I'm a successful politician.' Or that 'I'm a successful father.'"

That conversation became Bob Levy's reality slap. He couldn't save his marriage, he knew that, but perhaps he could become a better parent. He would abandon his political ambitions, spend more time with his sons. Perhaps he could rescue his law practice, or rejoin legal aid, or find a job at one of the larger law firms in the Annapolis Valley. Or, maybe, he thought, he might just find a good, secure government job that would offer him more time to spend with his kids. One day, he quietly approached Attorney General Terry Donahoe. "'You got any judgeships lying around?'" he joked. "I really was joking. I didn't expect that to happen. I was just interested in finding a job. And Terry was noncommittal."

He'd told Alexa about his marriage breakdown and that he was considering applying for a government job, but not that he'd broached the idea of a judicial appointment. But he did tell her he wouldn't re-offer in the upcoming provincial general election. He said he made that clear. On May 25, 1988, the final day of the last spring session of the last legislature before an expected provincial election, Levy spoke eloquently in the House about the Meech Lake Accord. Buchanan's Conservatives had pushed through a resolution supporting the constitutional deal. The Tories, Levy declared, demonstrated "the negotiating style of a schoolyard bully. . . . That is, maybe more than anything, a fitting way to end this session of the legislature and, perhaps, this general assembly, Mr. Speaker. This is the way history is written. We are not always favoured to be glorified and, in this instance, we don't deserve it."[79]

Levy sat down, turned to Alexa. "That's it, then," he declared with finality.

"My last speech in the legislature." Remembered Levy, "She gave me a look. We didn't talk about it then, and I think maybe she thought she could change my mind."

For her part, Alexa remembered Levy as mercurial, and not always easy to read. At times, she said, "He'd just be really, really down in the doldrums, just discouraged, kind of defeated feeling, 'Oh we're never going to be able to make a real impact.' [He was] not an easy person, a restless person." She shrugged. "Sometimes those qualities also go with being an in-your-face New Democrat."

Levy might have made the same point. "I remember somewhere along the line, Alexa and I were in her office. She was discouraged. Things weren't going well. And she said something about stepping aside. 'Why don't you take over, Bob?'" Levy said he had no interest in the leader's job. "I had a family to feed and leading the NDP was not the best meal ticket." McDonough never raised the subject again.

Whatever he'd said about his intentions, whatever he'd intended to convey, he allowed years later, didn't seem to register with Alexa. "She even sent her father to twist my arm," he said. "Lloyd didn't seem to get it either. Of course I wanted to run again. I wanted nothing more. But I couldn't."

In mid-July, Donald Cameron, Buchanan's minister of industry, trade and technology, telephoned Levy.

He didn't make him an actual job offer until later that month, when he phoned again to say Buchanan was about to call the election. The government was prepared to name Levy a judge of the family court but only if he would agree to accept the position right away. Becoming a family court judge was a long way from being an MLA, but a lot closer to issues like those faced by the boys at the Shelburne centre. And it would leave him more time with his own boys. He accepted the offer. Oh, and by the way, Cameron added, the government had a document it wanted him to sign and fax back. The document, which he dutifully signed and sent back, declared he had asked for the appointment. The Tories were leaving nothing to chance.

Decision done, deal made, Levy called McDonough to confirm he wasn't running. It was perhaps a sign of the disconnect between them that Levy insists he was "blown away" by McDonough's "furious" reaction. "Up until then, I thought we had a friendship, I thought there was mutual respect. But her reaction was like a grenade landed at my feet. I didn't intend to do that to Alexa, or anyone else. I thought, 'What's going on here?'" He paused. "You know, if I were to live to be a thousand years old, I will never have made a better decision. I didn't think I was being dishonest at all...."

12

Knowing the election would be called sometime on Saturday, July 30, in the middle of a provincial holiday weekend, Alexa had been forced to share a Halifax Natal Day parade reviewing platform with an already gloating Premier John Buchanan.

Rather than wait for the election shoe to officially drop, Alexa left town that afternoon for a previously scheduled pre-campaign stop on Chapel Island, a sacred Indigenous site in the middle of Cape Breton's Bras d'Or Lakes. She had to be rowed to the island, which had no phone lines or electricity, and, luckily, no reporters asking questions about Bob Levy. Despite entreaties from O'Connor, who was already being inundated with calls from journalists, Alexa refused to change her travel plans. The next morning, she attended a church service with her mother in nearby Inverness, her maternal family's ancestral home, before returning to Halifax.

In response to the government's public announcement of his appointment, Levy had issued a terse statement asking for understanding. "My highest duty, now more than ever, is to my children to whom I owe a life and a lifestyle with which political life is inconsistent." But journalists were quick to remind voters that Levy had, as a Canadian Press report put it, "made a career of blasting the government for the way it appoints judges. He once joked that Premier John Buchanan could give him a judicial appointment to earn his silence."[80]

And now he had.

By the time Alexa arrived back in Halifax for a planned Sunday afternoon photo-op outside Ray Larkin's house — she was to plant an "Alexa!" sign on his lawn while the cameras clicked and whirred — the only questions reporters asked were about Levy.

The scrutiny didn't ease the next day, when the NDP issued its first, ill-timed but long-planned policy statement about ending political patronage in the province. The party promised — still unheard of in Nova Scotia — that an NDP government would post all civil service jobs for open competition as they became available, outlaw discrimination in hiring and firing based on political beliefs, and punish anyone convicted of improperly influencing employment decisions with fines of up to $75,000 or two years in prison. "This election," Alexa declared, "presents a historic opportunity to shake off a wasteful, rotten, corrupting style of politics."[81]

She even did her best to turn Levy's appointment into a teachable moment. She slammed it as "exactly the type of political manoeuvre the average Nova Scotian is really fed up with," argued "nothing ever changes" so long as voters continue to choose the two mainstream parties," and insisted "an NDP government would not appoint an MLA of any political stripe to the bench on the very eve of a long-expected election."

But she was ultimately forced to concede to one reporter: "Whatever I say now [will] be interpreted either as Pollyanna-ism or sour grapes."[82]

•

The NDP's electoral strategy had been built on two pillars: Alexa's un-questioned personal popularity and integrity, and the party's principled attack on the province's patronage system. The strategy, of course, hadn't contemplated Bob Levy's unexpected defection, which "shot a big hole in our big issue," O'Connor acknowledged.

The NDP's strategy also failed to account for John Buchanan's political resilience. As his governing party was being buffeted by scandals, Buchanan hunkered down, delaying an election call beyond his previous three-year term standard and riding out the worst of the storms. Then, in the lead-up to the election call, his government began issuing a blizzard of tender calls for new highway construction, new schools, $600–$800 million worth of new spending in all, including a new power-generating plant for Cape Breton and a new coal mine for Pictou County. Sods were turned, more new projects announced. There were initiatives for senior citizens, increased allotments for welfare recipients, even un-ironic promises to reform the justice system. In metro Halifax, where the battle for the hearts and minds of urban voters was expected to be between a surging NDP and the Tories, Buchanan announced a $195-million federal-provincial agreement to clean up Halifax's sewage-saturated harbour. Finally, in the ten days leading up to the election call,

Buchanan orchestrated the resignations or retirements of four veteran cabinet ministers, including the disgraced Edmund Morris, allowing the premier to present a fresh(er) face to the electorate.

In the end, his party would boast it had nominated twenty new candidates, allowing Buchanan to claim the party he led was the "New PCs" and even promising, straight-faced, to clean up his own government by publicly tendering all government contracts, opening up competition for civil service jobs, and creating a code of ethics for politicians. All, of course, came directly out of the long-time NDP policy book. Buchanan's *mea culpa* promise to do better led to what the *Globe and Mail* would describe as Buchanan's "understatement of the campaign: 'We do not live in a perfect world.'"[83]

And then, of course, John Buchanan appointed Bob Levy to the bench.

The question of how to handle Levy's departure became a "huge preoccupation," O'Connor recalled. "Bob had been respected, beloved, so we couldn't go after him." In the end, however, figuring out what to do about Bob Levy was not the worst of the party's problems that summer.

•

CBC TV reporter Paul Withers's explosive report for the provincial supper-hour news program opened on a silent wide shot of an idyllic rural bungalow, its front yard featuring a prominent orange-and-green "Waiting for Fairness" NDP election sign. "Rumours that this house was the scene of a drug bust spread around political circles like wildfire today,"[84] Withers's voiceover began. That day, a week before voters went to the polls, the RCMP had charged Steve Skipper, who lived in the house, with growing thirty marijuana plants in the backyard. His wife, Julia Skipper, a "Catholic Sunday School teacher," insisted she knew nothing about any of it. "The only fault of mine is that I'm going to stand by my man." But the "fault" for the NDP was that Julia had agreed to be its last-minute, "out-of-the-goodness-of-her-heart" candidate in Colchester South, as traditional a rural two-party bastion as there was and one the NDP probably wouldn't have won even if everyone in the riding were stoned.

Nonetheless, the drug bust story—eagerly promoted to reporters by Liberal Leader Vince MacLean—became yet another dark cloud scudding low over the NDP's fading hopes. While Alexa insisted, "I am not about to ask Julia Skipper to withdraw as a candidate" because of something her husband had done, she also quietly instructed Skipper to suspend personal campaigning for the rest of the election.

Not that that could have salvaged anything at this point.

The NDP's decision to run candidates in all provincial ridings and campaign seriously in each of them had been crafted as a see-we're-serious gesture during the optimistic spring of 1988. Twenty-two of its candidates—the highest number ever—were women, thanks in part to a special fund Alexa had set up in 1987 to encourage more women to run for political office. But the Skipper saga only highlighted that most of those women (and many of the male candidates), were placeholders, designed to make the party appear both more inclusive and stronger than it really was.

By the time Buchanan had rewritten the playbook in the months leading up to the election call, remembered Ray Larkin, the then-rookie head of the NDP's election planning committee, the plan to compete provincially already seemed wildly off base. They needed to focus on the seats they could actually win. But, as the campaign suddenly swept over them, organizers found it difficult to recalibrate.

The candidate news wasn't all bad. Alexa herself had persuaded Allan O'Brien, the popular former mayor of Halifax (and Shaw family friend who had introduced her to her city social planning boss Harold Crowell twenty years before), to run under the NDP banner in South End Halifax. Well-known actor John Dunsworth (later internationally famous as the bumbling Mr. Lahey on the *Trailer Park Boys*) signed on as a star candidate in suburban Bedford. Future female NDP leaders Helen MacDonald, a university administrator, and Maureen MacDonald, a social worker, ran. So did teachers Eileen O'Connell, another future MLA, and Bill Estabrooks, a cabinet minister in the province's first NDP government. They all lost, but their presence offered the party immediate credibility while they each picked up valuable experience.

Besides Julia Skipper, there was Raymond Ethier, the party's candidate in Argyle. The week before the vote, Ethier publicly abandoned the race to fly to Toronto for a two-week spiritual retreat. He announced he would return to Nova Scotia—if he won.

And then there was Brenda Thompson. Many in the party and beyond considered the welfare mother a heroine for taking Social Services Minister

Alexa on the campaign trail in Nova Scotia's Annapolis Valley
during the 1988 provincial election (courtesy of Michael Creagen)

Edmund Morris to court and winning; however, others, inside and outside
the party, saw her potential candidacy as an attempt by Thompson, and the
party, to capitalize on her notoriety.

"We have to have a meeting," Larkin told Dan O'Connor after learning
Thompson planned to seek the party's nomination in Dartmouth North.
"This is going to be disastrous." The party had been carefully building
voter support in Dartmouth North and South, two key metro ridings,
O'Connor recalled, and there was concern that, no matter how righteous
Thompson might have been in her Brenda-and-Goliath battle, conservative
Nova Scotians "were just not going to accept an uppity welfare mother, who
probably didn't deserve the money anyway, running for the NDP."

An urgent election planning committee meeting to discuss her potential
candidacy, O'Connor remembered, turned into "a big, long, tough debate."
Under the NDP's constitution, the leader couldn't simply revoke a candidate's
nomination, but she did have that power under the Provincial Election Act.
"Alexa didn't say much one way or the other," O'Connor remembered. "She

let the debate rage back and forth." In the end, however, Alexa refused to intervene, and Thompson's candidacy stood.

Whatever moral high ground McDonough had chosen, it created one more electoral calamity for her party, which had its worst showing in years in both Dartmouth ridings, and "was hurtful everywhere else," O'Connor said. The hurt was amplified after a reporter, who'd accompanied McDonough on her door-knocking rounds, reported the Brenda Thompson issue had been raised, and negatively, by virtually every voter at virtually every doorstep.

And then, midway through the campaign, provincial organizers suddenly realized Alexa might be in trouble in her own riding. While Alexa, O'Connor, and a driver had been criss-crossing the province, showing the flag and helping local candidates get out the vote, even in ridings where the party didn't stand a chance, the outside organizer who'd been brought in to oversee the campaign in Alexa's own Chebucto riding had failed to do much organizing or overseeing.

"Alexa was such a strength provincially, we needed her out there," O'Connor acknowledged, but it was equally clear she had to win her own riding if she and the party were to claim even a moral victory from the shambles of 1988.

Enter — again — Cliff Scotton, the former NDP federal secretary, "friend of the Shaws" and "a teacher, a campaign genius, and a mentor" to party organizers across the country. It had been Scotton who'd convinced Alexa to run in Halifax Chebucto in 1981. Now Scotton and his wife, Joyce, returned to Halifax for a last-minute rescue mission. "They phoned every one of her family members," marvelled O'Connor. "They said, 'You have to get out there and help save her seat.'"

Husband Peter, who continued to be publicly supportive even as their twenty-two-year marriage frayed at its edges, was featured in one local newspaper profile campaigning his way through the Chebucto riding, cheerfully introducing himself to voters as "Mr. Alexa McDonough."

"I really enjoy campaigning," he told *Chronicle-Herald* reporter Peter Moreira. "It's a bit easier for me because I can introduce myself as Alexa's husband."

For her part, an upbeat Alexa praised her husband's "wonderful sense of humour and very good perspective. The most important contribution from my husband during campaigns, before campaigns, and after campaigns is keeping me human."

While doing their best to keep the extent of the potential debacle in Chebucto from Alexa herself, the Scottons made sure her campaign organizers scheduled her to spend the final weekend of the campaign in Bayers Westwood, a public housing neighbourhood in her district. "While they knew people there traditionally didn't come out to vote," O'Connor recalled, "they also knew that those who did vote would almost certainly vote for Alexa."

It worked. Barely. After a recount, Alexa defeated Clair Callaghan, an engineer and political neophyte, by just twenty-six votes. There were fifty-three spoiled ballots, including several with anti-abortion slogans scrawled on them.

Provincially, there had been a strong anti-government vote. The Tories' seat count dropped from forty to twenty-eight, just one more than the number of seats required for a majority. Most of that anti-government vote ended up being siphoned off to Vince MacLean's Liberal party, which more than tripled its seat count — from six to twenty. Paul MacEwan, running as an independent again, won his own seat. John Buchanan, by winning his fourth term in office, became Canada's longest-serving current premier. And Vince MacLean could legitimately claim to be premier-in-waiting.

The NDP was reduced to just two seats: Alexa's squeaker victory in Chebucto and John Holm's re-election in Sackville, by a much narrower margin than 1984. When early returns that night indicated Holm might actually lose, Alexa confessed later, she "thought it might be best if she lost too, instead of returning to the House alone."[85] The NDP's overall percentage of the popular vote remained depressingly static at just 16 per cent.

Publicly, Alexa, as always, did what she could to make defeat seem like victory. "The main objective of the main parties was to level us, wipe us out so they could once again fight over whose turn it was at the public trough,"[86] Alexa told despondent supporters. They'd failed, she insisted. The NDP wasn't going anywhere.

But what about Alexa McDonough? As *Chronicle-Herald* reporter Rob Mills put it in a post-election profile, she had gone to bed on election day, "knowing that after eight years of gut-busting work, after 2,638 days of living and breathing politics, her efforts were worth a twenty-six vote victory over a rookie opponent."[87] After three tries, she'd only managed to nudge her party from one seat to three and now back down to two. Was it time to face reality and find some other, more rewarding way to spend the rest of her professional career? And what about the future of her marriage? Was it past time to face that reality too?

NEW BEGINNINGS

1

Dan and Valerie O'Brien arrived at the McDonoughs' doorstep one morning in the spring of 1990 with happy news they wanted to share with their friends, Peter and Alexa. The families were close: Dan had been a professor at the Maritime School of Social Work when Alexa was a student and, later, a colleague on the faculty; Dan and Peter were kibitzing tennis-court rivals; the couples each had two sons of about the same age who were also friends; the families spent summers together on Shaw Island, lived a few blocks from one another in Halifax. Who better than Peter and Alexa to tell their news to: Dan had just been appointed president of St. Thomas University in Fredericton, New Brunswick.

But Alexa seemed nonplussed. She congratulated Dan, of course, but then seemed uncertain what to say next. Finally, she blurted it out. "I'm afraid Peter isn't here to share your news. . . . He's moved out."

It was a shock. But not a surprise. There were those, even among their friends, who'd never quite understood Peter's and Alexa's initial attraction to each other, or how long their love had managed to endure. Peter, the gregarious, quick-witted life of the party; Alexa, the earnest, over-thinking do-gooder. Peter, the small-and-big-*l* Liberal, the downtown real estate lawyer; Alexa, the NDP leader, the social worker, the university professor, the feminist.

Publicly, Peter was still the supportive political campaigner who wore his orange Alexa badge over his heart "just below the embroidered polo player on his Ralph Lauren shirt," as one reporter noted. They were supportive of even their political differences. "He's always been prepared to say he's not going to let his career crowd my politics, or certainly compromise my politics," Alexa explained. And vice versa.[1]

But, in private, their relationship had become complicated.

She was, without question, no longer the stand-by-your man woman who would choose being Mrs. Peter McDonough over all else. She had become single-mindedly obsessed with politics and policy, admitting to one interviewer she would happily "give up the chance to see a play just to read another policy paper."[2] Her friend Betty Muggah recalled many conversations in the waning years of the McDonough marriage when Alexa ruminated on ways to repair her relationship. They'd even tried marriage counselling. "She continued to be deeply in love with him, but the idea of giving up politics at this point would have been very difficult for her."

Peter had changed, too, in ways some might not have expected. Though they both doted on their teenage sons — it would continue to be their constant and their connecting tissue — Peter had become the more present parent. On the soccer-field sidelines and on the tennis court, at home and at school meetings.

"Perversely and because of the perceived inferior status of women, the husband of a female politician is often viewed as kind of a wimp," Alexa confided to journalist Sharon Fraser in an unpublished, for the historical record interview in the early 1990s.

> I think that even though my husband was always able to use his sense of humour to fend off those kinds of innuendoes and implications, and sometimes they were quite explicit, there's no question this created a real tension for him and for us around his role. He was never comfortable with the idea that he would be my tagalong. People were prepared to make allowances for him but most often it was, "Poor Peter McDonough. How does he cope with this awful situation where something is expected of him because of having an aggressive wife in public office?" I won't pretend it wasn't a constant strain in our marriage, the continual search for answers to the same old questions: what things was he comfortable doing? what things was he not prepared to do? what were the expectations of the constituents and the

media? We both understood that I never believed he should feel
he had to perform various functions as my spouse because I don't
think anyone should have to do that, but it was very difficult.

The less comfortable Peter was, the more immersed Alexa became in her
political career, and the less time they spent together. Many of his wife's
NDP colleagues, Peter suggested years later, "had no sense of humour," so
his enjoyment level was "not totally enhanced by spending time up close"
with them.

Politics was part of it, of course, but only part. While Alexa didn't have
to look further than Bob Levy, who'd decided he must choose between
politics and family, to know how difficult that life could be, marriages were
also breaking up all around her. Their marriage was not alone in suffering
the consequences of changing roles and expectations. "First Claudia and
I split," John Duckworth told me, beginning a mental roll call of the
marriage breakdowns of Peter's and Alexa's group of close friends from the
1970s. "And then Peter and Carolyn [MacGregor]. And Burpee and Joann
[Hallett]....And then Peter and Alexa."

But there was no escaping the ways in which politics—and the public life
Alexa led—intruded on their home life, and outside perceptions of it. Even
Peter's assumption of more of the parenting responsibilities did not come
without a psychic cost. Alexa remembered one of her son's teachers saying,
"'Well, I see you didn't get your homework done again this weekend. No
wonder. I read in the paper this morning that your mother was off to Ottawa
again.'" She stopped, considered. "A totally absurd thing to say and I don't
think it would be said of a male politician at all. The strongly held belief is
that it's the mother's responsibility to be all-attendant on the home front. If
she's not, then she's the one who's bucking her normal role and duty." She and
Peter, she acknowledged, "still struggled with the notion that [his parenting
role] was something unusual; there was an attitude of, 'Isn't it wonderful that
he's *willing* to do these things,' rather than a natural understanding that this
is the kind of joint parenting that makes sense in our society."

Alexa and Peter may have come of chronological age in the sixties, but
experientially, they were more children of the fifties who'd smacked up
against societal expectations and gender realities of the eighties. None of that

made real life easier. Friends began to notice. "I saw it on a couple of visits to Halifax," said Betty Muggah. "More and more, their values did not line up. She was so dedicated, and so earnest. Peter was more light-hearted. He had confidence and charisma, but you had to be wary. His way of winning an argument could be hurtful. He could be publicly cutting, ridiculing Alexa and her earnestness. She was still in love with Peter, craving a closeness. In those last few years, she was living in the same house with him, but she was very lonely."

No one knows, of course, what goes on inside any marriage. We only know what we see, and what happens. What happened with Alexa and Peter was that they drifted apart. As their relationship frayed, each began to lead more independent lives. Somewhere along the line, Peter began going to the YMCA every morning at 6:00 a.m. to work out with others in what became known as the "Early Morning Group." It was a tight-knit crew of men and women who'd exercise together, have coffee, and "solve the world's problems" before heading off to their respective offices for 9:00 a.m. The instructor was a woman named Suzanne Kushner. She and Peter became friends, and then more than friends, and then Peter moved out.

•

Alexa was scheduled to attend a conference at the Canadian Auto Workers' Family Education Centre in Port Elgin, Ontario, the week after Peter left. She debated cancelling but eventually decided against it. Instead, she called her friend Betty and arranged to visit her and her husband at their house in Hamilton before heading off to the conference.

"I remember she arrived, and we were in the kitchen, and she just fell apart," Betty said. "She'd been holding it all in, and now she just let it out." Over the course of the next two days, they talked, and cried, and laughed, and talked some more. "It was important for me to be there for her."

Even as she tried to come to terms with the collapse of her marriage, Betty remembered, Alexa also kept up her frenetic work pace. "We'd talk until one in the morning and then she'd be back up at 5:00 a.m., working on the computer or going over speeches in longhand. I don't think she would allow herself to mourn or grieve."

Betty and her husband, Henry, drove Alexa the three hours from Hamilton to her conference in Port Elgin. "I remember we drove in this long driveway and we pulled up to a wooden structure," Betty said. Outside, a small group of men stood around in bathing suits. "Well," Betty joked to Alexa, "look at those three good-looking guys. Things are looking up."

Alexa recognized one of them, a Nova Scotian trade unionist named Les Holloway, though they'd never met. He recognized her too.

To the men, Betty said: "Look after her."

They did.

•

Les Holloway, the executive director of the Halifax-based Maritime Marine Workers Federation, had been invited to Port Elgin to meet with Bob White, the president of the Canadian Auto Workers Union, who was trying to woo the small regionally based shipbuilders' union to join the CAW, one of the country's largest and most powerful unions.

Like Alexa, Holloway was on the rebound from a failed relationship. But that, on the surface, was all they had in common. Holloway, who was nine years younger than Alexa, had grown up "dirt-poor" in North End Halifax. His father was an alcoholic and a Conservative, his mother a Liberal. In high school, he was shunted into the non-academic stream, which he only discovered in grade 12 when a guidance counsellor asked him what he wanted to do with his life. "I said, 'I want to go to university. I want to be a lawyer,'" Holloway recalled. "She looked at me funny. I said, 'What's wrong?' She said, 'You're in general. You can't go to university.' It took the gut right out of me."

Instead, he turned a summer job at the Halifax Shipyard into a career and, ultimately, a cause. The cause was workers' rights. While working on the refit of a coast guard vessel, Holloway, then the shop steward, asked whether he and his fellow workers were breathing in asbestos from the ship's insulation and building materials. The superintendent dismissed his concerns and then suspended him. "You guys never want to work. Go home." Holloway grieved and won. And the worksite tested positive for asbestos.

By the mid-1980s, he'd become a union executive and member of the federal government's national strategy on shipbuilding, frequently travelling to Ottawa. "You came back from Ottawa, thinking it had been a good meeting and then you'd see a guy, a very senior guy working in the shipyard, and you'd say, 'How you doing?' 'Not too fucking good. I just got laid off.' He and six other guys working in the yard.... It grounded you."

When he wasn't working, Holloway worked out, including at the YMCA where Peter McDonough was a regular. "I used to see him at the Y," he remembered, "him and Suzanne. So I wasn't surprised."

That night at the Port Elgin centre, Holloway and a few friends knocked on Alexa's door. "Come for a midnight swim?" they asked. Why not? "I can't remember whether he said, 'Come over and have a glass of wine,'" or whether he said, 'I'll come over and bring a glass,'" Alexa recalled, "but there was wine involved."

Over the next few days, they swam, they talked, they played tennis, and they drank wine. By the time they flew home to Halifax, they were an item.

2

"Girls' Night Out" — or GNO as it became known — began sometime in late 1986 or early 1987. All its members worked for Alexa: Pam Whelan was Alexa's full-time executive assistant; Mary Jane White had become provincial organizer; Nancy Bowes had taken over Mary Jane's duties as constituency assistant; and Marie-Paule LaForge, who'd been lured to the NDP from the Fédération acadienne de la Nouvelle-Écosse to improve the party's links with the Acadian community, had recently begun work as the caucus assistant for the party's three MLAs.

They were all women with young families or about to start them. Their husbands had demanding jobs or were busy studying to launch careers. The chance to spend social time with one another, even for an occasional night out, "was a wild experience." It began with an after-work drink, then a casual dinner, and quickly became institutionalized as a once-a-month-or-so night away from husbands and family for dinner at a local restaurant to enjoy each other's company, gossip about work and politics "under the cone of silence," share news about family, and talk about life and whatever else struck their fancy. "It was an opportunity," Whelan said. "We relished it." While GNO's existence "wasn't a dark secret," it also wasn't "widely advertised, shall we say, at our workplace."

But when Alexa learned about their dinners, joked Bowes, "she begged for an invitation to join in." While there were fleeting questions about the wisdom of inviting a boss among the workers, they were quickly laid to rest. Alexa became a GNO member in good standing, the quartet became a quintet, and the personal relationships among the women deepened into permanent friendship.

That became especially important later, when life sometimes caught up with them. In the early 1990s, of course, that was Alexa's separation from Peter. The split was public and the subject of some "cruel items" in *Frank*, the local gossip magazine. "Of course, Suzanne's role as fitness instructor made the descriptions of her and Peter's 'activities' that much more cheeky...and hurtful. We attempted to play supportive roles throughout, as friends would. Lots of conversations, gatherings, propping each other up, and where possible, some levity and laughs."

Navigating through the breakup of Alexa's marriage, and her new relationship with Holloway, provided a template for an even more painful journey a decade later: Mary Jane White's battle with breast cancer and her death in 2005. The day Mary Jane died, Whelan recalled, she and the other members of GNO, along with Mary Jane's family, participated in a Run for the Cure cancer fundraiser on behalf of White and another friend, White's late sister-in-law, Eileen O'Connell. O'Connell, one of the many women attracted to the NDP by Alexa's example, had served as an MLA from 1996 until her death from breast cancer in 2000. During Mary Jane's memorial service, recalled Whelan, "Alexa spoke eloquently on our behalf." Then, in the spring of 2006, the surviving members of GNO gathered to plant a tree in Mary Jane's honour in a park near where she'd lived with her husband and children.

There would also, of course, be many brighter moments over the years as their lives and careers diverged, but their connection endured. There would be "glorious" getaways at someone's home or cottage, including at Shaw's Island, "cooking for one another" and catching up on family, friends, and life. For Alexa's fifty-fifth birthday, in 1999, they went tidal bore rafting in Maitland, Nova Scotia; for her sixty-fourth, in 2008, it was San Francisco; and then, in 2009, a week of hiking at Gros Morne National Park in Newfoundland. "Alexa broke her toe on day one when we were unpacking our bags at the cabin we'd rented," Whelan recalled. "We still hiked every imaginable trail, including Gros Morne. Alexa was one serious trooper!"

GNO, of course, was one of Alexa's two core circles of female friends—the other was the group of women she'd known since her days as a Canadian Girl in Training at First Baptist Church.

3

"She was blowing smoke," Robert Chisholm would acknowledge with a laugh, years later, of the late 1990 pizza-night conversation with Alexa McDonough that launched his political career. She'd confidently told him he could actually win an upcoming provincial by-election in former Conservative premier John Buchanan's riding of Halifax Atlantic, a riding Buchanan had won with more than 50 per cent of the vote just three years before and where the NDP candidate in the race had finished a dismal, distant third. "It was all smoke," Chisholm agreed. "But she was good at it."

Like others who would play key roles in the later success of the Nova Scotia NDP, and who were inevitably also objects of Alexa's ever-optimistic smoke, Robert Chisholm's political roots were not in the NDP, nor especially political. The youngest of five children of the operator of a small Annapolis Valley insurance agency, Chisholm's father had once been a PC candidate. While conservative politics was a staple of dinner table conversation, Robert remained apolitical, more interested in hockey than politics—or education. After an injury during his first year of university hockey, he dropped out of school entirely. In the spring of 1981, he followed his new wife, Paula Simon, to Vancouver where she'd landed a job as a social worker. During their three years in BC, he "picked away" at his undergraduate degree, then signed up for a master's degree in sociology at Carleton University after Simon landed a job in Ottawa.

Studying sociology had been "a huge awakening.... I learned about inequality, fairness, justice, and I realized there were all these social justice questions that needed to be answered." After graduating in 1987, he landed a job in the Ottawa research office of the Canadian Union of Public Employees (CUPE) and became immersed in union politics. Two years later, he returned to Halifax as CUPE's Atlantic representative for Nova Scotia and Newfoundland.

"I didn't immediately become involved with the NDP," Chisholm offered; by then, he considered the party "more conservative than I was." Still, as a CUPE rep, he served on a number of joint labour-NDP committees, including one with Mary Jane White, the NDP organizer. White encouraged him to seek the party's nomination in an upcoming by-election in Halifax Atlantic.

"Novice mistake," Chisholm joked. "I said I'd think about it."

The electoral opening existed because the man widely known as "Teflon John" Buchanan abruptly resigned as Nova Scotia's premier on September 12, 1990, to take a senate appointment. In the two years since his crushing victory in the 1988 provincial election, Buchanan's non-stick surfaces had turned into too-egregious-to-ignore scandal catchers and reputation clingers. In June 1990, a former deputy minister and government insider named Michael Zareski told the province's public accounts committee about a sordid history of "corruption and cronyism throughout the Buchanan government," tying Buchanan himself into the allegations of wrongdoing.[3] His disclosures prompted RCMP investigations and, eventually, revelation that a secret trust fund had paid off more than $1 million in Buchanan's personal debts during his time as premier.

Although the Tories, who'd quickly scheduled a leadership convention for February 1991, were clearly in disarray and public disfavour, so too were the Liberals. It turned out Liberal leader Vince MacLean's $82,000 MLA's salary had also been secretly topped up by $47,000 a year from yet another private party trust fund, this one allegedly financed by bribes liquor companies had paid to the Liberals during the 1970s to get their products on the shelves of the provincial liquor commission.

Suddenly, it seemed, Alexa McDonough had an opening — again — to try to change Nova Scotia's traditional political conversation. An Omnifacts poll in the fall of 1990 showed the NDP with an unprecedented 29 per cent support among decided voters, the Liberals with 27 per cent, and the governing Tories now pulling up the distant rear at just 11 per cent.

There was even better NDP news in Ontario, where Bob Rae's provincial New Democrats had stunned the nation, and themselves, by winning the first NDP majority government in Canada's largest province. And the federal NDP was once again leading in national polls.

No wonder the 450 New Democrats who gathered in a Halifax hotel in November 1990 to toast the tenth anniversary of Alexa McDonough's election as party leader were ready to celebrate—and dream. So was Alexa. But, as she admitted to *Maclean's*, "I would be lying if I did not admit the whole thing is a little unreal."[4]

That was the question: was it real? Once again, the NDP was enjoying a mid-term bounce as scandal-weary voters declared a pox on both traditional mainstream alternatives. But what would happen when they actually had to make a ballot-box choice?

Their first opportunity would come with the Halifax Atlantic by-election that the Conservatives seemed intent on putting off for as long as possible. Given the NDP's lack of previous electoral success in that working-class constituency, Alexa and Dan O'Connor were keen to nominate someone as soon as possible so that person could begin building an organization and start the hard work of vote building.

Confirming that candidate's willingness was the larger purpose of that smoke-blowing pizza dinner at Salvatore's, a popular pizza parlour on South Street. The diners included Alexa and her new beau, Les Holloway (a "good friend" of Chisholm's), and Robert and his wife, Paula, who had been one of Alexa's basement tenants as a student at the Maritime School of Social Work. It was a decidedly who's-your-father Maritime evening. And it worked. Alexa was encouraging, flattering, confident. Chisholm acknowledged he didn't need a lot of flattery or encouragement. He and Paula had already talked. "We were at that point in our lives," he remembered, "when, if you believed in something, and we did, then you should do it. Regardless of the odds."

Despite Alexa's smoke-blowing, Robert Chisholm knew the odds still weren't riding with him.

•

When he was officially nominated in February 1991, Robert Chisholm barely knew the boundaries of the riding he'd set out to win. At the same time, few inside or outside those boundaries had any idea who Chisholm was. Despite the NDP's recent province-wide polling numbers, no one believed a neophyte politico could win the conservative, white-working-class district folksy John Buchanan had owned for more than two decades. Among the political cognoscenti, Chisholm barely merited mention. As late as the week before the August 27, 1991, vote, Acadia University political scientist Agar Adamson would confidently predict an angry, "damn-the-Tories" electoral mood would inevitably send the Liberal candidate, a popular county councillor named Randy Ball, to the legislature.[5]

But the NDP had a number of unexpected advantages. After the Tories chose Donald Cameron as their new, anti-patronage leader at a convention in early February, he needed time to put his own stamp on the party and to stamp out, to the extent possible, Buchanan's recent scandal-plagued history. But Cameron's Tories didn't help their cause in working-class Spryfield when the centrepiece of its first legislative session became a two-year public sector wage freeze. Which helped explain why the Tories waited nearly a full year before calling the by-election.

That gave Chisholm, an energetic and telegenic thirty-three-year-old, time to knock on doors and make his presence felt. Better, because it was a by-election, the NDP could target scarce resources to the campaign. Mary Jane White and Maureen Vine, an experienced local organizer, "went in very early to the lowest-income areas to make personal contact with everybody who lived there and talk up the NDP and get them to know Robert," O'Connor said. "They did that tremendous advance groundwork you need to do to get turnout."

Best, of course, was the party's not-so-secret weapon: Alexa McDonough, the province's most admired and trusted political leader who viscerally understood how to connect with people where they lived. Brenda Taylor, the former director of the Council of Christians and Jews who'd since enrolled in law school, attended the opening of Chisholm's campaign headquarters with her husband, Jack Stewart, who'd volunteered to distribute signs. "There were lots of people from Spryfield there, many of them living close to poverty" she recalled. "They knew Alexa from the TV. But she talked to them directly about how important it was for them to get involved. And they responded."

They also responded to Chisholm whose anti-patronage message was straightforward. "People are honest, hardworking, and trying to make ends meet, and then they see this stuff happening,"[6] he said, explaining he understood there was a lot of "loyalty out there" to the leader Buchanan had once been, "even though people do feel he betrayed them."

When the votes were counted, Robert Chisholm had been elected with nearly 40 per cent of the votes cast and, in the process, transformed Donald

Cameron's majority government into a minority. There were twenty-six MLAs, including the Speaker, on the government side. Former Tory deputy premier Roland Thornhill was now sitting as an independent while he fought criminal charges against him.[7] The Liberals held steady at twenty-two seats, and the NDP now had three seats in the legislature again.

There were a number of ways to look at the outcome. One was that the NDP now held the balance of power in the legislature. Another was that the NDP — after eleven years of ups and downs under Alexa McDonough — still couldn't win more than three seats.

There was no question how Alexa McDonough looked at it. "It strengthens our position considerably," she "bubbled" to reporters at a victory party. "It puts the government in the situation where they're darn well going to have to be accountable for what they do."

4

Jane Wright knew within a month of landing her job at the Nova Scotia Department of Labour she'd made a terrible mistake. She'd just come off two-and-a-half years at the Nova Scotia Office of the Status of Women where she had "an amazing woman boss" named Debi Forsyth-Smith and an important role in helping promote pay equity legislation. Becoming the labour department's first pay equity officer had seemed like a natural next step, but she quickly discovered a gaping chasm between the government's declared intent and departmental execution. She found herself with little to do. "People were photocopying pages of novels so they could appear to be reading a 'report' instead of a novel."

She spent her own time urgently applying for other jobs, which was how she came to interview for a position in the NDP caucus office in the fall of 1991. The party needed to fill at least four different positions — researcher, writer, communications person, and librarian — but only had the resources to hire one. Wright had a Dalhousie degree in library science. She'd grown up on a farm near Ottawa, spent three years studying English at Carleton, dropped out and moved to Vancouver Island, where she found work as a waitress, then drifted back to Ontario in 1979 where, still only nineteen, she'd enrolled at Trent University. In a second-year sociology course she was assigned *Karl Marx, Volume I.* "I read it cover to cover, got an A on the paper, and never saw the world the same way again." By the time she arrived at the NDP office for her interview with Dan O'Connor and Pam Whelan, she would have described her politics as more international socialist than NDP.

Alexa wasn't directly involved in the hiring process, Wright recalled, although she learned later she hadn't been the leader's first choice. "I wasn't a New Democrat. I wasn't known." But Wright quickly made herself known—and valued. In that pre-Google era with just three NDP MLAs responsible for twenty-six critic areas, Wright's wall of filing cabinets jammed with meticulously organized clipping files and records became an invaluable resource.

During legislature sessions, Wright's workday began at home at 7:00 a.m. with a quick conference call involving O'Connor and the party's three MLAs. By then, she'd watched the previous night's supper-hour news shows, the late-night regional TV news, and read all three morning newspapers to help get a handle on the day's key issues. After getting her two children breakfasted and off to school, she would rush down to the caucus office and begin flipping through her Rolodex. "Alexa really wants to know about..." she discovered was the best way to get deputy ministers' attention. By 10:00 a.m., she would have prepared briefing notes for the MLAs who would then begin the process of organizing and assigning questions and resolutions.

During House sessions, Wright followed legislative debates on a TV on her desk. The written Hansard, she quickly realized, didn't record everything said inside the Assembly. On more than one occasion when Alexa would be making an argument, Wright remembered distinctly hearing "an honourable member" say loudly enough to be heard but inevitably not to be recorded in Hansard: "Oh, you're cranky today. Must be your period."

When the legislature wasn't sitting, Wright would sometimes travel with Alexa to meetings and speaking engagements. Once, she remembered driving Alexa on a Cape Breton press tour. "I was driving her car and I remember backing up outside the radio station in Port Hawkesbury and backing right into a telephone pole." She was mortified. She had barely begun the job. "Don't worry about it," Alexa said. "It doesn't matter. Let's just go." Wright, who would go on to launch one of Halifax's most successful restaurants, said, "I learned to be a better boss from my experiences with her. She thanked everyone every single day. There was no budget for overtime, but it was easy to do the work because you were appreciated. It made you want to come back the next day."

She also got to see how her boss interacted with others, both the powerful and the usually unacknowledged. "I remember once we stopped to eat at a Wendy's. At some point, Alexa excused herself to go to the washroom. I waited and waited for her to return. We were going to be late for the next event, so I finally went to see what had happened. And there she was deeply engaged in a conversation with a cleaner. She connected with everyone on a very personal level."

5

On a May night in 1992, seventy men, and one woman, crowded into a basement meeting room in the Heather Motel in Stellarton, Nova Scotia. Outside, it was a pleasant spring evening; inside, the atmosphere was thick with sweat, tears, anger, grief, regret, recrimination, rage, exhaustion, frustration, fear. Especially — or at least it seemed that way to the woman taking it all in — fear.

The woman was Alexa McDonough. Twelve days before, at 5:18 a.m. on Saturday, May 9, 1992, a methane gas explosion had rocketed through the coal dust–laden innards of the Southwest 2 tunnel at the Westray mine in Plymouth, just a five-minute drive from tonight's meeting. The explosion, which sent boiling gas and flame through the tunnels at high speed, had trapped a full shift of twenty-six men at the far end of a 1.6 kilometre shaft, 350 metres beneath the Earth's surface. Every one of those men — the youngest twenty-two, the oldest fifty-six — was now dead.

Mining was a dirty, dangerous business in the safest, best-regulated circumstances. Coal miners rarely enjoyed a comfortable retirement. If rheumatoid arthritis didn't shorten their lives, black lung from breathing in coal dust too often turned their last years into a fight-for-breath hell. Worse, the alternative to a slow, agonizing death was too often a sudden, tragic end of life. Since 1838, more than 500 Nova Scotia coal miners had died doing their jobs, 270 of them here in Pictou County. Risking death, many believed, was the price miners had to pay, dying for their living. Many willingly paid;

the risks seemed an acceptable trade-off for a well-paid job in places where there were far too few to go around. Except...sometimes those mines turned out to be poorly managed and even more poorly regulated, and the risks beyond reckless.

On the eve of the 1988 provincial election, a vote-seeking John Buchanan triumphantly announced a plan to restart mining in Pictou County and create up to two hundred jobs. The province, he boasted, had struck a deal with Clifford Frame, an Ontario-based mining promoter, and his company, Curragh Resources, to open the mine and sell its low-sulfur coal to the Nova Scotia Power Corporation.

Frame's plan, championed by the local Tory MLA Donald Cameron, then the province's industry minister, now Buchanan's successor as premier, was costly. Buchanan's Tories agreed to provide Curragh with its mining lease, pony up a $12 million loan and guarantee to purchase 275,000 tons of its coal every year for fifteen years. When even that turned out not to be enough to make the project reality, Cameron telephoned Prime Minister Brian Mulroney, whose government sweetened the pot with an additional $85 million federal loan guarantee as well as an $8 million interim loan. When all was counted, governments had put up $105 million of the mine's $130 million cost.

When the mine officially opened on September 11, 1991, of course, there were plenty of glad-handing, back-patting politicians sharing in the mining revival glory story.

But none of them, it turned out, had paid attention to what was happening. The company had quietly rejigged its original plans, pushing the mine's pathways through major geological faults—the coal seam was considered to be "among the most dangerous in the world because of its high methane content"[8]—in order to get to the coal faster. The politicians weren't paying attention either when officials in the department of labour questioned the company's inadequate training, its lack of an emergency plan, and its failure to submit requested designs for roof supports. And they certainly weren't in the mine after it opened to experience the frequent roof falls and cave-ins, or to see just how much highly combustible coal dust had been allowed to build up on the mine's floors and walls with no stone-dust to neutralize its explosiveness.

The miners saw it all. Although they understood the risks baked into their job descriptions, what was happening at Westray was of a different magnitude. The company seemed to be callously endangering their lives. If they complained, they were told they could leave. Some, experienced miners, did. Others swallowed their fears and hoped government would do its oversight job. It didn't. On April 29, just ten days before the tragedy, a mining inspector noted the dangerous levels of coal dust in the mine — again — and ordered the company — again — to remove it immediately. Failure to do so, he said, could result in a $10,000 fine or a year in jail. But no one followed up. And then the mine exploded.

Five years later, a public inquiry would conclude that, from beginning to end, Westray had been "a story of incompetence, of mismanagement, of bureaucratic bungling, of deceit, of ruthlessness, of cover-up, of apathy, of expediency, and of cynical indifference."[9]

Within an hour of the explosion, Alexa McDonough was awakened with news of the unfolding tragedy. By that afternoon, she was in Pictou County, 170 kilometres northeast of Halifax, meeting with the miners' families still desperate for news of their fates. She remembered meeting one young woman, suddenly made a widow with two preschool-aged children. "She recognized me," Alexa said. "And she said to me, 'Promise me nothing like this will ever happen again.'" She promised.

Two days later, Nova Scotia's legislators bowed their heads for a minute of silence to remember the eleven miners so far confirmed dead. Each of the party leaders spoke sombre words, offering sympathy to the families and praising the bravery of the men risking their lives in a frantic, futile search for survivors.

Alone among the leaders, wrote Dean Jobb in *Calculated Risk*, Alexa McDonough, "whose party had been critical of the government's poor record on labour issues, served notice that the gloves would come off in the days ahead."[10] After a Westray spokesman suggested "Mother Nature cannot be anticipated," Alexa fired back in the legislature. "The fact of the matter is that this is a disaster that was not an act of God. We have a responsibility to say that we must learn from this situation, and in the future, hopefully, it will be possible to prevent similar tragedies, similar losses."

Learning from the situation was why Alexa, Robert Chisholm, John Holm, and Dan O'Connor had come to Stellarton that night. This private meeting with the miners had been organized by officials from the United Steelworkers, the union trying, before the tragedy, to convince the men to sign union cards.

So far, the company, with the complicity of the RCMP who kept journalists away from the families of the dead miners, had managed to control the flow of information. When reporters raised rumours about potential safety issues, a company spokesperson batted them away as "unfounded and an affront to our people."

For three hours inside that meeting hall, however, the miners—supposedly "our" people—made clear those allegations were well founded. The miners told graphic horror stories about conditions in the mine before, and after, the tragedy. Smashed equipment, coal dust, and the constant threat of explosion. The company was still sending men underground, even as methane levels continued to rise, to "rehabilitate" the mine so it could reopen quickly. Miners who refused to work, they said, were told to "hit the highway."

Alexa didn't say much. "It was more compassionate listening," remembered O'Connor. Although there were four of them, "there was no question who was in charge on the NDP side." Alexa was there "to listen and try to make sure their story and their concerns were drawn out." Knowing how fraught the situation was and how fearful the men were, Alexa made it clear she would only make their concerns public if they agreed. They agreed.

So the next morning, on May 22, back in the legislature in Halifax, Alexa arrived armed and ready. She went after Labour Minister Leroy Legere for his department's failure to follow up on the April 29 inspection and, worse, allowing the company to "harass" men into returning underground even though "the conditions in that mine are unsafe; they're life threatening." Given the potential for yet another disaster, she told reporters, Legere would have "blood on his hands if he doesn't take some responsibility to put an end to what's going on there."

All that week, Alexa had been pressing the government to change the terms of the announced public inquiry to give official standing to the miners and the families of the dead. Now she backed that up with a letter from forty-five miners demanding a say in ongoing investigations. Labour department investigators, the men wrote, hadn't even contacted the three surviving members of the mine's health and safety committee to participate in the department's investigations, "despite the fact that those rights are enshrined in the Occupational Health and Safety Act."

Alexa also tabled a company memo dated eight days after the explosion. Titled "Security Measures," it not only warned employees not to use cellphones because they could be monitored or leave papers on their desks, but it also outlined "shredding" procedures. Alexa told the legislature what she'd been told by those who'd witnessed what was happening to company documents. "We're not talking several garbage cans" of papers being shredded. "We're talking about several buckets on sizable loaders."

6

It was the middle of the night, and Travis McDonough was frightened. He was in his early twenties, the "hell-raiser" brother, "the major risk taker who pushed Mom to the brink. I had a long rope and I used it. Drinking, or drugs, or women, I was burning the candle at both ends." But tonight, what he wanted most was to talk through his fears with his mother.

He was in grade 12 when his parents split up. By then Justin was a student at Queen's University, and Travis was, as he explained with a laugh, "already kind of crazy." While their parents' divorce may have "burst the bubble of security," he is quick to point to other factors that led to his own behaviour. "I had this raging form of cocktail of [undiagnosed] dyslexia and ADD. Academically, I was a disaster. I spent way too much time doing things I shouldn't have. And Mom was remarkably tolerant and was remarkably understanding and non-judgmental in those years of anarchy."

Which may explain why he wanted to talk to her that night.

Despite the fact he was slight of stature and wispy of weight, Travis had taken up competitive boxing. It began with the occasional bar fight in college, and the even more occasional call home from a police lock-up. Dan O'Connor remembered one such incident. Alexa only told him about it "in case any reporter got wind of it." But O'Connor was intrigued by her reaction. It turned out Travis—one of the few whites on his high school basketball team—had been "standing up for a Black friend who was the object of abuse," and words soon turned to fists. "Alexa felt Travis had done the right thing," O'Connor said. "She was proud of him."

He'd since graduated from bar fights to the gym where his fearless Jack Russell persona earned respect. In 1992 and 1993, Travis represented Nova Scotia in Canada's national amateur championships.

So, when a boxing team from the US military visited Halifax for a friendly competition with the locals, Travis was naturally tapped to fight in a match. But his opponent, he'd discovered, would be a veteran US Army sergeant with more than 350 official fights to his name. At the time, Travis had just six.

"I couldn't sleep I was so nervous, so I went in to see Mom in the middle of the night." He asked his mother, who had grown up studying ballet and was anything but a boxing aficionado, what he should do. Her response, "not in a callous way," was: "You've committed to this, you've got to do this." Looking back years later, Travis would be grateful. "What that did to build inner grit and resilience was way more powerful than if she'd said, 'Oh you're right, you know, throw in the towel.' She had this tough-love type of parenting style. She wasn't going to throw me a life preserver." He paused. "Those are the great builders I still rely on today and those come from a place that it's hard to figure out."

7

In January 1993, having won airline tickets in a charity draw, Alexa decided she and her two now-adult sons — Justin, twenty-three, had graduated from Queen's in May 1992 and taken a job with London Life, while Travis, twenty-one, had finally, happily settled into a kinesiology program at Dalhousie University — should enjoy "ten glorious days in Hawaii" together to be "fortified... for the demanding year ahead."

She didn't know the half of it.

By the end of January, when they landed back in Halifax, where Alexa's father, Lloyd, was already in a nursing home suffering from the Alzheimer's that would take his life later that year, they discovered that Alexa's mother, Jean, was in the hospital awaiting open heart surgery after a severe angina attack.

And there were other "demanding" moments Alexa already knew awaited her, including an election. Donald Cameron, almost certain to be defeated in a confidence vote if he recalled the legislature for its spring session, waited until three days before the House was to meet before pulling the trigger on an election for May 25, 1993.

"I dreaded the campaign in the lead-up," Alexa confided in a letter to a former McDonough cellar-dweller named Sine MacKinnon, "trying to imagine getting through it without Peter, Dad, and Giff...."[11]

MacKinnon had first encountered Alexa in the early 1980s while covering the NDP's annual convention for the *Antigonish Casket*, her local community weekly. A family friend mentioned to Alexa that Sine would be heading to Halifax that fall to begin journalism studies at the University of King's College. "I didn't have anywhere to live," MacKinnon remembered, and Alexa's basement apartment was vacant. "It was all just happenstance." MacKinnon would drive sons Justin and Travis and their friends to and from soccer matches, occasionally help with their homework, set the table for breakfast, and generally be available as needed. In exchange, she could live rent-free. "It was pretty remarkable, and Alexa just automatically, as she does with people, embraced me and made me part of the family. It never felt like an arrangement, even though it was; it felt like family."

MacKinnon's late father had been a Progressive Conservative MLA during the Stanfield era. She herself had been the Tory prime minister — "red Tory," she clarified — in her high school's model parliament. But, like others before and after, she soon became part of Alexa's larger NDP family. She and another King's student named Darrell Dexter, who would become the province's first NDP premier in 2009, relaunched the moribund King's-Dal New Democratic Youth club. "I had always been interested in politics," MacKinnon recalled, "but she took me under her wing and introduced me to lots of people and encouraged me and helped me."

After the NDP formed government in Ontario in 1990, MacKinnon took a job with a cabinet minister and had since become Premier Bob Rae's assistant press secretary. "I'm in the back seat of Bob's car and we're coming back from an event and the phone rings," she recalled. "Bob answers it and then he turns to me and he says, 'It's for you.'" It was the Nova Scotia NDP campaign office asking how soon she could get to Halifax. She immediately took a leave of absence to become whatever Alexa needed her to be.

"From the moment you arrived," Alexa later wrote in a thank-you note, "I felt relaxed and confident we knew what we were doing, and if we didn't, we could laugh our way through it, which we did."

By 1993, Alexa McDonough had become the longest continuously serving political party leader in Canada. In that thirteen-year period, she'd faced off against Tory premiers John Buchanan and Donald Cameron, and competed for votes with Liberal leaders Sandy Cameron, Vince MacLean, and now John Savage.

Savage's decision to seek the Liberal leadership in 1992 had been a crushing blow. The Welsh-born Savage, who'd immigrated to Nova Scotia in 1966, seemed cut from New Democrat cloth. A "bearded hippie" family doctor who'd run a detox centre in Dartmouth and a free medical clinic in North Preston, a nearby Black community, Savage ran for his local school board after failing to convince its members to launch a school sex education program. He went on to serve as mayor of Dartmouth from 1985 to 1992.

Although Savage had twice unsuccessfully run for office as a Liberal in the 1970s, Alexa convinced herself, and attempted to convince Savage, his real sympathies were with the NDP. In early 1992, in fact, she attempted to recruit him to run for the party in the next provincial election, even suggesting she'd be willing to step aside if he decided to run for party leader. Instead, a few weeks after their private meeting, Savage announced his own candidacy for the Liberal leadership, which he won in June 1992. "When Savage won the Liberal leadership," declared political scientist Agar Adamson, "the longest face in the room was Alexa McDonough's."[12] By the time the election campaign began nine months later, polls showed the Liberals with a commanding lead over the Tories and the NDP "lagging far behind."[13]

It was an all-too-familiar story. Three years before — in the deepest depths of the Tory scandals, but at a time when voters didn't have to make a real choice — the trend lines had been very similar to those in the lead-up to the 1988 election. Polls showed the "soaring" NDP with 38 per cent support, running neck-and-neck with the declining Vince MacLean–led Liberals, and well ahead of the decimated Buchanan Conservatives. "I think the Tory government and the Liberal opposition are doing their part to help drive people in our direction," explained Alexa, who "could scarcely hide her delight."[14]

But now, with real government on the line, both Liberals and Conservatives boasted new leaders preaching new old sermons, both earnestly proclaiming themselves clean-government evangelists, not to mention job creators and deficit slayers.

An increasingly desperate Cameron, who'd won the Tory leadership with his promises to end patronage and to step down if he couldn't balance the province's books in three years, suddenly began doling out tender-free goodies from a treasury that now seemed bottomless. Savage, who would impose massive government cuts as premier a year later, campaigned on the promise of open government and new jobs in a province battered by 13.6 per cent unemployment. "What people are telling us is that they're ready for a change," Savage told Canadian Press reporter Alan Jeffers, adding pointedly of Alexa McDonough's NDP: "What most of them are saying is that the change that they prefer is the middle-of-the-road Liberal government."[15]

The NDP had decided to focus on a few winnable seats and tout a message that was less about grand policy schemes and more about the simple idea "the NDP might not be perfect, but we're better than the other two. That was really what it came down to," recalled Dan O'Connor. Alexa, he said, initially wasn't happy with what she perceived as "such a negative message. When she first heard it, she couldn't imagine ever possibly campaigning with it. But the whole team begged her to give it a try." After test-driving the approach in the 1991 by-election Robert Chisholm won handily, "she discovered it worked like a charm."

But 1993 was a different campaign. Chisholm himself remembered "just hanging on" after the Tories gerrymandered his riding, carving off his strongest areas of support in advance of the election. "We'd won by five hundred votes in 1991," he said. "In 1993, the margin was twenty-three."

One of the pro-NDP neighbourhoods moved out of Chisholm's riding ended up in Halifax Fairview, a new riding that encompassed most of Alexa's Halifax Chebucto district, a sure sign the government had given up on personally defeating her. Not that the NDP itself was taking any chances this time.

Sue Dodd, a former intern and another one-time cellar-dweller now serving as Alexa's constituency assistant, recalled that "twenty-six votes" — the paper-thin margin by which McDonough won in 1988 — became a "mantra" for everyone working on the campaign. "Whenever you'd think it was time to go home, someone would say, 'Twenty-six votes,'" and you'd go back to work." In the end, Alexa won her new constituency with more than 40 per cent of the vote.

Alexa, flanked by Liberal leader John Savage (left) and the
Progressive Conservative premier Donald Cameron (right) taking part
in the televised leaders' debate during the 1993 provincial election.
CBC host Jim Nunn (standing) fields questions.
(Republished with permission from the *Chronicle Herald*.)

But that didn't change the outcome. Within twenty minutes of the polls
closing, the television networks called the election for the Liberals, who ended the evening with forty seats, compared to nine for the PCs and just three,
again, for the NDP, which claimed, again, just 18 per cent of the popular
vote. Dan O'Connor did his best to turn defeat into at least a variance of
victory, slicing and dicing the results to show the NDP had come second in
ten ridings. "Dan did the figures," Alexa explained later, "and they showed
that, if something like 2,068 votes in the closest ridings had come our way,
we would have been the official opposition."[16]

But they didn't, which rekindled the flame of the perennial question: was
it time for Alexa to move on?

"I never know how to deal with people's obsession with, 'What are you going to do when you get defeated?'" Alexa confessed to Halifax *Mail Star* political reporter Judy Myrden. "Well, I don't know," she answered her own question. "I only know there's a whole world out there of things worth doing."[17]

8

The ceremony, on June 14, 1993, in the chapel at the St. Vincent's Guest House, a nursing home in central Halifax, was a poignant reminder of both who Lloyd Shaw had been and also what had become of him in the years since he'd disappeared from the public stage.

In 1990, he was diagnosed with Alzheimer's, the insidious, mind-sapping disease that had claimed his own father thirty years before—and was not yet done with the Shaw family. In the years that followed, Lloyd's deterioration had been swift and inexorable. By the winter of 1993, when he was named to the Order of Canada, one among the small number of Canadians each year honoured for their "extraordinary contributions to the nation," he had trouble speaking and walking and was no longer capable of travelling to Ottawa for the investiture ceremony. Instead, Lieutenant Governor Lloyd Crouse came to St. Vincent's, Lloyd Shaw's home for the past year, to make the formal presentation.

To prepare for the event, Alexa spent time reading to him the letters of commendation his six non-political nominators had written in support of his appointment to the order. "He was attentive and approving," Alexa would remember. "When I told him about the folks coming to celebrate, he was pleased."[18]

More than three dozen close family and friends attended. Crouse presented his medal and read out the citation. "He rose to the occasion," noted Alexa, "leaving us with some wonderful photos of memorable moments.... But throughout the celebration itself, he kept searching. With almost non-existent vocabulary, he was signalling, 'Where is he?'" Later, when she showed him photos of the event, "he kept pointing at himself and nodding approval. It was clear he no longer had any sense of who he was, but he did know who Lloyd Shaw was, and it was evident, he quite liked his old friend."

Lloyd Robert Shaw died on October 16, 1993, at the age of seventy-nine, with Alexa and Robbie at his side. "Mercifully," Alexa would joke in her own annual Christmas letter to family and friends, "he was spared ever knowing of the NDP devastation at the polls [in the federal election] one week later, though he would surely have found some basis for optimism in the aftermath, as he always did."

But could Lloyd's daughter and the inheritor of both his political passions and his endless optimism continue to find optimism in a reality that didn't offer much? "NDP Provincial Council know that I will be informing the 1994 convention whether I'm prepared to lead the party into another election," she noted in her letter. "As I grapple with that decision, I come to the end of 1993 uncertain about what the future holds, but more certain than ever of the importance of family and friends, and immensely grateful for the privilege of serving my community and the social democratic cause. The struggle for a more caring, compassionate society is surely more, not less relevant, than ever in these troubled times."

9

"You know," Les Holloway said finally, "this isn't going to work." It was mid-February and he and Alexa had decided to go for a walk, and have "the talk," as they strolled along Barrington Street near his apartment.

In truth, there were any number of good reasons why this — whatever their relationship was — should not have worked. And yet it had. Until now.

They came from different worlds and different world views. When Alexa would boast her father had sold his company to its workers, Les would volley back, "He sold it to his *management* workers." After Les's mother died, Alexa recalled having dinner with Les's alcoholic father. "You know she's a communist," he'd declared, pointing hard at Alexa. "You can tell by her name: Alexi. A socialist like that Gorbachev, with the mark of the devil on her." Les told his father he'd make his own mind up, thanks.

But there was no question he often felt he'd stumbled into a life and a lifestyle "way over my pay grade." He and Alexa spent time in Naples, Florida, visiting Alexa's parents at their condo, enjoying a lifestyle "I never expected to be able to do" as a kid from the poor end of town. Sitting on the condo's balcony with Alexa's "Boston relatives" watching the sun set, he would remember asking himself, "Why would anyone need a swimming pool when they're right next to a beach?" But he swam, played tennis with Alexa and with her father. "He was still a real good tennis player." Later, as Lloyd's Alzheimer's progressed, he remembered a Christmas with Alexa's family. "One year, Travis gave Lloyd tennis balls, and he seemed to be trying to figure them out. It was funny, but it was also touching."

Les admired Alexa. "She didn't have to do what she did," he would say. "She was born into the family she was born into, and she lived in a comfortable way, but she always cared about making sure other people were treated right." He also loved her. "I'll always love Alexa," he said many years later. "She was different than other women I'd known. She understood me when we talked."

"I think the world of you," he confessed to her that day on Barrington Street. But... Les Holloway was pushing forty. He wanted children of his own. His "biggest regret" was that he'd never had a child with his former partners. Although he was now involved as a mentor with Big Brothers, he still wanted to be the father his father wasn't to his own children. "I knew that wasn't possible with Alexa."

Their love affair was over. But, as with many of Alexa's relationships with men, the relationship itself would never end.

10

"I think every single person in this room knows me well enough to know what a tremendously difficult decision it was for me," Alexa McDonough confided to the sixty members of the NDP's provincial council who'd gathered in a Kentville church hall for what was supposed to be a routine meeting. There were tears in her eyes. "I obviously do it filled with emotion. But I do it with joy and with no sense of regret whatsoever."[19]

No one was surprised, but everyone was shocked. On November 19, 1994, fourteen years and one day after she'd won the leadership of the Nova Scotia New Democratic Party, Alexa McDonough resigned from the job. She was fifty years old.

She'd made the decision quietly, on her own, months before. The people she'd told in advance were mostly just those who needed to know: the party president and fellow MLA John Holm, who was about to be appointed interim leader. The night before, the media had been advised she would be making a "special announcement" at that Saturday's provincial council meeting. Sensing news, they drove the hundred kilometres from Halifax to hear it.

Given all that had gone before politically and personally — her father's death, a recent breakup — quitting wasn't nearly as easy a decision as it should have been. "I wasn't frustrated, or fed up, or burned out,"[20] she told a journalist later. "I loved my job."

She still seemed to. Despite everything. Less than six months earlier, Nova Scotians, in their haste to send what Alexa called the "Bu-Cameron" Tweedledee government packing, had passed over the NDP, again, and instead chosen the Tweedledum Liberals under John Savage. He had, just as predictably and even more quickly, transformed himself from Nova Scotia's vote-seeking, no-new-taxes, jobs-focused saviour into a Donald Cameron sound-alike deficit slayer. He'd slashed government spending while introducing $78 million worth of new taxes in order, he said, to tame the Tories' out-of-control spending.

When government workers, university professors, and students massed outside the provincial legislature in October 1994 to denounce those draconian and unexpected moves, the protestors booed both Savage and interim Conservative leader Terry Donahoe, but "loudly cheered" when Alexa took the mic. For a woman who'd seemed awkward and unsure as a public speaker when she'd begun her political career a decade and a half earlier, Alexa was now "considered one of the ablest opposition members to grace the House."[21]

Inside the legislature, she'd made her small three-member caucus the province's real opposition, challenging the government not only on its economic austerity programs and attacks on workers' rights but also on its consultation-free plan to impose amalgamation on Nova Scotia's largest municipalities and its scheme to make casino gambling the province's economic salvation. Halifax *Chronicle-Herald* cartoonist Bruce MacKinnon had even dubbed the NDP MLAs the "FiliBusters" in recognition of the "long, long hours of debate they forced on the other parties," said chief of staff Dan O'Connor. "Alexa threw herself into the fray with enthusiasm, forcing the Liberals into amendments to end the weeks of debate on each piece of unpopular legislation." As usual, "she did her own research and used her own contacts, not relying only on the small caucus staff." Voters again seemed to be paying attention. Just two months before she quit, a public opinion poll showed the NDP with 24 per cent support. Alexa herself was, as she had been many times before, Nova Scotians' most popular leader.

Why quit now? Why not? "It was just time. For me and for the party. I didn't have the energy to take the party over the next hurdle," she explained of the thinking that had gone into her decision. "And I'd become a liability to the party. I know that sounds like a contradiction when you look at that poll, but the myth made it hard for people to see just how strong this party really is. It's not just me. The party has outgrown me. But in order for people to see that, the Alexa Myth has to be buried," she said, breathing new life into the old myth. Selfless...self-deprecating...Good old Alexa.[22]

Party members didn't want to see her go, Pam Whelan said later, but they were happy for her too. "We were all elated for her to be making this decision for herself. To heck with the uncertainty it threw anyone's way. No matter." Alexa had more than earned her right to decide the right time to leave.

That night, the faithful gathered in a room at the nearby Old Orchard Inn for a "serious party." Noted Joanne Lamey, a member of the provincial council, "There were a lot of tears shed. I do remember a bunch of us acting out with Alexa that evening — maybe some wine, dancing on the beds, country music..."

•

Alexa returned to the legislature two days after her resignation to stirring tributes and a standing ovation as she sat in her new seat in the chamber's second row, behind interim leader John Holm and MLA Robert Chisholm. Premier Savage declared, "She has earned the respect and admiration of not only her colleagues, but also her foes, through her passionate commitment to the people she represents, and her ability to focus clearly on issues that may be at times uncomfortable — but are also very important." Interim Conservative leader Donahoe added, without irony, her longevity in the House said "a very great deal about her tenacity and determination."

In response, Alexa began by thanking her nemesis, the New Democrat turned spiteful independent turned leader of his own party turned independent again turned Liberal and now Speaker Paul MacEwan for "not ruling this out of order."

She allowed that it was "the one and only time I'll hear such kind words from all corners of the House." But she couldn't help recalling her days as the only New Democrat and lone woman in the House. There were now five women in the legislature, a modest improvement she could have but didn't take credit for. Instead she chose to focus on the work still to be done. "We all know that sexism is still alive and well in this province and in this House."[23]

As if to prove her point, the Liberal House leader Richie Mann, in a scrum with reporters outside the chamber that night, speculated Alexa had decided to quit because she was planning to remarry.

"He must know something I don't know," Alexa joked when reporters asked for comment. Then she turned serious, describing it as a "typical reaction to a woman. He thinks, 'My goodness, she has been single now for five years. If she is going to do something significant, she is probably going to go off and get married.'"[24]

Alexa certainly had no plans to remarry. But what were her plans?

Alexa McDonough speaking in the House of Commons, c. 1998
(courtesy of McDonough Family Collection)

THE NATIONAL STAGE

1

When Alexa McDonough announced on May 30, 1995, that she intended to seek the federal NDP's top job not even seven months after resigning the Nova Scotia NDP leadership, no one was shocked. Politics, it seemed, was simply the sum of who, and what, Alexa McDonough had become. But both before and after her resignation as provincial party leader, Alexa had seriously considered two very different new career paths.

Seven months before she quit, she quietly applied for a job as Africa regional director at the Inter Press Service (IPS) News Agency, an international non-governmental agency providing news stories and analysis from the world's poorest regions. She even flew to Bonn, Germany, in April 1994 to meet with IPS officials on the sidelines of the World Summit on Social Development to discuss the position in more depth. She later told journalist Sharon Fraser she came away from those meetings, with a better understanding of "how critical it is to recognize [global economic] problems can't be solved domestically anymore. But neither will they be solved internationally by G7 leaders or by multinational corporations." She talked about a new kind of people's internationalism that, on the face of it, seemed to lead her away from partisan politics. Despite that, for reasons that she never made clear, she withdrew her IPS application months before she announced she was stepping down as NDP leader.

Then, two months after she resigned, she applied to be director of the school of social work at McGill University in Montréal. "It feels like an opportunity for me to come 'full circle,'" she wrote in her January 30, 1995, cover letter. "It would appear to represent a remarkable convergence of many of my lifelong passions, preoccupations and professional commitments."[1]

Less than a month later, the CBC invited her to fly to Ottawa to be a panel commentator discussing federal Finance Minister Paul Martin's second budget. Watching Martin from the parliamentary sidelines in February 1995, Alexa was beyond shocked and appalled. By the time Martin had finished laying out his draconian neoliberal plans for the country's economy, Alexa had already privately snapped shut any further thought of seeking an escape hatch from public life.

Martin's second budget reversed many of the progressive promises the Liberals had made to win their landslide majority in 1993. In the name of deficit reduction, Martin announced $25 billion in spending cuts and decimated programs for the country's most vulnerable: the unemployed, the elderly, those on welfare. Foreign aid would be cut dramatically. There were even threats to Canada's flagship medicare program.

What made that even more appalling for a social democrat like Alexa was the shocking reality so many Canadians seemed to agree with the government. An Angus Reid poll taken shortly after Martin's speech indicated two of three Canadians approved of the budget, and overall support for the government increased 5 per cent to 63 per cent following the budget presentation.

In part, Alexa believed that was because the parliamentary opposition was in disarray. Canadians had been so eager to get rid of Brian Mulroney they took out their anger on his successor Kim Campbell and the party he'd left behind, reducing the Progressive Conservatives from 154 seats to just 2 in 1993. The 177 Liberal MPs — governing from the right, after campaigning from the left — stared across the House of Commons at a divided but predominantly conservative opposition. The Bloc Québécois, led by a former Tory cabinet minister whose ultimate goal was separation from Canada, formed the official opposition. The Western-based, right-wing Reform Party, led by Preston Manning, claimed the mantle of "loyal" opposition.

And after winning forty-four seats under Ed Broadbent in 1988 — the NDP's best showing ever — the party had simply collapsed. His successor, Audrey McLaughlin, the first woman to lead the federal party, had led it to its worst showing in thirty-five years. Winning less than 7 per cent of the popular vote, the NDP elected just nine MPs, five of them from Saskatchewan, effectively reducing it to a regional rump. Worse, the party had fallen three seats short of official party status, so it didn't qualify for public funding; its members weren't appointed to official parliamentary committees and rarely got opportunities to put questions to the government in Question Period.

There were plenty of explanations for what had gone wrong, not least that the NDP had simply become roadkill as voters rushed to rid themselves of the Tories. Many moderate NDP voters, determined to drive a stake through the heart of the evil Conservatives, had at least temporarily shacked up with Jean Chrétien's progressive-sounding Liberals. Some populist protest voters had even skipped past their traditional home in the NDP to embrace the brand of Western alienation espoused by Reform's Preston Manning.

There was another truth too. Audrey McLaughlin had failed to capture the Canadian political imagination. A social worker from the Yukon who'd first been elected to Parliament in a 1987 by-election, McLaughlin had been re-elected in the general election a year later. Just one year later, she won her party's leadership over former BC premier Dave Barrett on the fourth ballot.

McLaughlin had not been Alexa's first choice as leader. In fact, she'd been part of a high-powered lobbying campaign by what journalist Michael Valpy called the NDP's "blood royal" to convince former Ontario NDP leader and UN ambassador Stephen Lewis to seek the job. He had politely declined.[2]

Many then shifted their attention to Alexa, who was widely respected and personally popular inside the party. But she had demurred too. Politically, she was still shaking off the ashes of her disastrous 1988 provincial campaign and, personally, she was well aware of the toll political life had taken on her family life.

Although Alexa had been publicly supportive of McLaughlin's leadership, there was never much chemistry between the two. She confided to friends she found the federal leader aloof.

When McLaughlin announced her resignation in mid-April 1994, Alexa wasn't ready to commit to seeking the job. But she'd clearly begun having second thoughts about her future. A few weeks before McLaughlin quit, the Nova Scotia NDP staged a thank-you celebration to mark Alexa's retirement. Organizers, who'd set out 450 chairs for the event, found themselves scrambling at the last minute to add extra chairs as a boisterous crowd over-filled the auditorium. "The thought of living without politics," Alexa mused to a reporter that day, "is a bit like asking me to live without oxygen. I don't know what I'm going to do."[3]

But what ultimately changed her mind was a sentiment she had begun hearing bubble up inside her own party. "I was so sick of hearing people say, 'We can't have another woman leader because this one didn't work out,'" she explained. "I was appalled to think how rampant the sexism would have to be in the party. We've had all-male leaders, always. When a male leader didn't take the party to great heights, nobody said, 'Oh, we can't have another male leader.' And that struck me as so bizarre and twisted. I thought, 'I'll be damned if the party I care about is not going to have a woman leader in the race.'"

•

It was early June 1995, and the National Union of Public and General Employees (NUPGE) had just wrapped up its annual convention at a hotel in downtown Halifax. "A few of us we were just sitting around congratulating ourselves on our successes, having a few drinks, a few folks smoking a little weed," remembered Skip Hambling, the union's communications director. "It was a little like sitting around at the cottage—and then she showed up."

She was Alexa McDonough, recently declared candidate for the leadership of the federal NDP. She'd asked for an opportunity to meet with the union's leadership to make a pitch for their support. This was that opportunity. "No one really wanted to listen," Hambling acknowledged later. "She wasn't getting deference from anyone, but she didn't let that bother her. She just rolled with the punches, and she connected with people. James liked that, liked her informality."

James was James Clancy, the national president of NUPGE, one of Canada's largest unions. NUPGE had never been politically affiliated but the union, which represented more than 350,000 mostly public sector workers, was political—and powerful.

Clancy had never met Alexa, but he very quickly decided he wanted to help. "She was down to earth. There was no hubris, no bluster, no bravado. She was practical, and I thought she could contribute to the party. Besides, she was a woman. And an underdog."

She was certainly an underdog. Most union leaders—a significant power base within the NDP—had already lined up behind one of Alexa's two main rivals, maverick Svend Robinson and Lorne Nystrom.

NUPGE became the first major union to endorse Alexa McDonough.

•

"Listen, guys." Lawrence McBrearty did his best to make himself heard above the din, tamp down the obvious enthusiasm around the table. "We really can't pass a motion like that."

It was the late spring of 1995 and McBrearty, the Canadian director of the United Steelworkers union, had travelled from Toronto to Trenton, Nova Scotia, for the annual get-together of leaders of Steelworkers' locals across Atlantic Canada. It was an opportunity for the union reps to spend a few days discussing common concerns. Somehow, the conversation this day had turned to the question of who should be the next leader of Canada's NDP.

There was no doubt inside the room the correct answer was Alexa McDonough. No one had forgotten her compassionate advocacy after the Westray mining disaster three years earlier. Alexa had been there for union members in their worst days, and now the union reps wanted to be there for her. Finally, one of them proposed they pass a formal resolution of support for Alexa as the NDP's next leader.

Which was when McBrearty realized he needed to step in. It was not up to local union reps to endorse candidates for national office. That was the responsibility of the national executive. "Why don't you just tell me, 'Look, Lawrence, this is what we'd like,'" he said, "and I'll bring it to the national executive."

In truth, McBrearty wanted the same thing. He'd begun his career as a seventeen-year-old miner in Noranda's Quebec copper mines in 1960. A decade later, he was president of his local and head of its safety committee when a young miner was crushed to death in the mill. McBrearty was among those who brought his body out "in a basket," and had to console the widow, who was pregnant with their first child. Although a coroner's inquest determined the company had been negligent, Quebec's justice minister refused to prosecute. "Seeing that, knowing what happened," McBrearty recalled quietly many years later, "it stays with you. You never forget."

Now, as the Steelworkers' national director, he was in a position to do something to advance his union's — and his own — safety agenda. A few days later, he called Alexa, whom he'd known in the mid-eighties while he'd served as the union's Atlantic director.

"Let's meet," he said. They met in the Air Canada lounge at the Toronto

International airport. McBrearty brought along Harry Hynd, the director of the union's powerful Ontario District 6. He and Hynd had already contacted other major private sector unions so he knew there was support for Alexa's candidacy.

McBrearty quickly came to the point. "I think I can get enough union support to make you the number one candidate in the race."

2

They called themselves Thelma and Louise, and they spent much of the sweltering summer of 1995 criss-crossing the country in a green station wagon, laughing, talking, stopping off at backyard barbecues, dropping in on rollicking kitchen parties, sitting around in earnest living-room *kaffeeklatsches*, handing out leaflets, talking, listening, talking some more, eventually collapsing for the night, often into a shared bed in someone's spare room, waking up, moving on, another day, getting lost, finding their way, laughing some more, arriving at yet another event in another somewhere, taking another opportunity to make a first impression with maybe a dozen or so potential supporters.

For Alexa McDonough and Sine MacKinnon, the 1995 NDP leadership campaign became an extended shared road trip adventure. MacKinnon, who'd been Alexa's "everything" during the 1993 provincial election campaign, returned to reprise her many roles — driver, advance woman, publicist, speechwriter, campaign liaison, confidante, friend — during the federal leadership race. After Bob Rae's Ontario NDP government was defeated barely a week after Alexa announced her candidacy, MacKinnon took her six months' severance as Rae's press aide and arrived in Halifax a few days later.

By then, "the gang was already there," MacKinnon recalled. Mary Jane White was running the show as the official campaign organizer. She and other supporters set up their first headquarters in an office in the back of the Lord Nelson Hotel and immediately shifted into national campaign mode, making fundraising calls, preparing new campaign literature, planning tours, and organizing media and events in places they'd never been. Judy Wasylycia-Leis — known affectionately among the Halifax crew as "Judy Alphabet" — the former Manitoba NDP cabinet minister who'd first encouraged Alexa to run for office back in 1979, set up shop as the campaign's national coordinator in her Winnipeg basement with just a phone and a fax.

Meanwhile, Alexa and Sine set off on the campaign tour in Alexa's car. The first events were small. A supporter would invite a few friends to meet Alexa and hear why she wanted the job, what she'd do if she became leader. Alexa talked, but she also listened. "She really, really listened," MacKinnon recalled. "She wanted to hear what everyone had to say." That, of course, often, and not atypically, pushed the end of one event into what was supposed to be the middle of the next. The pace was relentless, the schedule intense. Between events, Alexa would be on the phone, doing interviews, hustling campaign contributions, picking the brains of policy experts. "It was all-absorbing," MacKinnon said. "You could never get enough sleep." After a full day of campaigning, Alexa would inevitably put in a few more hours cramming for the next day's events, then wake up before dawn for phone strategy sessions with White and others back in Halifax. Alexa even found a way to "sleep-talk" the hours in between, MacKinnon joked. "It was exhausting but it was also energizing because Alexa got her energy from people, and she was indefatigable." Still, she added, "campaigns are relentless, and this was a long campaign."

•

Reinforcements eventually arrived. NUPGE, which had agreed to rent an RV for the campaign, also volunteered the services of Louis Fournier, a staff member of the Ontario Public Service Employees Union, to act as Alexa's driver and advance man.

They became Thelma, Louise, and Louis, and dubbed the new camper their "Win!-nebago." While Louis drove, MacKinnon wrote press releases and speeches or strategized with the campaign back in Halifax while Alexa prepared for the next event. Some nights they'd billet with supporters; other nights they'd sleep in the camper. "Alexa didn't care if Louis saw her in curlers or in various states," MacKinnon said. "She was unself-conscious in a kind of ego-less, self-effacing way."

Fournier, a large, "blue-collar guy" from New Brunswick who'd worked as a youth counsellor before joining the staff of the union, had a reputation for "getting stuff done. He knew how to work a room," noted Skip Hambling.

He also had a knack for bringing even the most reluctant voter around to his point of view. NUPGE set up one event for members of the Canadian Auto Workers Union's largest local in Hamilton, Ontario, Hambling remembered. After Alexa spoke to two hundred union members, "Louis worked the room, pitching for all he was worth. It was a quintessential blue-collar crowd and not everyone was on board. Louis kept at this one guy until he finally gave in. 'Well, I'll tell you, I ain't voting for the thief (Nystrom had once been arrested for shoplifting) and I ain't voting for the queer (Robinson), so I guess I'll be voting for your broad.'"

•

No one who knew anything about politics believed Alexa would win. For all her personal charm and charisma, her electoral record was hardly inspiring. Nova Scotia itself was an NDP wasteland. Just 79 of close to 2,000 leadership convention delegates would come from Atlantic Canada.

Alexa's chief rivals for the job were experienced federal politicians with power bases in NDP strongholds — three-quarters of the party's 80,000 members lived in Ontario, British Columbia, and Saskatchewan — and they'd been campaigning for months before Alexa announced.

British Columbia's Svend Robinson had been a media-savvy, nationally known federal MP since Alexa's first failed try at elective office in 1979. The first openly gay MP, Robinson had positioned himself on the left flank of the party's ideological spectrum. His goal was to knit together what he hoped would be a "rainbow coalition" of minorities, gays, lesbians, students, seniors, and the disabled, and combine their voices with those of various interest groups to create a new progressive majority. He had the backing of a number of high-profile progressives, including David Suzuki and Judy Rebick, as well as the full-throated endorsement of Buzz Hargrove, the prickly president of the Canadian Auto Workers, one of Canada's largest and most powerful private sector unions.

Saskatchewan's Lorne Nystrom, the youngest MP in Canadian history when first elected in 1968, had spent twenty-five years in the House of Commons. A Prairie pragmatist and former finance critic whose focus was the deficit and debt, he represented the conservative Western wing of the party. When he was only twenty-seven, he'd been a credible third-place finisher at the 1975 leadership convention won by Ed Broadbent. He believed he was ready for the big job now. So did others. He arrived at the convention with endorsements from seventy NDP MPs and Western MLAs, more than the combined totals of his rivals.

Both men, however, also carried some burdensome political baggage. Nystrom, who had been defeated in his own riding in the 1993 election, was considered bland (former Ontario NDP MP Steven Langdon compared him to "cold French toast") and unlikely to resonate much beyond the NDP's shrinking Western base. Robinson, the party's most militant MP, had a reputation for criticizing his own provincial colleagues, choosing the wrong side of current law at logging protests, and involving himself in the murky assisted suicide of a constituent. He was, suggested the *Toronto Star*, "a self-aggrandizer who put self ahead of party, a mortal sin in the NDP."[4]

Some of the initial pressure on Alexa to run, in fact, came from anyone-but-Svend and someone-other-than-Lorne party insiders. They desperately wanted a leader who could not only rebuild the shattered party from the inside but also reach out to disaffected Liberals and red Tories.

Many within the party's inner circle considered Alexa the candidate best positioned to achieve both goals. She'd spent close to thirty years on the party's national council and had what former strategist Ian McLeod described as "significant status among NDP moderates."[5] Although the NDP in Ontario had been devastated by its defeat that June after just one term in office, key figures, including now former premier Bob Rae and former provincial leader Stephen Lewis, pledged their support. So did other provincial NDP leaders, such as Manitoba's Gary Doer, Newfoundland's Jack Harris, and New Brunswick's Elizabeth Weir.

The cognoscenti remained unimpressed. "No one seriously believes Alexa McDonough, a silver-spooned socialist from Nova Scotia, has a hope of victory," sniffed Robert Fife, the *Ottawa Sun*'s parliamentary bureau chief, summing up the prevailing conventional wisdom going into the convention.

The *Hill Times* front-page feature on the eve of the convention declared flatly: "The NDP leadership is a two-way race between Lorne Nystrom and Svend Robinson." Nystrom himself felt the same. "A distant third," is where he predicted Alexa would wind up.

After describing her as "feisty and telegenic," the *Toronto Star* also dismissed her. "She has the misfortune of being a woman with the same initials as the outgoing leader, and if New Democrats are united on one point it is that McLaughlin was a mistake.... That judgment is rubbing off on McDonough."

Just before the convention began, the *Vancouver Sun* invited Alan Whitehorn, the co-author of an upcoming book *Political Activists: The NDP in Convention*, to opine on the leadership race. He had no trouble outlining the barriers: "The harsh reality is that she has no experience in the federal parliament. She is also handicapped by coming from one of weakest regions of the party. Many speculate whether the party is willing to embrace another female leader." And he wasn't done: "McDonough's organization was slow to become operational, and she did not initially appreciate the importance of the membership direct ballot in setting the momentum for the campaign."[6]

And yet—after declaring the race between Nystrom and Robinson too close to call—Whitehorn wrapped up his "historian's handicap" with an intriguing but unexpected question: "Will McDonough pull off a surprise?"

3

Two days before delegates were to choose the next leader of the New Democratic Party, Alexa McDonough's campaign rolled into the Ottawa Congress Centre on Thursday, October 12, 1995. At that point, as she would confide to reporters later, "our campaign was sinking like a stone."[7] Or at least that's the way it appeared from the outside. Which was just fine with those inside, working feverishly to make that stone walk on water.

The party had constructed an awkward, two-tiered voting system to select its leader. Even before the convention, would-be candidates had to run a gauntlet of American-style primaries in each region, as well as a separate popularity contest among the party's trade unionists. To be on the ballot at the convention, candidates had to win one of those contests or take at least 15 per cent of all the votes cast in the primaries. Lorne Nystrom had won the labour vote, as well as his home prairie primary by such an overwhelming margin he arrived at the convention with 45 per cent of the overall popular support. Robinson had won three contests—British Columbia, Ontario, and Quebec—so his 32 per cent support still gave him the bragging right to claim his was a more broadly based national coalition. Alexa had won only one primary, in her home region of Atlantic Canada, and her overall share of the vote, an anemic 18.5 per cent, was only slightly above one of the benchmarks for moving forward.

But the truth was the only real function of the primaries was to get candidates on the ballot at the convention.[8] Alexa's organizers knew she would win the Atlantic primary so the real contest, and the one they focused on, became the trenches battles for the hearts and minds of voting delegates. More significantly, they sought second-choice, second-ballot commitment if a delegate's first choice was eliminated on the first ballot.

Mary Jane White had created a sophisticated database to track every delegate. Some of what it showed might have seemed, at first blush and to someone unfamiliar with Alexa's own history, surprising. In New Westminster–Burnaby, for example, a constituency cheek by jowl to Robinson's own, the majority of delegates came to Ottawa committed to Alexa. That was largely because the riding's former MP, Dawn Black, was among many in the national party who'd pressed Alexa to seek the leadership. Their relationship dated back to the 1984 federal election when Black was assistant to MP Pauline Jewett. Alexa had called Black "out of the blue" to say she was in British Columbia and volunteered to do some door-knocking for Jewett. "I was just so impressed by her manner of meeting people," Black recalled. "She talked to, and listened to the women who were stuffing envelopes, and she just had such a warmth and interest in people, really listened to them, really engaged with them." The two became friends, and allies.

White's database recorded each delegate's first ballot commitment as well as their preferred candidate if their first choice got knocked out. Those results were striking, and significant. While the numbers showed Robinson would most likely emerge from the first ballot with a modest lead, the race for second place between Alexa and Nystrom was too close to call. If Alexa finished third and was dropped from the second ballot, close to half of her supporters, many female and young, would choose Svend and assure him victory. But, if Alexa finished second and Nystrom had to drop out, the vast majority of his supporters would come over to Alexa, guaranteeing her victory. The key for Alexa was to come out of the first ballot in second place.

In the Thursday night debate she performed well, making the pitch that she among the three contenders was best positioned to lead a progressive popular alternative to the mainstream right and righter parties. She also made a strategic jab at Robinson. He was not "a team player," she said, an argument that played well with Nystrom's anti-Svend supporters.

Her "strong performance" on the debate stage "gave her floor workers the encouragement and the arguments they needed to begin serious arm-twisting."[9]

The next day, when the ninety Steelworkers' delegates caucused to decide whom to support, they voted 95 per cent to back McDonough. The decision, of course, was a tribute to the work of Lawrence McBrearty and his arm-twisting team.

Inside their own war room in the convention centre hotel, NUPGE churned out three pro-Alexa newsletters a day. At one point, when they realized it had become "hot as hell" inside the convention centre, they decided to make cardboard "Alexa" fans. *Who do you get to print fans — and where do you buy several thousand tongue depressors to hold them — at 6:30 on a Friday morning?* They managed to do both. "The subliminal message was, 'Elect a leader who can turn on a dime,'" Clancy explained. "And, no matter who they were supporting, we knew every delegate would want a fan." He laughed. "But if they were waving an 'Alexa' fan..."

Meanwhile, Alexa agents buttonholed Nystrom supporters on the floor and in the corridors, making the case Nystrom couldn't win — *do the math!* — and so, if they didn't want Svend Robinson as their new leader, they needed to either vote for Alexa on the first ballot or simply not vote at all. According to Olivia Chow, one of Robinson's political advisors, "dozens" of Nystrom supporters "left the convention floor without voting" after discussions with Bob Rae on voting day.[10]

Still, it was not a sure thing. As everyone waited for the announcement of the first ballot results, Rod Dickinson, now an Alexa floor manager at the convention, hovered near Nystrom's table with a "Lorne" button in his pocket. Just in case.

Finally, the results were announced: Robinson, as expected, had finished first with 655 votes. Alexa was 89 ballots behind with 566 votes, but 52 ahead of Nystrom, who ended up with 514 votes.

It was all over, and everyone who was anyone in the rival camps knew it. Alexa volunteers materialized beside Nystrom's section. "The Nystrom supporters were grabbing for Alexa stickers faster than they could be peeled off the sheets," reported the *Globe and Mail*.[11] Nystrom himself made his way to Alexa's table to signal he too was backing Alexa. The scene was set, and it was just a matter of waiting through a second round of balloting to confirm the result and allow Alexa her moment in the solo spotlight.

In the afterglow of the first-ballot announcement their candidate was, at least temporarily, in first place. Robinson's mainly young and mostly less strategically sophisticated supporters cheered loudly. So, too, had Robinson, "raising his fist in the air like a warrior leading his charges into battle," as his biographer, Graham Truelove, put it. "But he knew that by the end of the night he would not be leader of the NDP."[12]

Robinson and his key advisors, including Chow and her husband Jack Layton, retreated to a hallway to consider their options. Bill Siksay, Robinson's campaign manager, reminded them that the bitter 1989 leadership contest between Audrey McLaughlin and Dave Barrett had left "deep divisions" in the party. "Why not stop that from happening by making a pitch for party unity?" someone suggested. For the leading candidate to drop out in the middle of a convention and throw his support to the second-place candidate would be unprecedented. But, with the outcome preordained, what did he have to lose? And, practically, there seemed something to gain. Robinson would not only appear magnanimous but, finally, also a team player.

When Robinson arrived at Alexa's table after a slow walk across the convention floor, he was still freelancing. Nothing about his decision had been discussed with his passionate young supporters. Alexa herself wasn't sure what to make of his presence. She suggested they wait to talk until after the second-ballot results were announced, but he cut her off. "Alexa, I'm telling you we don't have to wait for a final ballot," he declared as the cameras rolled, and the reporters took notes. "I'm here to support you. I want to pull this party together, and you've done a superb job. You'll be a great leader and I'll be proud to work with you."

Alexa McDonough was the new leader of the federal New Democratic Party. But Svend Robinson, as usual, was the centre of attention. "Only Svend could snatch the front page from the jaws of defeat," Marcus Davies, a Saskatchewan-based employee in the party's federal wing, deadpanned to the Toronto *Sun*.[13]

•

"Where's Justin and Travis?" The post-convention partying had stretched late into the Ottawa night as Alexa's supporters savoured their sweet victory. But Alexa herself was distracted. She'd been accompanied throughout the convention by her mother, Jean, and her two sons, and now she couldn't find the boys. They should be here with her, celebrating.

They were, in fact, at another party in another part of the city, a significantly less happy gathering of Svend Robinson's supporters. While Robinson and Nystrom raised Alexa's arms in victory on the convention stage and while Alexa praised Robinson for his "typically courageous" decision, the passionate young idealists in Robinson's "rainbow coalition" who'd venerated him as a politician unlike the rest, were in tears, shocked, angry, and hurt.

"I know many of you feel a sense of anguish and betrayal," he'd told a gathering of his supporters after the results. "I share that. But I plead with you, we must all come together in solidarity and unity."

Many weren't having any of it. A few booed, some tossed their Svend pins on the floor. "You set us up," shouted one.

"People were just distraught," Justin McDonough remembered later. Although he and his brother had supported their mother and her political dreams since they'd first stood beside her on the stage at the Lord Nelson Hotel in 1980, they were not especially partisan themselves, developing lives and careers outside the political arena. "So that convention was an eye-opener to me," he said, "the passion just burgeoning over. I highly respected these were people with conviction, people of principle." Many of Svend's young supporters were their own age, people they could connect with. And they did. Just the way their mother had taught them. "Not only is my mother compassionate, but she's also very practical. She had proven over and over that the best way to mend fences is to be transparent and get people to open up and talk with one another." So that's what Justin and Travis did. Until deep into the night.

When Alexa heard later where they'd been and what they were doing, she confided to friends it was one of her proudest moments as their mother.

4

"Ms. McDonough," the man said, "you don't know me, but I know who you are." Alexa had just walked out of the Shoppers Drug Mart in the Rideau Centre near the Château Laurier Hotel. She'd been staying there during the convention. It was the morning after the night before, and her day had already been full of such "you-don't-know-me-but" moments.[14]

It had begun that morning with a wake-up call from a woman with a Cockney accent. "You don't know me, but my name is June Aston. Can you come over and visit our condo today?" She laughed. "You need to see it because you're the one who's going to be living here!" It turned out that Aston and her husband, Geoff, a retired couple, were decamping to Florida for the winter in two days and needed someone to condo-sit their place overlooking the Rideau Canal, a fifteen-minute walk to Parliament Hill. They'd watched on television as Alexa won the leadership. They liked the looks of her. And the timing seemed ideal. So why not? "It was the perfect location," as Alexa discovered when she visited, "so I never looked anywhere else."

She really hadn't expected to win; in fact, she'd booked a flight back to Halifax in anticipation of her loss. Since she'd only packed what she thought she would need during the convention, she'd had to stop at the Shoppers on her way back to the hotel. Shampoo, pantyhose, a refill for a prescription. She'd left the actual form back in Halifax but managed to talk the pharmacist into giving her what she needed.

"And you are?" The man seemed familiar. At some point, Alexa was certain, he and her father had worked together on . . . what was it? The Atlantic Provinces Economic Council? She'd seen him on TV too; she knew he was a politician, though not a New Democrat.

"David," the man answered. "David MacDonald." MacDonald was indeed a politician. A United Church minister, he'd begun his political career as a Progressive Conservative MP from Prince Edward Island thirty years before in 1965. At the time, MacDonald was just twenty-nine, John Diefenbaker was in his final tumultuous years as Conservative party leader, Tommy Douglas was leading the NDP, and Alexa Shaw was still a university student.

When Joe Clark's Tories formed the government in 1979, MacDonald became minister of communications, secretary of state, and minister responsible for the status of women. But Clark's administration, and MacDonald's

time as a cabinet minister, were short-lived. Defeated personally in 1980—as
was Alexa—MacDonald was re-elected in 1988, and then defeated again in
1993. But his CV boasted much more than getting elected and unelected.
He'd launched Canada's African Famine Secretariat, served as Canada's
ambassador to Ethiopia, Sudan, and Djibouti, chaired a panel on environmental issues, headed up a parliamentary committee on AIDS, and chaired
a global panel on food security. He was currently commuting from Ottawa
to Montréal, where he was an adjunct professor at Concordia University,
teaching courses with titles like "Impediments to a Sustainable Society"
and "Pizza Parliament." Perhaps not surprisingly, MacDonald—among the
self-described "brightest red" of red Tories—found himself isolated in what
had become an increasingly right-wing Progressive Conservative party.

After offering his congratulations on her victory the day before,
MacDonald turned earnest. "I think the most important thing that has to
happen in Canadian politics is for the NDP to re-establish itself as an official
party," he told her. "Anything I can do to help, I'd really like to do that.
Please call me."

Alexa promised she would.

•

"You'll never guess who I just met," Alexa offered breezily as she officially
met the nine members of her parliamentary caucus for the first time later that
day. When she suggested, as was so often her wont, that MacDonald might
be a potential NDP convert, Bill Blaikie, the veteran MP from Manitoba,
was dismissive.

"He just wants to date you," he joked. It was a joke, and it was not a
joke—and not just because MacDonald would eventually ask Alexa for a
date.

"The caucus gave her a rough time from the beginning," remembered
Mary Morison, her first Nova Scotia chief of staff, who'd agreed to act in
the same capacity again in Ottawa for three months while Alexa settled into
her new job. "They didn't think she should have won." There was sexism
too. "They didn't grant her the respect they'd customarily grant a male,"
said Morison, who stayed with Alexa in her apartment during her stint in
the new leader's office and often commiserated with her on the backroom
manoeuvring.

As evidence of that lack of respect, the *Ottawa Citizen*'s Paul Gessell reported that, six months after she won the leadership, Alexa still had to use up a good deal of political energy "battling her parliamentary caucus to formulate policies and strategies.... Some MPs and their aides have taken to swiping at McDonough in off-the-record interviews."[15]

Alexa hadn't helped her cause inside the caucus when she declared — on the day she'd announced herself a candidate for the party's leadership — she'd felt "sick" after learning all but one member of the NDP federal caucus had voted against the Chrétien government's gun registry. She was "personally...absolutely in support of strengthening our gun control measures," Alexa explained, suggesting the MPs had "capitulated to the ferocity of the right wing" because of the party's "leadership vacuum."[16]

British Columbia MP Nelson Riis remarked, "It's an interesting way to start out your campaign by alienating the sitting caucus members."

Not a single member of that caucus had backed her leadership bid. The only NDP MP who'd supported tighter gun control legislation, in fact, had been Svend Robinson. And, notwithstanding his "you'll be a great leader and I'll be proud to work with you" convention pledge, Alexa understood she could not look to him for support. "There's a theory among some New Democrats that Svend Robinson is waiting for Alexa McDonough to screw up," wrote Jane Taber in the *Ottawa Citizen.* "Her leadership collapses and he triumphantly marches back in to rebuild."[17]

Alexa also appeared to diminish her new caucus's importance in her first post-convention press conference. "Politics just doesn't take place across the street in the House of Commons," she said. "Politics takes place in people's backyards, in their workplaces."[18] Vowing to "launch a grassroots campaign to rebuild and revitalize the party as an alternative," she added she would spend her foreseeable future "living out of a suitcase all over Canada."[19]

She had also decided not to seek a seat in the House of Commons in a by-election, she told reporters, but did intend to run in the next general election in Halifax, a riding the NDP had never won. For some in the caucus, that was the good news. They would soon have another chance to choose someone else.

•

In the six months following her surprise victory, Alexa McDonough did indeed seem to disappear from the Canadian political consciousness. It was both a calculation and a consequence of her decisions to focus on grassroots organizing and internal restructuring to remake the leader's office in her own image and to prepare for the next election — all of which occurred beyond the glare and the interest of the Ottawa media.

When Alexa began casting about for someone to run her Ottawa office, Dan O'Connor, who'd been her Nova Scotia chief of staff for close to a decade, expressed tentative interest. Alexa was initially hesitant. So was O'Connor. Despite the years they'd spent working together, O'Connor acknowledges, "We didn't always have an easygoing relationship." O'Connor believed Alexa instinctively distrusted the party's paid staff, wondering "what are they trying to put over on us now." Alexa confided to others she believed O'Connor often undermined her behind her back. That said, there was a comfort level in their familiar discomfort — "Alexa knew the office would run smoothly," O'Connor explained, "leaving her plate clear to do whatever she wanted" — so, in January 1996, O'Connor moved to Ottawa as chief of staff.

While O'Connor beavered away shaping the leader's office, Alexa criss-crossed the country, meeting with small groups of supporters in their kitchens, attempting to re-energize the party base. It wasn't easy.

There was mistrust between the powerful labour-focused Ontario NDP that had championed Alexa's leadership bid and the equally powerful rural-based Saskatchewan NDP that had mostly supported Nystrom. Many in the Ontario camp saw their Saskatchewan brethren as Liberals in disguise, while the Westerners could point to the failure of Bob Rae's Ontario government as evidence where that brand of socialism led.

Alexa's personal connections with all factions helped bridge those divides. "People have had honest differences," she allowed at the time. "There have been tensions within the left, sometimes within the party, sometimes within the labour movement, sometimes within the broader social democratic partnerships. But over the last couple of years, the assaults on the things that really matter to all of us have been so severe that people have understood that it's when we work together that we can win these battles."[20]

While that behind-the-scenes boosting and massaging would prove important for the coming campaign, it barely registered a blip with the media. If she wasn't being ignored, she was being pilloried. The Saskatoon *Star-Phoenix* declared her decision not to run in a federal by-election in Hamilton against Sheila Copps "the real story of why the party has stagnated under her leadership and is headed for the political dumpster."[21] At another point, when Alexa did call a press conference in Ottawa to denounce federal tax breaks to corporations, just two of the more than one hundred accredited press gallery reporters showed up to cover it.[22] In what seemed the unkindest cut of all, an *Ottawa Citizen* editorialist dismissed her as "Audrey McLaughlin without the charisma."[23]

Alexa McDonough needed some good news.

·

During the year after they'd met outside Shoppers, David MacDonald would occasionally forward newspaper clippings he thought Alexa would find interesting, often enclosing encouraging notes. In the fall of 1996, he sent her an op-ed he'd written for the *Montreal Gazette* criticizing Canadian policy on Africa. Alexa picked up the phone. "This is really interesting stuff," she told him. "You should talk to Bill Blaikie, our foreign affairs critic."

"I'm happy to talk with Blaikie," MacDonald replied, "but I'd be happier to talk with you. Why don't we have lunch?" They agreed to meet for lunch at Bibliothèque Café, a cozy book-filled restaurant in downtown Ottawa. Alexa went "for business," as Juliet O'Neill reported. "He had other interests."

Although Alexa would tell her secretary that day that MacDonald was the first really interesting man she'd met in years, she had no intention of pursuing a relationship. She thought he was still married, "and that's the last thing I need." But when she mentioned it to her brother, Robbie told her: "Are you crazy? He's been separated for five or six years."

A few weeks later, on a Sunday morning, they met for tennis. "And we've been together ever since," Alexa happily told the writer Silver Donald Cameron in the fall of 1997. As left-leaning political junkies who both understood and accepted the demands of the life they had chosen, they were, in many ways, much better matched than Alexa and Peter, or Alexa and Les. That Christmas, she invited MacDonald, who had four adult children from his marriage, to meet her sons in Halifax. "They want to interview you," she said.

"About what?"

"They just want to make sure you're OK. If this is getting serious, they want to know about you."

So MacDonald sat in Alexa's living room for an hour one December morning with Justin and Travis. "It was a real conversation," he remembered, "but they were checking me out."

Although MacDonald was happy to support Alexa's political ambitions, "the only restriction I put on my political activity was, 'Don't ever ask me to run. I've run eight elections, and I really don't need to run the ninth time to prove anything.'"

That changed in the lead-up to the 1997 federal election after the Tories' new leader, Jean Charest, released his party's platform. "I picked up a copy and read it, and I was appalled," MacDonald recalled. "All the stuff we had worked on for years, having to do with regional development, cultural policy, foreign affairs, international development, stuff that I was deeply involved in as a parliamentarian, was just thrown out the window, and they brought in.... It was really a kind of Reform-lite."

He called Alexa. "I'm taking off the table what I said," he told her. "I am prepared to run as an NDP candidate. Anywhere you want me to run, I will be the candidate." Within twenty-four hours, the NDP riding association in Rosedale, the wealthy Toronto constituency MacDonald had represented as a Conservative, called to ask to meet with him. Later that spring, during the NDP convention in Regina in April 1997, Alexa alluded to her own—and the party's—changing circumstances in a speech to the convention: "I've adopted a new political slogan," she explained. "Rebuilding our support, one red Tory at a time."

MacDonald, who was sitting in the audience, laughed at the memory: "Of course, the place went wild, clapping and hooting." It was now "completely clear I was not simply going to be her companion. I was going to be an activist in '97, which, of course, I was."

5

As he approached Alexa McDonough's campaign headquarters in Halifax that spring morning in 1997, Anthony Salloum had a decision to make. He was thirty-one years old, a political junkie no longer at home in a party in which he'd invested more than a decade of sweat, tears, and dreams.

He'd arrived in Nova Scotia with his family in 1980, refugees from a deadly Lebanese civil war where "you never got involved with politics because you could be killed." Three years later, he'd watched, "flabbergasted," as Tory leader Joe Clark, who'd just won 67 per cent support in a leadership review, declared the result not clear enough and called for a leadership convention. "It was so civil, so peaceful."

But because then Liberal prime minister Pierre Trudeau had opened doors to family reunification, allowing the Salloums to settle in Canada, he joined the Liberal party. "It just became my passion," he remembered of the 1984 election. "I said, 'I can go to that rally. I can go to that debate. I can go put up lawn signs. I can help you print brochures and drop them in mailboxes.' I wanted to experience it all." By 1997, however, he was disillusioned. Liberal Prime Minister Jean Chrétien had reneged on federal promises about free trade and the Goods and Services Tax (GST). Nova Scotia Liberals had dumped John Savage, a premier "who really wanted to change the political culture."

Salloum wanted to be part of the upcoming federal election, but how? He knew — and admired — Alexa McDonough. She and her son Justin met every week for breakfast in the small restaurant Salloum ran in the basement of the office building where Justin worked. "I thought, 'Alexa McDonough is amazing. She deserves to be the MP for Halifax.' I made a deal with myself." Alexa's campaign headquarters was on his route to work. "When I got there, I'd either walk into her office and offer to help her, or I'd continue walking and not get involved with any campaign at all."

"Hi," he said to the woman at the entrance, "my name is Anthony Salloum and I've been a Liberal all my life, but I want to help Alexa."

"Anthony!" a voice boomed from the back of the room. It was Justin McDonough. "Welcome. Come here. We're going to put you to work." They did. After Alexa won, Salloum became her Halifax constituency assistant.[24]

•

That Alexa McDonough would choose to stage the penultimate rally of the 1997 federal election campaign—a celebratory ceilidh on the day before the June 2 vote in the Steelworkers' Hall in Sydney, Cape Breton—seemed pure Alexa, yet one more triumph of perpetual Pollyanna over hard-learned conventionally correct wisdom. The NDP had not won a single seat on the island, federally or provincially, since Alexa became its public face seventeen years before.

So, when the party's new provincial secretary, Ron Cavalucci, who'd previously worked in Ontario and Manitoba, reported what he considered signs of a "real breakthrough" on the island in mid-campaign, more experienced Nova Scotia NDP hands were skeptical. Veteran provincial organizer Mary Jane White, "who had seen so many false hopes about Cape Breton," urged the federal campaign not to "get drawn into another wild goose chase." She wasn't the only one, said Dan O'Connor, one of the party's four national campaign organizers. "The federal director of organization sternly told me to shut down all that Cape Breton talk."

Although Alexa herself had confidently predicted at the outset that the NDP would "send more members to Ottawa than ever before," no one, including Alexa, really believed that—or that Cape Breton would be among the ridings sending NDP MPs to the nation's capital.

Going into the campaign, the party's real objectives were considerably more circumscribed: win at least the three additional seats needed to regain official party status and make sure one of those seats belonged to Alexa McDonough. They could rebuild from that base for the next election. The party's savvy new advertising agency, NOW Communications of Vancouver, had come up with a modest, but pointed "Wake Up the Liberals. Shake Up Ottawa." The pitch targeted traditional NDP and progressive voters who'd abandoned the party in 1993 to rid the country of Brian Mulroney's Conservatives only to discover Jean Chrétien's Liberals were really also draconian conservative wolves cleverly disguised as social democrats for vote-getting purposes.

Billboards bearing the party's new message began showing up across the country even before the campaign officially began, each accompanied by a portrait of a relaxed, confident-looking Alexa. That too was the result of a clever ruse. "Alexa could barely tolerate most photos of herself," O'Connor explained. In the past, she'd "left her provincial campaign teams with a miserable selection of candid photos that featured an array of hairstyles." This time, however, with advice and encouragement from long-time assistant Pam Whelan, Alexa had opted for what *Toronto Star* columnist Rosemary Speirs positively described as a "new, stylish haircut [that] has brightened her greying hair to an attractive blonde."[25] Better, the campaign's photographer managed to trick Alexa into relaxing for the lens. "The photographer suggested that, before she changed clothes and fixed herself up, he try out some different spots in the studio and a few different poses just to give him an idea of what would work when they moved on to the real photo session," O'Connor recalled. "And, of course, it was photos from that 'dress rehearsal' that were by far the best, with Alexa relaxed . . . without tensing up for the ordeal of trying to look right."

The real problem, according to the pundits, was not the leader's photograph but the party's time-worn policy messages: cut the country's 10 per cent unemployment rate in half, eliminate the GST, expand medicare to cover drugs and home care, enhance education, reduce Canada Pension Plan premiums, increase employment insurance benefits, restore reductions to federal transfers to the provinces, create thousands of new daycare spaces, reinvest excess bank profits in communities. . . . "Canadians have been indoctrinated with a deficit-fighting mentality," columnist Barbara Yaffe in the *Vancouver Sun* dismissed. "They're looking forward to a balanced federal budget and musing about the day they'll finally get a few tax breaks. In 1997, McDonough's NDP, with its traditional socialist platform, is out of touch with the times."[26]

On the same day, on the other side of the country, the Halifax *Chronicle-Herald*'s Dale Madill, who'd spent the previous week trailing the NDP leader across the country, saw something different. "McDonough's biggest asset in this campaign is not what she says, it's who she is and her uncanny ability to touch people. Her personal appeal is compelling, even among those for whom the campaign is not a cause but a job."

To bolster his argument, Madill spoke with Sgt. Jean Auclair, one of Alexa's RCMP bodyguards "who towers over her and is never more than a few strides away."

"Madame McDonough is a wonderful woman," the thirty-five-year policing veteran told Madill. "I am very glad I got to meet her. I think she is very smart and very courageous for doing the debate." He was referring to that week's party leaders' French-language debate. Despite spending weeks living with a family in Jonquiere, Quebec, trying to turn her high school *français* into something approximating fluency, Alexa's French was still hesitant, so she'd been mostly marginalized in the high-stakes debate. "That's not easy," Auclair allowed.

As with debating in French, Alexa refused to back away from her party's — and her own — socialist beliefs. She told *Our Times* Julia Bennett,

> You know, fifteen years of relentless right-wing propaganda
> has kind of numbed people from believing that you can have
> Medicare, a decent unemployment insurance system, decent
> public pensions. But the reality is that there is more wealth
> in this country than there ever was.... The problem is that
> the wealth and the resources are increasingly concentrated in
> the hands of the super-rich, who are getting richer and richer
> because everyone else is paying for it!... Why shouldn't we
> amend bank policy in this country? Why can't we put limits
> on how much money can be taken out of Canada by pension
> plans? Why can't we change our tax policy so that it rewards
> employers for keeping employees, rather than what it does now,
> which is essentially reward major corporations for laying people
> off. You know what I'm saying? It's not rocket science.[27]

But none of that seemed to resonate with voters — even those who claimed to be impressed by Alexa personally. With less than two weeks before voting day, the *Vancouver Sun* reported the latest national poll showed the NDP with just 9 per cent of voter support, awful enough to rank fourth among five competing parties, and barely even in national support with the nationalist Bloc Québécois, which was only fielding candidates in Quebec. The newspaper quoted a Wilfrid Laurier University political science professor whose projections showed the NDP winning just seven seats, two fewer than its dismal showing in 1993.[28] Agar Adamson, the Acadia University political scientist who had incorrectly dismissed Alexa's chances in a number of previous provincial elections, remained consistent, suggesting the party's only hope in Atlantic Canada might be in McDonough's Halifax riding, but even that was no sure thing.

O'Connor and others in the party's inner circle, especially those with Nova Scotia connections, never doubted Alexa would win her riding, but no one wanted to take anything for granted. Especially not up against two worthy veteran opponents in Mary Clancy, the feisty two-term Liberal incumbent, and Terry Donahoe, the long-time provincial Tory cabinet minister. As a result, Alexa—who criss-crossed the country so often she'd travelled the equivalent of one-and-one-half times around the world by voting day—still spent part of each week campaigning in her Halifax riding. Which made it harder for her to be in the forty other ridings that the campaign believed its candidates had at least a chance to win.

The national campaign continued to be skeptical about Cape Breton, so Cavalucci dipped into the provincial party's line of credit to print signs. Then he drove down to Cape Breton to poster the two island ridings and "did everything else he could to generate public evidence of the momentum that he was certain existed," O'Connor recalled. When the party's pollsters expanded their Nova Scotia polling in mid-campaign, O'Connor recalled, they were shocked to discover there were actually six competitive seats in the province, including both Cape Breton Bras d'Or and Sydney-Victoria. "It was too late to invest much on the ground, but that big Ceilidh was approved."

For Joanne Lamey, an Alexa loyalist who'd relocated from Halifax to Cape Breton to manage local lawyer Peter Mancini's campaign, organizing a leader's-tour ceilidh event at the end of a long campaign was a "pain in the ass." The national tour staff wanted to know everything: measurements of the hall, the stage, how many steps from where the tour bus stopped to the building's entrance, the number of stairs to the second floor where Alexa would go to freshen up, re-edit the speech she'd given hundreds of times already, and prepare for her final brief moment in the spotlight. A local volunteer had even been tasked with building a set of steps behind the podium so Alexa would be seen from the waist up. "I think we faxed them the information twice," Lamey explained later with a laugh. "Finally, I told one of them that Alexa could probably answer all their questions since she had been to the Steelworkers Hall many times."

In the end, those details became far less important than the sense of excitement and anticipation in the hall that night as four hundred Cape Bretoners gave *their* leader a "thunderous" welcome home.[29] There was music, there was dancing, there was one last speech by a clearly exhausted but totally energized Alexa McDonough. On an island where one in four residents couldn't find work, she ridiculed Jean Chrétien for claiming he understood the pain of unemployment, having been out of work for four months as a young man between his law school graduation and opening his practice. "Let him tell the children who go to bed hungry at night that he's so proud of his Liberal record on the economy," she chided, adding for good measure a swipe at Liberal Health Minister David Dingwall, who was running for re-election in Cape Breton. "How can someone who delivers the biggest health-care cuts in Canadian history call himself your friend?" she demanded. And then, finally, she circled back to her campaign's key message. Simply replacing Liberals with Conservatives, the traditional Atlantic alternative, wouldn't change anything. "The Tories paved the way for Liberal policies." The only way the Liberals, who were almost certainly poised to return for a third term, could be held accountable for their actions, she implored, was for them to send more New Democrats to Ottawa. Including from Cape Breton.

•

Alexa McDonough had "felt it on the ground." But she had been disappointed before. Many times. "I had to question whether my optimism was based on anything other than that I am a relentless, unapologetic optimist," she would acknowledge after the actual votes were cast.[30] But during the campaign's final weekend, she'd grown even more upbeat, "Still, when her campaign team insisted "we're really going to do it. We have all the evidence," she resisted. "I thought: 'Well, that sounds pretty interesting, but, no, I don't want to believe it because I don't want to be disappointed.'"[31]

She wasn't. June 2, 1997, would be, by her own account, the best night of her career, "truly thrilling."

•

"I've never voted for anybody who won before," a stunned partygoer marvelled to Halifax *Daily News* columnist David Swick, summing up the general mood of "happy shock" that evening. Close to one thousand New Democrats gathered in the ballroom of the Lord Nelson Hotel in Halifax — scene of generations of funereal election-night moral victory parties—and "celebrated the incredible.... The NDP was leading in Halifax West, in Cape Breton, in New Brunswick, in Bonavista, Newfoundland. Cheers exploded with each new report. Then came the first Halifax result—with Alexa on the road to a landslide. Cheers turned to foot-stomping.... The room picked up a delirious buzz, with fists punching the air and screams of 'Yes!' and 'Omigod!' Someone in the room let loose a peal of maniacal laughter."[32]

Alexa McDonough hadn't just won her Halifax riding. She'd captured a remarkable 50 per cent of all the votes cast—and won 180 of the riding's 193 polls—in what the experts predicted would be a too-close-to-call four-way race.

Her party not only swept all four metro Halifax ridings but its candidates also picked up both Cape Breton seats too, defeating David Dingwall, and Vince MacLean, the former provincial Liberal leader who'd served as mayor of Sydney. Alexa's regional coattails proved far stronger than even her most ardent supporters could have hoped, adding two more seats in New Brunswick and almost another in Newfoundland.

"Well, friends," Alexa had to shout to be heard over the ballroom din as jubilant supporters continued to chant her name, "the very first thing I want to do is welcome you to the NDP riding of Halifax." She was joined on stage by Justin and Travis, who'd shared this same stage with her seventeen years and another lifetime ago, and by her mother, Jean, now eighty-two. She was especially "delighted" her mother was there to share the moment with her, Alexa told reporters later, "considering that she and my dad went to a political convention on their honeymoon sixty years ago this summer, and she's worked ever since to make that federal breakthrough in Halifax and in Nova Scotia."

By its own ambitions, the party had dramatically overachieved. Alexa had won her place at the parliamentary table. She would be joined by twenty more New Democrat MPs, whose elections from coast to coast offered the party at least the image of being truly "national." Their numbers not only restored the NDP to official status and, with it, public funding and visibility, but also created the critical mass necessary to hold the government accountable.

Alexa was just as proud of the fact that 40 per cent of the NDP's new caucus would be women, and more generally delighted to see that there would now be sixty-four women in the new Parliament, up from fifty-three in 1993. The National Action Committee on the Status of Women released a statement, saying it was encouraged by the number of women who'd won a seat in the Commons, but singling out the NDP and its leader for special praise. "The successful campaign run by Alexa McDonough...is a victory for women's groups across Canada."

And yet, for all the election-night jubilance, there were troubling canaries hidden in the numbers. The NDP's share of the national vote was still an anemic 11 per cent—better than its 7 per cent in 1993 but barely half of the 19 per cent the Ed Broadbent-led party had won in 1988. Although the party had experienced its first-ever breakthrough in Atlantic Canada and managed to hold its own in the face of a Reform sweep through Western Canada, electing MPs in three of the four Western provinces, the NDP found itself completely shut out in seat-rich Ontario. Its highest-profile candidates—Jack Layton, Olivia Chow, and David MacDonald—all went down to defeat.

While the party had hoped to capitalize on voter frustration with the spending cuts imposed by Prime Minister Chrétien and Ontario Tory premier Mike Harris, the *Toronto Star* columnist Thomas Walkom found a villain closer to home—Bob Rae's one-term NDP government. "The most common reaction to the Rae years among voters who refused to come back to the NDP was that his government had somehow just blown it," he wrote. "Some of these criticisms are justified. Some aren't. No matter. The ironic result of the NDP's one-term of government in Ontario is that it has left voters with a bad taste in their mouths, a taste that McDonough will find hard to dispel."[33]

But that was an issue for a future day. For tonight, it was enough to be surrounded by celebrating New Democrats. "Tonight, friends, is about making history," proclaimed Alexa. "The next four years are going to be about making a difference. The New Democratic Party is back!"

•

Even before he and Alexa met for breakfast the morning after the election-night celebration, Dan O'Connor knew what was coming. Back in Ottawa in mid-campaign, he'd accidentally walked into a meeting and overheard a staffer ask, "Well, has she given us any idea who she might want as chief of staff?" He remembered going home and telling his wife, "'I think I'm going to be fired.' She didn't believe it." He spent the rest of the campaign wondering when the axe would fall. On election night, he'd been with Alexa. "I wrote her statements. I was the main liaison with her, so we were together for all the celebration and seeing the victories and how they were happening and what it all meant, and what's to be said about it, working as closely together as we possibly could . . . and I knew I was gone."

Years later, he said he still wasn't sure why. Alexa didn't explain her decision beyond saying she wanted to go in a different direction. He put it down to "Alexa's restlessness." No matter. "I wasn't going to fight it. I told her I thought it was a mistake, but she had every right to do it."[34]

A few years later, Alexa called O'Connor out of the blue. "We hadn't had a lot of contact," since his firing, he remembered, and they were never personally close in the ways she was with some of her women staff, but she told him now she wanted to set up an educational trust for his young son William. Though he hadn't said so, she had to know he had taken a huge financial hit when she fired him. "We had just bought a house in Ottawa. I had to sell that house, buy one here." In the process, he'd racked up close to $40,000 in added expenses. "So, she just stepped up in the nicest way," he remembered.

•

Anne Marie Foote stared out at the empty parking lot. Where was everyone?

It was February 1998 and Foote, a former civilian employee with Canada's Department of National Defence, had just been hired as Alexa McDonough's new federal constituency executive assistant.

Alexa was scheduled to attend a one-hundredth birthday celebration for a constituent at a local church hall in South End Halifax. Foote, who'd made the arrangements, chauffeured Alexa to the venue. But the church was deserted. Foote got out, checked all the entrances. No response. She walked back to the car. "I have no idea what's going on," she told her new boss. She pulled out the itinerary. "See, this is the church, here's the civic address. . ."

Alexa looked the piece of paper. "Except the event is tomorrow, not today."

"I thought, 'Oh, my God!' My first week on the job, and I'm going to be fired!"

Instead, Alexa laughed. "She's lived to be a hundred years old," she joked, "so I'm sure she'll be around for her party tomorrow night. We'll come back."

Now Foote can laugh too. "What a way to make a new staff person feel like she's not such a big screw-up."

For the next decade, until Alexa retired in 2008, Foote would continue as her executive assistant. "It was never like you were staff who worked for her," she recalled. "You were a colleague who worked with her. And then you became a friend."

6

On November 27, 2000, just three years, five months, and twenty-five days after the last federal election, Canadians returned to the polls. But this time there would be no poll-defying election-day breakthrough, no new history-making.

Just about everything went wrong.

Having brought the party back from its 1993 brink, Alexa had been eager to use her hard-won leader's leverage to reimagine the future of her party. "We are not interested in just being the conscience of the nation," as she put it at the time, "but putting forward solid policies and leadership that will gain power."[35]

That ambition first showed itself on August 31, 1998. Fresh from a week-long, cross-country train trip with her caucus, Alexa emerged at a press conference in Halifax to unveil a new and seemingly much more fiscally conservative New Democratic Party. This new NDP committed itself to balancing the country's books, applying one-third of future budget surpluses to paying down the debt, one-third to targeted tax cuts, and one-third to social spending. Even the party's plans for spending — $2.5 billion for health care — came carefully framed as an investment because, as Alexa told reporters that day, "good health is an essential to full participation in the community and the economy." There would be no more rote calls for across-the-board tax increases on the wealthy either, but a careful cost-benefit analysis of each of the many tax perks the rich enjoyed to determine which actually stimulated investment in jobs and the economy. And the party would reach out to the private sector, particularly small business, creating a new caucus position for a business spokesperson. "The NDP has not always acknowledged the importance of the role of the private sector to the extent that is appropriate and necessary," she acknowledged, adding the party itself had, "unwisely, and perhaps somewhat unwittingly," contributed to its own past anti-business image.[36]

This was no Saul-like conversion on the train to Halifax. Alexa's business world view had been shaped by her socially responsible business family where workers' rights were respected, and profits reinvested in both the business and the community. And then too, she could point to her own NDP role models. Iconic Tommy Douglas, as premier of Saskatchewan, had not only introduced Canada's signature medicare program, but he had also kept his province's books balanced. More recently, Roy Romanow's Saskatchewan government, inheriting a budget deficit, had turned that into six straight years of balanced budgets coupled with tax cuts and health-care investments.

After close to twenty years in politics, Alexa was frustrated to be still watching from the sidelines. Rival Liberal politicians inevitably talked from the left to win votes and just as inevitably governed from the right. She wanted the opportunity to finally govern from the left too.

In a little-reported February speech to the Canadian Labour Congress, she had challenged unions to stop blocking inevitable and perhaps even positive economic trends such as the move to self-employment, already a reality for one in five Canadians. The next month, she travelled to Europe to study the success of social democratic parties there as they found innovative and collaborative new ways to govern from the left. Thirteen of fifteen EU countries, she reported enthusiastically on her return, were governed by social democratic parties or by coalitions in which social democrats played the leading role. In Holland, government, workers, and business had all come together to set the country's economic and social goals. Why not in Canada?

"Any movement that pretends things can go back to the way they were," she publicly declared in May, "is dooming itself to irrelevance."[37] And her party took another major step into uncharted territory, declaring it was no longer unalterably opposed to all free trade deals, but would judge them on their individual merits. "Globalization is not by definition some kind of disaster," she said. "Globalization is a reality."[38]

The party she led hadn't completely abandoned its roots or its causes, of course. In Parliament, it was still calling for the Liberal government to make job creation its top priority by investing public funds to cut unemployment and to restore transfers to health care. But the NDP's voice on those issues was still barely heard amid the deficit-cutting din from the right.

That all began to change—and not necessarily for the better—after Alexa's post-train-trip press conference. Less than a week later, she was the featured guest on the Labour Day edition of CBC Radio's national call-in show, *Cross Country Checkup*, where she answered questions about Canada's modern labour party.

Buzz Hargrove, the president of the Canadian Auto Workers Union, one of the biggest financial supporters of the NDP, was among the callers. He lit into Alexa, angrily excoriating her for selling out their party's principles for popularity and claiming the small business community Alexa was trying to woo were "the biggest enemy of working people."

When he finally finished his public dressing down, Alexa calmly replied—correctly—that 70 per cent of Canadians were employed in small business.

Hargrove's personal attacks were no surprise. He'd been a vociferous supporter of Svend Robinson's bid for the leadership in 1995. By the fall of 1998, Hargrove also had a personal interest in publicity. He was promoting his own book, a memoir called *Labour of Love*. In laying out his own poor-boy pedigree, Hargrove noted pointedly, "No one in the Hargrove household ever gagged on a silver spoon." Hargrove described the book, in which he openly mused about strategically voting for Liberals to defeat the Conservatives, or even launching a new political party to challenge the NDP, as "a wake-up call to the left."[39]

Alexa downplayed the personal nature of Hargrove's stinging attacks, telling the *Vancouver Sun*'s Barbara Yaffe, "I have a hide like a rhinoceros. The other thing," she added, trying to turn her party's in-house rough-housing into a plus, "New Democrats are a bit crazy. We thrive on debate. We do it all out there publicly."

Three months after their national radio dust-up, Hargrove and Alexa met for lunch in Halifax to see if it was possible to patch up their differences. It wasn't. Alexa asked him to stop his public attacks; Hargrove refused. "No one listens if you whisper in the corridors," he explained. "Vintage Buzz Hargrove," Alexa told reporters. "He thrives on controversy."

But Alexa herself inadvertently fanned those flames later that month when she sat down for a wide-ranging interview with Robert Fife, the Ottawa bureau chief for Conrad Black's *National Post*. The headline on Fife's December 21 front-page story ran: "NDP's McDonough Hopes to be Like Blair." According to Fife, Alexa claimed the remaking of Tony Blair's British Labour party offered Canada's NDP a "new pro-business model with a social conscience."

Blair's approach, known as the Third Way — a somewhat fuzzy governing philosophy "in favour of growth, entrepreneurship, enterprise and wealth creation but also in favour of greater social justice [with] the state playing a major role in bringing this about"[40] — had become ideologically trendy in the nineties. Even Jean Chrétien's Liberals claimed to be following a Third Way. It was also controversial, especially on the left, where the Third Way was often considered a betrayal of traditional progressive values and a capitulation to capitalist reality.

For Hargrove, Fife's putting Third Way words in Alexa's mouth was chum in the water, and he was quick to ratchet up his attacks. "I think this will cause a lot of people to re-evaluate their commitment to the party over the holidays," he told the *Post* just one day after Fife's story appeared.

Alexa's rejoinder was published as a letter to the editor on December 28, 1998. In it, she noted she and Fife had discussed all manner of social democratic government initiatives in Europe, including reduced work weeks in France, new forms of job security for part-time and contract workers in the Netherlands, and sustainable job development in Germany. "It was surprising then to read that the *National Post* had interpreted that as an attempt to remake the New Democratic Party in the image of another country's political party." But her letter's message got lost in the Christmas break shuffle, and Alexa found herself tagged as a Tony Blair Third Way wannabe.

Buzz Hargrove was not Alexa's only critic, of course. To others, like Bob White of the Canadian Labour Congress, a long-time Alexa ally, her new New Democratic Party sounded suspiciously like the Liberal Party. "To say I am troubled would be to understate my feelings," he wrote in a letter to her. While many trade union leaders, like the United Steelworkers' Lawrence McBrearty, did support Alexa's attempts to modernize the party, the concerns from those within the labour movement — many of whom claimed to be blindsided by the party's new direction — could not be ignored. After all, the modern party had been the result of a 1961 merger between the old CCF and the labour movement, and unions continued to play a vital role in its policies and to pay much of its expenses. The irony was that more and more rank-and-file union members actually voted Liberal, Conservative, and even Reform.

Alexa did have the support of much of the NDP caucus, including many Western MPs who'd initially been skeptical of her. The debate over the party's future, suggested veteran Manitoba MP Bill Blaikie, "needs to be about substance and not about who will get into left-wing heaven and who will not."[41] Alexa helped her cause among those party pragmatists (while hurting it with purists) by appointing Ed Tchorzewski, Saskatchewan's former deficit-fighting finance minister, as her new senior advisor.[42] In the early 1990s, Tchorzewski had closed rural hospitals, cut spending, and raised taxes as his province became the first in Western Canada—ahead of oil-rich, right-wing Alberta—to achieve a balanced budget. He'd also lowered sales and income taxes, but as he was quick to point out, he'd "actually increased spending in social services in very specific areas.... A social democratic party is, by its nature left of centre," he insisted. "The principles and values don't change."

•

The battle to define those principles and values for the future came to a head in August 1999, when seven hundred party activists gathered in Ottawa in the middle of a summer heat wave for their national convention.[43] Many of the delegates proudly sported neon green stickers reading, "Third Way—No Way."

In her keynote speech, Alexa did her best to thread the needle. "We must lay out a new way for Canadians to navigate in the twenty-first century," she declared. "Not an old way, not a Third Way but a made-in-Canada way, our New Democratic way.... It's time to change. Why change? Because we must. Because there is too much at stake not to change. We must begin with the new economy. We need economic growth in Canada. It's desirable for all our sakes, but not for its own sake." New Democrats, she added, "must offer to Canadians both the enduring principles on which to build a better, more humane society and the positive practical solutions for how we can achieve it. Solutions that say supporting a market economy does not mean supporting a market society."[44]

Alexa prevailed... mostly. The delegates voted for key economic resolutions embracing balanced budgets, debt reduction, a cut to the GST, and tax cuts for low- and middle-income Canadians, and they agreed to the establishment of a small business caucus headed by Western MPs to develop an election strategy aimed at winning the support of entrepreneurs. They also passed a resolution with echoes of a battle Alexa had waged earlier in Nova Scotia to allow the party to accept donations from business "under certain conditions" and as a "supplementary source of income." But—at the urging of labour leaders—they sent a jobs creation policy paper back for more study because it failed to recognize the importance of public sector job creation, the right to strike, and the need for strong labour standards. And they overwhelmingly distanced the party from any association with the Third Way. Alexa, who'd already publicly rejected the label, publicly voted with the majority. And then the delegates also even more overwhelmingly acclaimed Alexa as their leader for two more years.

That outcome, of course, didn't mollify Hargrove. Even while the 2000 election campaign was unfolding, he continued to undermine Alexa. Although the CAW had agreed to provide the NDP with $150,000 and some staff support, he told reporters he "wasn't doing it enthusiastically," and predicted the party would take a "real beating" when the votes were counted.[45] Two days before voting day, in the *Globe and Mail* Hargrove was listed among those "ostensible" NDP supporters "preparing for the worst [and] putting distance between themselves and their leader's campaign." The party's mistake, Hargrove insisted, "was failing three years ago to begin planning for rebuilding social programs. When Reform (now the Canadian Alliance) emerged as the party of tax cuts, the NDP had a chance to distinguish itself by going in the other direction."[46]

In the end, however, Hargrove's attempts to undermine Alexa's leadership probably had less to do with the ultimate electoral outcome than the Chrétien government's clever positioning of itself as the only option to prevent a newly energized right-wing Canadian Alliance (the former Reform party under a new leader, Stockwell Day) from slipping into power if progressives split their votes. "The choice that everybody has is if the Liberals don't form the government," Chrétien warned an audience in Corner Brook, Newfoundland, "what will happen is we'll have Stockwell Day," whose party had vowed to further tighten already restrictive unemployment insurance requirements and put an end to regional development institutions like the Atlantic Canada Opportunities Agency. "We will not let them destroy all these programs that ensure there are opportunities for everybody," Chrétien promised.[47]

This might have seemed rich coming from the same prime minister whose government had imposed such massive cutbacks after 1993 that the Liberals lost all but one seat in Atlantic Canada in 1997; however, the Liberals argued all that painful deficit-cutting, surplus-creating budgeting was allowing it to "reinvest" now. In June, the Liberals announced a new $700 million economic development program aimed at Atlantic Canada and then, in the budget they'd introduced but not passed by the time they chose to call the election, promised another $500 million to boost payments for seasonal workers like those on the East Coast. That they'd targeted Atlantic Canada wasn't accidental; it was cynical. The year before, Chrétien had temporarily appointed former Nova Scotia Liberal cabinet minister J.B. "Bernie" Boudreau to the Senate to allow him to "use the upper chamber as a taxpayer-funded base to organize a Liberal comeback in Atlantic Canada."[48] Liberal strategists targeted half a dozen Maritime seats, most of them held by first-time NDP MPs, hoping to offset expected losses in Ontario.

In the face of all of that, Alexa McDonough did what she always did. She put on a happy, optimistic face. "Does this look like a party that's going to shrivel up and blow away?" she asked days before the campaign began. "I don't think so. . . . We're going to win significantly more seats than we have now. I absolutely believe that is well within the achievable range."

It wasn't. And she knew it. But that didn't mean she couldn't make this, perhaps her last campaign as leader, fun.

7

The hotel room door opened. "Madame" stuck her head out. "Where are you going, Linda?" she asked.

Sgt. Linda Martell didn't need this. Not now. She'd been on duty twenty-four/seven for who knew how many days. Back and forth across the country: touch down, motorcade, event, interview, back on the plane, sometimes three different cities in three different provinces, all in the same day. It was her first assignment protecting a political party leader during a national election campaign. She and another female RCMP officer had begun serving as the personal protective detail for the NDP leader the day the election was called, and their duties wouldn't end until after the last votes were counted six weeks later.

It was exhilarating, but it was also exhausting. Some days started at 4:00 a.m., waiting in the candidate's hotel room while she got dressed, going over her day's itinerary, liaising with her staff and with local law enforcement offices wherever events were scheduled. On the aircraft, she and her fellow officer had designated seats between Madame McDonough's team and the media. She hung two cloth monkeys from the luggage bin above them with a sign that read "RCMP," which was the accepted signal the reporters could go no closer to the candidate without an invitation. Martell tried to keep the mood light. Just before takeoff, she'd yell, "Who let the dogs out?" And the reporters, and everyone else, would chant back the next line from the Baha Men song: "Woof, woof, woof, woof!" Sometimes, during long flights, she'd stage trivia contests. Whenever someone answered correctly, "I'd throw candy out over across the seats to them. It was a lot of fun."

Not that the fun changed her careful approach to her job. She and Madame McDonough had pre-arranged ways to communicate. Near the end of a speech, the candidate would glance at the Mountie. If Martell moved her head in a certain direction, it was a signal "something's up. 'Just for safety's sake, please, follow my directions.'" If they needed to move or get out of a situation for some reason, "I would place my hand on the small of her back just lightly, and she knew it was me and she had to move on."

Luckily, there'd been very few such incidents on this campaign. Oh, there was that time in Bedford, Nova Scotia, when Alexa was going through a crowd shaking hands. Martell walked just ahead of her, scoping out potential threats. "I spotted this little, little guy sitting in the front row getting ready to shake hands with her. And I saw him open up a napkin, take his teeth out. He wiped them down, and he put them in his mouth." She tried to signal the candidate not to take the man's hand but just tap him on the shoulder. Too late. The candidate shook his hand. Back on the plane, "we had a really good laugh over it."

The two women were together all day every day. Martell recalled, "I was there for every speech. I was there for every consultation. Everything. I was in the room with her when she spoke on the radio. I was with her constantly." They developed a "bond that's a very trustworthy bond," and not just because Martell had signed a confidentiality agreement before beginning the assignment. "She confided in me in several things, things I will go to my grave with."

In the process, Martell also became a fan of the woman she still couldn't help but call "Madame." She would "give me heck many times for calling her that," Martell remembered. "But it's just…I just respected her. I just didn't think it was right for me to say, 'Alexa.'" She knew all too well there were VIPs who would have treated her differently. "'Here, fill my glass, off you go.'" She paused. "She treated people the way she wanted to be treated. She had time for anybody, good or bad. She was just a lovely, lovely person, just a lovely human being."

By the time their day wrapped up, after twelve, fourteen, sixteen, or more hours of campaigning and Martell had said goodnight to her charge—"it was like putting your kids to bed for the night"—she was usually more than ready for the night team to take over and stand guard outside Alexa's hotel room door until morning.

But today, the campaign plane had arrived early in Calgary. Since there were no events scheduled for the evening, Martell and some friends had arranged to go line dancing. "Everybody had brought their cowboy boots and jeans and whatever hat they had, and we were going off to the nearby club." They were waiting for the elevator when Alexa McDonough's door opened, and she asked where they were headed.

"Line dancing," Martell said.

"Give me ten minutes," Alexa responded, "I'll be with you."

"So, I went, 'Oh, no,'" Martell remembered. It wasn't that she was unhappy to have Alexa join them. She was delighted. But it meant she was now also officially, unofficially back on duty. "I went in my room, got all geared up, with my weapon and my earphones and mic and all that, and threw a jacket over the top of it. And we all went line dancing." Martell had a great time; so did Madame. "I remember watching her saying into the mic, 'Okay, everybody to the left, two steps, kick.' And we were all just laughing."

While they were inside having fun, however, "some lady who was impaired" drove her car into the back of the leader's limousine. Without letting on what was happening, Martell slipped out into the parking lot, arrested the woman for impaired driving, and arranged for the local police to replace the limo. "When Madame McDonough came out after line dancing, everything was in place. She never knew a thing." A job well—and happily—done. "She was just somebody I truly admired. We all did."

•

In truth, Alexa's final election campaign would be more notable for its lighter moments and for its camaraderie than for its moments of high drama or tension about the outcome.

Alexa surrounded herself on this campaign plane with aides she was comfortable with, including Jane Wright, the former provincial researcher who'd moved to Ottawa to join Alexa's staff just six weeks before the election call, and Phyllis Larsen, who'd become one of Alexa's Halifax constituency assistants in 1999. They were both members in good standing of the second tier in Alexa's inner Girls' Night Out circle.

"She wanted me on the plane with her," Larsen recalled. "I was surprised. But Alexa has a light and sometimes it shines on you. She was always so curious about new people, identifying their skills and finding opportunities for them. The light happened to shine on me then." Her role? "Personal support, help her with her wardrobe, do her hair, and the rest." The rest could include everything from being her six o'clock-in-the-morning confidante, to getting Saskatchewan premier Roy Romanow on the phone, to arranging a quiet conversation with her family back in Halifax. "My job was to make it all happen." Although Alexa was her boss, Larsen said, "she also became a really good friend."

The campaign offered Larsen insight into her friend's steely determination. Alexa wanted the plane to make a stop on Prince Edward Island to support the party's candidates there, and Larsen was designated to make the case to the national campaign staff. They pushed back; there were no winnable seats on the Island, they argued. But Alexa was insistent. "She said she'd run four times before she was elected," and it was important to show loyal candidates "some love." Alexa prevailed. "She could be persistent when she wanted something," Larsen said.

Wright, who'd become close to Alexa while working in the party's small caucus office in Halifax, couldn't help but lament that "a lot of the personal stuff" had been lost in the translation to federal politics. "She was never as 'managed' in the provincial days." She watched Alexa endure days of debate preparation in an Ottawa hotel. She stood at a mocked-up podium trying to anticipate questions as well as other leaders' responses. "She'd get eight words into her answer and someone would say, 'No, no, don't say it like that.' So, she'd try it again. And they'd stop her again. She needed to stay on message. She'd go through that over and over." Wright shook her head. "If that was me, my self-esteem would be completely gone. But she never stopped, never let on."

Larsen remembered the debate too, the discussion over how to dress. Should Alexa wear an NDP-orange jacket, or was that too cliché? "It was always a fine line, and occasionally she'd push back. In the end, it was about making sure the leader was comfortable."

The media, of course, was often more interested in what she wore — or who she was with — than in what she said. It was news when David MacDonald joined her on the plane, and when her "handsome sons"[49] showed up in the last days of the campaign.

Alexa was not averse to campaign fun and games. When the satirical CBC comedy show *This Hour Has 22 Minutes* decided to play on the Canadian Alliance's promise to hold national referenda on matters of serious interest by staging its own referendum on whether Alliance leader Stockwell Day should legally change his name to "Doris Day," Alexa was happy to offer her two cents. "I think we all know how goofy Stockwell Day looks in a wet-suit," she told reporters, riffing on Day's much-mocked appearance at a news conference in a wetsuit. "Well, I'm not sure he'd look better in a sweater set with pearls."[50]

And then there was the tattoo. As part of its own lighter-side campaign coverage, the *National Post* asked all the party leaders a number of non-political questions, including, "If you had a tattoo, what would it be and where would you put it?" While Jean Chrétien, Stockwell Day, and Joe Clark were all quick to offer up a uniform and clichéd "Canadian flag over their heart" — proving, according to Alexa, they all thought alike — Alexa answered mysteriously she already had a tattoo but didn't reveal any details, including where it was located. So, the *Post* asked its readers to guess. More than 50 per cent of the more than five hundred readers who responded suggested Alexa's tattoo would be found "on her butt." Alexa's chest (12 per cent), shoulder (10 per cent), hip (9 per cent), and ankle (8 per cent) all also got votes. In the end, as the *Post* revealed just two days before actual voting day, Alexa's eyeliner was actually her permanent tattoo. She was partially blind in one eye and couldn't wear makeup.[51] It was another fine, fun moment in a campaign everyone understood would not end well.

On November 27, 2000, the NDP lost much of the ground it had regained after its calamitous 1993 defeat. The party slid back down the slick electoral pole, holding on to just thirteen seats, barely sufficient to maintain its status as an official party. And its share of the popular vote once again dipped below double digits; only 8.5 per cent of Canadians would choose to vote for the NDP.

Privately, Alexa would remember the 2000 campaign as the lowest moment of her political career. Although she believed the NDP had organized "great events and photo ops" to showcase their policy positions, reporters covering the campaign couldn't get past her poll numbers and were always asking how she would feel leading her party "into oblivion." "It's like— I won't say it out loud—but it's just like f-off," she lamented years later. "I mean, the degree of perversity and cynicism just blew my mind."

Publicly, of course, Alexa saw the glimmer of light, as she always did. The NDP had elected its first member from Ontario since 1993. "We now represent working families in six provinces from the Atlantic to the Pacific," she told reporters, adding, "we're going back to Ottawa to fight for health care, cleaning up our environment, making education affordable...."[52]

Would she stick around to fight another campaign, she was asked? "I absolutely intend to take the mandate that we have been given...and do exactly what we said we would do during the campaign." It was not exactly an answer to the question, but perhaps it was.

Sgt. Linda Martell had watched election night unfold inside the suite in the Lord Nelson Hotel, with Alexa, her family, and her campaign team, as the results rolled in and over them. "That was very sad," she recalled. "It was sad to see someone who was the right person at the wrong time. I'll be honest," she confided, "it was the first time I voted NDP. And I voted for the person....I was very impressed in Madame McDonough's...how can I put it?...in her beliefs, in what she stood for. And what she really wanted for the people. That came across as genuine."

Still, even that was not enough.

8

Alexa McDonough began planning her exit as leader almost before the final votes had been tallied on November 27, 2000. "I think an important attribute of leadership," she would explain later, "is knowing when to pass the torch." And how to pass it.

Alexa didn't have to look far to understand the potential for political disaster if she waited too long. Despite winning a third majority government, the federal Liberals were already embroiled in an increasingly bitter internecine war between supporters of Jean Chrétien, a prime minister who had no interest in resigning, and Paul Martin, his finance minister and heir who had no interest in waiting. That said, there were no current credible rivals for Alexa's job, and few inside the NDP seemed eager to push her to the exits. Why would they? She continued to be more popular than the party she led.

At the same time, her bruised and battered party needed time to heal and prepare for the transition to a new leader. So, in February 2001, Alexa put in motion a renewal process to rejuvenate the spirits of the faithful and revitalize the party. During the eight months leading up to the November 2001 national convention, more than 10,000 members attended cross-country grassroots meetings to discuss reforms aimed at democratizing decision-making in the party, as well as reconsidering its links to organized labour and provincial parties.

Even though Alexa's electoral vision for the party had prevailed at the last national convention, the larger question of where the NDP should fit in the political spectrum had not disappeared. In fact, her call for party renewal had been quickly joined by a group calling itself the National Politics Initiative (NPI) that wanted the NDP to disband. Its proponents believed this could lead to the development of a new, more grassroots, inclusive, and left-wing political movement — more along the lines of the "rainbow coalition" Svend Robinson proposed in 1995. The effort, unsurprisingly, was spearheaded by Robinson, fellow British Columbia MP Libby Davies, activist and former National Action Committee on the Status of Women president Judy Rebick, and Alexa's long-time nemesis Buzz Hargrove, all veterans of Robinson's failed 1995 leadership campaign. Jack Layton, the Toronto city councillor, who'd been a Robinson supporter and would eventually succeed Alexa as national party leader, was not officially a member but he was considered sympathetic to its objectives.

"It seemed to many of us that the left needed an electoral party with closer links to the new energy in the grassroots social movements, to better unify our efforts, push our demands, win converts, and fight for change — both inside parliament, and outside," explained CAW economist Jim Stanford, another member of the group.[53]

By the time the issue came to a head at the party's national convention in Winnipeg, the NPI's call for a new party had been endorsed by close to 2,000 individuals and organizations, many but not all involved with the NDP.

The whole idea frustrated Alexa. "I just don't believe for a moment that people think we should cut our momentum dead," she told reporters, "that we should say, 'Now let's spend another couple of years talking about whether we'd actually like to put ourselves out of existence and start up in some new form.' I think we want to build on the momentum we've got."[54]

Once again, Alexa won the convention. The 1,200 delegates not only endorsed her ongoing renewal process but also rejected, by a vote of 684 to 401, the motion for the party to disband. She'd won, but 37 per cent of delegates agreed with Robinson: "Our members want a left turn, we don't want the mushy middle," he declared. After the vote, however, as had happened after the 1995 leadership, he once again urged his supporters to stay in the party and continue to fight for change.[55]

•

If the 2000 election result represented a low point in Alexa's political career, her moral leadership in the midst of one of the world's lowest points — 9/11 — offered a shining example of what authentic leadership looked like.

On October 2, 2001, less than a month after the terrorist attacks on New York and Washington, Alexa introduced an NDP resolution in the House of Commons. At one level, it was straightforward enough, adding the NDP's voice to worldwide condemnation of the attacks as "crimes against humanity" and joining in the growing international chorus demanding that any response to the attacks be made under the auspices of the United Nations.

But it was the third aspect of the NDP motion — "[to] direct the government to table in the House, within ninety days, a report setting out the steps Canada will take to implement an action plan, including detailed budgets and timetables, to fight the rising tide of intolerance and racism directed against Arab and Muslim Canadians" — that became, in Alexa's words, "the most immediate" and compelling.

The week before, she told the House, she'd met with two dozen Arab community leaders in Toronto. "These are people, some of whom have been here for generations and others more recent arrivals, who are fiercely proud to be Canadians, people who have often risked their lives to get here and people who are working hard to build this country," she said.

> Yet, in the aftermath of the September 11 terrorist attack, they are people themselves under attack for no other reason than their race, religion or ethnicity.
>
> Many of these people have been victims of violence in their own countries of origin and yet their response has not been to demand vengeance but rather to express sympathy, peace and to search out deeper understanding among all Canadians and all members of the human family. We must learn from their experience, and today we call upon the Canadian government to develop a detailed action plan that brings citizens together in a dialogue for tolerance. We must reinforce the best of Canadian values and strengthen the bonds of tolerance.

One of those Muslim community leaders, she said, told her how his twelve-year-old son, a boy named Osama, came to him in tears, "begging his parents to change his name to Michael." It wasn't the only such story she heard that day. There was the seven-year-old, also named Osama, whose teacher, "sensing the backlash and the growing tide of intolerance," informed him she would now call him Sam instead. "We need Canadians to know that Osama is a Canadian name," Alexa told a hushed chamber, "that Mohammed is a Canadian name, and that worshipping in a mosque is a Canadian tradition."

It was Alexa McDonough at her eloquent, principled, human best, and her words carried echoes of both CCF leader J.S. Woodsworth's public opposition to Canada's entry into the Second World War and Tommy Douglas's lonely stand against the imposition of the War Measures Act in 1970. Although they profoundly disagreed on issues, Prime Minister W.L.

Mackenzie King said of Woodsworth, a person of his principled calibre was "an ornament to any Parliament."

The same was true of Alexa McDonough.

•

On June 5, 2002, after nearly seven years as leader of the New Democratic Party, Alexa McDonough announced her resignation. It was not a shock, but it was a surprise. "I do not think I had ever seen her so pleased with herself," said Pam Whelan, who stayed with Alexa at her Halifax condo the night before and then walked with her through Halifax's Public Gardens to the Lord Nelson Hotel for the early morning press conference. "She was totally in charge of whatever was to come."

That afternoon, back in Ottawa for Question Period in the House of Commons, members of all parties saluted her with six standing ovations. Alexa McDonough would leave behind "a powerful legacy of defending Medicare, the Canada Pension Plan, the unemployment insurance system, advocacy on social issues such as equality and human rights, and reinvigorating the NDP."[56]

"Smiling broadly [and] looking like a big weight had been lifted off her shoulders,"[57] Alexa officially asked the party to begin planning a convention to choose her successor. "As you can see," her partner, David MacDonald, told reporters, "she feels very comfortable and very pleased. She's been looking forward to this day."

Two days after her resignation, Alexa's mother Jean died of congestive heart failure. She was eighty-seven years old. Eulogizing her in the First Baptist Church in Halifax, Alexa recalled the lesson she learned from her mother more than forty years before, when she and her friends first connected the injustices of apartheid to what was happening in their own community. "There's no excuse in this world to tolerate either racism or poverty in our midst." Jean Shaw's pride in her daughter, Alexa's brother, Robbie, told mourners, "quite rightly knew no bounds."[58]

But what next? Alexa McDonough was just fifty-seven years old. She'd been an elected public official for almost twenty-one years. And she wasn't ready to disappear quietly or completely into the political good night. She planned to continue as the MP for Halifax, she said, "as long as [my constituents] will have me."

David MacDonald already sensed what was to come. She had, he suggested, "put a lot of effort into opening doors to the whole Arab community in Canada. I'm sure these will continue to be genuine concerns of hers."

They would. On December 12, 2002, in her final Question Period as leader of the NDP, Alexa demanded the Chrétien government protect the rights of Maher Arar, a Canadian citizen in prison in Syria. Arar had been detained by American authorities on September 26, 2002, while changing planes in New York, en route to Canada after visiting family in Tunisia. He had then been "transferred secretly, via Jordan, to Syria, where he was held in degrading and inhumane conditions, interrogated, and tortured."[59]

"I asked this question today," Alexa told reporters, "because I think it desperately needs to be answered for the benefit of the young family, who are absolutely distraught and distressed, but also because it goes to the soul of Canada. If Canada can no longer stand up to the Americans, no longer can stand up against grotesque violations of international law, then Canada's soul is literally withering away."[60]

9

"Hello," the voice on the phone began, warm, concerned, kind. "It's Alexa McDonough calling."

Alexa McDonough? Monia Mazigh knew the name, of course, remembered she'd been the leader of the New Democratic Party back in Mazigh's home country of Canada. But Mazigh was at this moment, in mid-October 2002, in Tunisia, nearly 7,000 kilometres away, feeling more alone, more isolated, and more bereft than she'd ever been.

In June, Mazigh and her husband, a Syrian-born Canadian software engineer named Maher Arar, had travelled from their home in Ottawa to Mazigh's birthplace in Tunisia for their first family vacation in years. It had been a difficult year, and they wanted a chance to recharge, reimagine their futures back in Canada. As Muslims, they'd "sensed a feeling of creeping distrust" from their fellow Canadians after 9/11. Mazigh wore a head scarf, and "the way people were looking at me had changed from curiosity or ignorance to mistrust and suspicion."[61] Both Arar and Mazigh had experienced racial profiling by authorities. To make matters worse, Arar's consulting business

Alexa, Monia Mazigh (centre), and Nazira Tareen (right)
during the vigil for Maher Arar, December 2002
(Material republished with the express permission of the *Ottawa Citizen*,
a division of Postmedia Network Inc.)

was not doing well—the high-tech bubble had burst the year before—and Mazigh was on maternity leave.

In mid-September, a colleague from the Ottawa software company where Arar once worked called Tunisia with news: there was a "real possibility" Arar could land a new contract. They decided he should fly back to Ottawa immediately. The rest of the family would follow a month later.

On September 26, 2002, Maher Arar flew from Tunis to Zurich, spent the night and caught an American Airlines flight to New York. From there, he was scheduled to fly to Montréal, pick up his car, and drive home to Ottawa. He would call Mazigh from his mother's home in Montréal at 7:00 the next evening, 1:00 a.m. Tunis time. "You'll be awake, won't you?" he joked. She told him she would.

But he didn't call. Not then. Not the next day. Worried, Mazigh telephoned the Canadian embassy in Tunis and Arar's lawyer back in Ottawa.

But she wouldn't learn where her husband was until almost a week later, when her mother in Canada finally telephoned. Arar had called her from prison in Brooklyn, New York, but hadn't been able to tell her much.

The next day Mazigh spoke to Canadian consular officials in New York. US authorities had informed them Arar belonged to the terrorist group al Qaeda. He didn't, of course. He was an ordinary Canadian software engineer with a wife and two children who happened to be Muslim. Mazigh was stunned.

Six days later, Canadian officials went to visit Arar in prison, only to discover he was no longer there. And no one knew where he was. Two days later, the Canadian consul called again. Arar had been deported to Syria. Maher Arar had been born there but had moved to Canada with his family as a seventeen-year-old in 1987. He hadn't lived in Syria for sixteen years and had been a Canadian citizen since 1991. Why would US authorities dispatch him to brutal, authoritarian Syria, where he might be interrogated, and possibly tortured, in order to get him to confess to things he hadn't done.

On October 12, 2002, the *New York Times* reported "a Canadian citizen suspected of having ties to terrorist organizations was deported to Syria on Thursday, two weeks after he was detained at Kennedy International Airport as he tried to catch a connecting flight to Canada."[62] That same day, the *Ottawa Citizen* quoted a Canadian foreign affairs spokesperson saying Arar, who'd been travelling on his Canadian passport, had been "removed from the US due to an immigration infraction."[63]

Infuriated, frustrated, desperate, Mazigh finally contacted the office of her MP, Liberal Marlene Catterall. Two weeks later, Catterall called her back to tell her Canadian officials were "looking into the matter."

But then, unbidden, out of nowhere, Alexa McDonough had telephoned. "Her voice struck me as so natural, as if she knew me," Mazigh would marvel, even years later. "She was the very, very first person to reach out to me." She considered. "Alexa did not know who I was. But she reassured me, told me, 'We are here for you.' Alexa adopted me. I say God sent her to me."

•

After returning to Canada in November, Monia Mazigh visited Alexa McDonough's parliamentary office. She recalled admiring

> all the books and art works on the shelves. I smiled; I had never visited a political personality before. In Tunisia, such a thing was out of the question.
>
> When Alexa McDonough entered the office, she found me lost in thought. She was warm and there was compassion in her eyes. She put me at ease at once and listened with close attention. I told her about my efforts to get the government to move, and how disappointed I was to see so little action taken to bring Maher home. She understood what I was telling her and promised that this was a case she was not about to let drop. That sentence alone meant a great deal to me. It told me that, in my solitude, in the isolation I was experiencing, there were people who were with me, supporting me. . . . As long as I had people like her to rely on, I wouldn't stop.[64]

As Mazigh was leaving, Alexa did what she inevitably did. Made connections. Did Mazigh know Nazira Tareen?

"Nazira?" Mazigh repeated. "I don't know the name."

"She's an extraordinary woman, you must meet her." Tareen was a community activist and the founder of the Ottawa Muslim Women's Organization. Alexa met her at an event at an Ottawa mosque soon after 9/11 and had already discussed Arar's situation with her. "She's anxious to meet you," Alexa said.

A few weeks later, Mazigh was invited to a party for local Muslim women that Tareen hosted to mark Eid, the end of the month of fasting during Ramadan. After everyone had eaten and Tareen welcomed the dignitaries, including Alexa, she introduced Mazigh, "a courageous woman who is fighting to see her husband again."

As Mazigh told her story — "the disappearance, the anxiety, the imprisonment, the deportation, the appalling silence and the government's foot-dragging, the way my family's life had been turned upside down, the uncertainty" — she noticed the women in Nazira Tareen's living room who, "minutes before, had been carefree, happy, and laughing," now "blowing their noses and wiping away tears."

Alexa made the case the women must support Mazigh. Less than two weeks later, the first "Free Maher" vigil took place near the Eternal Flame in front of Canada's Parliament Buildings. Although Alexa's office sent email invitations to all federal MPs and their staffs, the only politicians Mazigh saw were her MP, Marlene Catterall, and Alexa.

"Never did I sense in [Alexa] the glad-handing, scheming politician taking an interest in this affair merely to score points against her political opponents," Mazigh would write in her memoir. "She was taking an enormous risk in supporting me. I didn't live in her constituency; she was under no obligation to help me. Since Maher was being presented by the media as a suspect with links to terrorism, why should she endanger her reputation, her career, and her good name for a cause such as his? I realized as the days went by that Alexa was not only defending the rights of Maher Arar, the individual, but was going beyond that: she was defending her vision of Canada."

10

On January 24, 2003, more than one thousand delegates to the NDP leadership convention in Toronto offered a heartfelt thank you to Alexa McDonough for her stalwart and steadfast stewardship during seven-and-a-half tumultuous years. Those years had been highlighted—for her and the NDP—by the party's unpredicted, unprecedented, and hopefully permanent electoral breakthrough in Atlantic Canada. There had, of course, been lowlights too, though no one wanted to dwell on them on this night.

In her own parting speech, Alexa tried, one last time, to bring together her party's disconnected threads. "The old, sterile debate over whether we're a party or a movement? It means exactly nothing to the people we serve," she declared. "A party that ignores social movements loses its connection to the source of our strength and principles. A movement that ignores politics and parliament surrenders the state to the right.... Our goal must remain to one day form the government in this country."[65]

The next day, Toronto city councillor Jack Layton won the party's leadership on the first ballot. And Alexa became, happily, the MP for Halifax.

In the Commons, she continued to focus on health and foreign affairs while serving as a kind of "senior statesperson" too.

She still had much to accomplish.

•

Promise me nothing like this will ever happen again. Alexa had never forgotten those haunting words from the newly widowed young woman with two school-aged children, whose husband had been killed in the 1992 Westray mine explosion. They continued to motivate her in the decade that followed the disaster. Alexa had teamed up with the Westray Families Group, and with Lawrence McBrearty's United Steelworkers and other labour groups to press Ottawa to introduce legislation to hold corporations accountable for their actions. Year after year, Alexa introduced private members' bills that went nowhere. She even crossed partisan lines to work with Nova Scotia PC MP Peter MacKay, who represented the district where the mine had been built.

Finally, on October 27, 2003, Parliament unanimously passed Bill C-45, "the Westray bill," to make those who "direct the work of others" legally responsible for taking reasonable steps to provide for the safety of their workers. If they failed to do so, they could face criminal charges.

The new law, declared Alexa at the time, wasn't just about Westray or even coal mining. "It is about the thousand men and women in this country who lose their lives in workplace accidents. It is about the close to one million . . . workplace accidents that occur on an annual basis in this country. At the end of the day, it is not a statistic or an array of statistics that we are talking about. What we are talking about are human lives shattered or terminated as a result of practices that could have been improved and accidents prevented."

•

Alexa McDonough's question in the middle of a telephone conversation stunned Monia Mazigh. In the year since Alexa first called her in Tunisia, much had changed. Most significantly, on October 5, 2003, Syrian officials had released Maher Arar from prison and he'd returned to Canada. He'd endured close to a year of interrogation and torture.

Over the course of that difficult year, Mazigh would remember, her relationship with Alexa "had developed into a kind of friendship. Alexa had become a teacher and guide, a tenacious woman in politics who'd overcome obstacles to reach the pinnacle of her party without ever losing her humanity or her openness."

And now, mid-conversation about "this, that, and the other thing," Alexa had shocked her friend by asking, "Did you ever think of going into politics?" Was Mazigh interested in running for the NDP in the next election?

On January 24, 2004, they met in Alexa's apartment so Alexa and one of her assistants could answer Mazigh's questions about what being a candidate would involve.[66] As she got up to leave, the telephone rang. It was Alexa's office. The federal minister of public security, Anne McLellan, was about to make a statement concerning Maher Arar, and Alexa should switch on the television. Almost from the day of Arar's release from prison, Alexa had been one of the leading voices demanding a full public inquiry into the role Canadian officials played in Maher Arar's detention and imprisonment.[67] Now she and Monia Mazigh watched as McLellan announced there would be an inquiry.

"Alexa turned to me; both of us were in tears," Mazigh remembered. "'What wonderful news,' Alexa kept repeating."

•

Monia Mazigh wasn't to be the only woman Alexa recruited to run in the 2004 election.

Alexis MacDonald was the director of an international initiative by St. Francis Xavier University's Coady Institute to respond to the HIV/AIDS crisis in Botswana and Rwanda. Alexa arranged to meet her in Toronto during a stopover on her way to Africa. MacDonald was flattered and intrigued, she told Alexa, but she wasn't ready. Not yet. She was only twenty-six. Maybe in a few years. . . .

Two days later, in an internet café in Addis Ababa, Ethiopia, MacDonald reread a follow-up email from Alexa, asking her to reconsider. Politics needed more women, Alexa wrote, and unfortunately, women often had to run two or three times before they could be elected. Why not start now? As a sweetener, Alexa promised to make sure Stephen Lewis — the iconic politician turned international AIDS activist Alexa knew MacDonald admired — would speak at her nominating convention.

MacDonald sat in the café. "You look around, you see your own privilege, you see how hard people work, especially, the women, and you know they will probably never have this opportunity.... That was the tipping point." A few weeks later, she returned to Nova Scotia to seek the NDP nomination in Central Nova. True to Alexa's promise, Stephen Lewis came to tiny, rural Plymouth, the site of the Westray mine disaster, to speak in a fire hall at MacDonald's uncontested nomination.

Unsurprisingly, MacDonald lost to Peter MacKay, the former Progressive Conservative leader who had represented the reliably Conservative riding since 1997 and had recently engineered a merger with the Canadian Alliance to form the new Conservative Party. But surprisingly, MacDonald picked up 28 per cent of the popular vote, finishing second in a riding where the NDP had previously barely registered a blip. She ran again in 2006, increasing her percentage of the popular vote to 33 per cent.[68]

•

Although David MacDonald would acknowledge he and Alexa had been "drifting apart" for some time, the end of their relationship came suddenly, in the spring of 2004 shortly before the election, and soon after *Frank Magazine* published a "quite nasty story on the front page — 'Alexa Alone Again,'" which suggested David was seeing someone else.

Their seven-year relationship had always been complicated. After David's divorce from his first wife in 1997, the Astons — the retired couple who'd invited Alexa to live in a bedroom in their condo after her 1995 leadership victory — invited David to share that bedroom with Alexa. "We used to call it one big pyjama party," David joked. Later, he and Alexa agreed to share the rent on a second apartment in the same building, but "we never really went that extra step," by which he meant getting married.

The question was how to define their relationship. In 1998, Alexa registered MacDonald as her "companion," so he qualified for free airline travel once reserved for politicians' spouses. Later that year, when the *Ottawa Citizen*'s Juliet O'Neill asked if they planned to marry, Alexa's response was quick. They were too busy to even consider it, she said. "We both lead insane lives." David's answer was more measured, and perhaps hopeful. "We're still in the process of getting to know one another."

While she was party leader, he recalled, "There were so many pressures on her I never felt it was appropriate to say, 'Well, I'm sort of your partner. I am your companion. I try to be a big supporter of what you're doing. But I'm not sure just where we stand.'" Alexa's "comfort zone was a kind of informal common-law relationship." MacDonald wanted "to formalize it. I wanted to know I was married, that we shared responsibilities."

Though they lived together when they were in Ottawa, travelled as a couple, spent summer vacations and occasional holidays with her family at Shaw Island — "her friends became my friends" — Alexa had long since developed a determined independence that would have seemed foreign to the Alexa Shaw of the 1960s, and certainly problematic to MacDonald's desire for "shared responsibilities."

After the NDP's losses in 2000 and the increasing likelihood Alexa would resign the leadership, Alexa decided "on her own," MacDonald recalled, that she didn't want to hold on to their shared apartment, "so we let it go." MacDonald rented another apartment in the same building; sometimes Alexa would stay with him, sometimes in the Astons' condo when they were in Florida. When Alexa decided to sell her Halifax family house and buy a condo, "I was never really consulted. . . . There were times when she would go off and do something, and I would say, 'You never even asked me whether I would. . .'" He paused. "I'm the type of person that if I feel something is not going forward, then I just say, 'Well, maybe there's a message in there.'" In the spring of 2004, they separated, at least temporarily.

Temporary became permanent after the *Frank Magazine* article. "Alexa said to me, 'Can you just not be seeing anybody else for the next couple of months 'til we get the election over with?' And I said, 'Is that the main reason I'd be doing it? Just so you get the election over? If that's all it means, no, I'm not going to put my life on hold because you've got a political campaign going on.' I said, 'I won't do anything to embarrass you. But I won't pretend something exists when it doesn't exist.'"[69]

•

In April 2008, Alexa, Jane Wright, and Phyllis Larsen — all veterans of the NDP's 2000 election campaign plane tour — travelled to Ontario's cottage country to celebrate the wedding of Linda Martell, the RCMP officer assigned to protect Alexa during the campaign.

Much had changed in the intervening years. Linda Martell was now Linda Davidson. From 1979 to 2004, she'd been married to a man. After their relationship ended, she'd come out as a lesbian and had invited Alexa and the others to celebrate her marriage. "It was very informal, seventy-five or eighty family and friends in front of a fireplace at a golf course here in Muskoka."

Alexa was among the guests offering a few words of support and encouragement to the newlyweds. "She didn't have to," Davidson allowed. "But I thought that was so nice, and very heartfelt. It touched me deeply that she thought so much of me. Madame McDonough will always be an inspiration to me."

She was. In 2015, Davidson — who'd endured decades of bullying, abuse, and sexual harassment, dating back to her first days as an RCMP officer in Grand Falls, Newfoundland, and who had suffered PTSD and come close to dying by suicide — would become the lead plaintiff in a class action suit against the RCMP. A year later, RCMP Commissioner Bob Paulson offered a tearful apology to Davidson and the hundreds of past and current female officers who'd experienced bullying and sexual harassment and announced the force had set aside $100 million to compensate them.

•

On June 2, 2008, the eleventh anniversary of her first election to Parliament, in a banquet hall at the Lord Nelson Hotel in Halifax, in the company of close to one hundred family and friends, political colleagues and party supporters, Alexa McDonough officially announced her retirement from politics. She was sixty-three years old and had been a politician for nearly thirty years.

Three of her six grandchildren[70] — Abbie Jean, six, Lauchlan, four, and Elizabeth, two — presented her with NDP-orange roses. Four provincial MLAs offered pink and red roses to mark her lifetime of work for feminism and peace.

"This is a pretty emotional moment for me," Alexa allowed when she took the podium. "I am deeply indebted to the people of this great city and province for the trust they have placed in me again and again." She was the first woman to win four consecutive terms representing Nova Scotia in Parliament, and only the second MP in history to have done so. "I don't know if I can fully explain it, but I know in my heart that it's time. It's the right time. It's time for the torch to be passed to the upcoming generations."[71]

There were tributes from near and far.

The then provincial NDP leader Darrell Dexter, who noted, "Alexa carries a status within the Nova Scotia party that is almost legendary and universally appreciated," recalled being recruited as a university student in the early 1980s. Within minutes of meeting Alexa, he said, she'd instructed him to prepare a research paper outlining financial problems students faced. Dexter would soon lead their provincial New Democratic Party to victory, forming Nova Scotia's first NDP government. "If it wasn't for Alexa, I doubt I would be where I am today," he said.[72]

Alexa's replacement as federal NDP leader, Jack Layton, sent along greetings too. He pointed out 41 per cent of the current NDP caucus were women, "which is the highest it's ever been, and that can be chalked up to Alexa's work." Layton's own slow building of the party he inherited would culminate in 2011, when he led the federal party to its best showing ever — 103 seats — enough to form the official opposition. Another milestone that might not have happened if not for Alexa's McDonough's efforts to keep the party from splintering.

In her own speech that day, Alexa herself didn't miss a last chance to be a beacon for political diversity. "We are challenged to take very seriously the need to increase the numbers of under-represented people in Parliament," she said. "That means women. That means visible minorities. That means people living with disabilities."

But she also talked about her desire for a less hectic, less partisan, more family-focused life. She wanted to hang out with her grandchildren, maybe pick up a few racquetball games with her sister-in-law, and "get a few good nights' sleep." She recalled her grandmother, Winnifred MacKinnon, a single parent who'd raised four kids in Boston. "She worked as a secretary to a bank manager, but always took time each summer" to visit Halifax and spend time with her grandchildren. She would stay with the Shaws in their tiny basement apartment across from the Public Gardens, where they'd lived when they first arrived from Ottawa and on the same site where Alexa herself now lived in a condo. "My first and longest lasting favourite memory," she said, "is of running around in the Public Gardens with my grandmother. Now my favourite thing is to run around through the Public Gardens with my grandchildren."

"Hopefully," said Justin, looking around at his own children, "she'll enjoy some of the smaller things in life that are probably the most important things in life, and that's hanging out with these guys."[73]

Her brother, Robbie, was less certain. He predicted a "difficult adjustment and I think she knows that. . . . You can't be a politician for nearly thirty years and not find the adjustment tough."

•

For Alexa McDonough, tonight's nomination meeting, just three months after her resignation, was the culmination of a lifetime's effort to convince more women and visible minorities to seek office, but it also represented a personal dilemma. Six hundred local NDP supporters met to choose the person who would replace her as the Halifax NDP candidate in the 2008 federal election.

Three people wanted the nomination: two women and a Black Nova Scotian man. The man was Irvine Carvery, one of the children from Africville who'd attended the summer camp Alexa and her friends organized in the early 1960s. Carvery was now a leading spokesperson for the former residents' fight for compensation for the loss of their community. One of the women seeking the nomination was Alexis MacDonald, the young international development worker Alexa recruited to run in the 2004 and 2006 federal campaigns.

"Despite our friendship," MacDonald remembered, "Alexa didn't endorse anyone. She wanted an open and fair convention, and she always stood by her values."

In the end, the third candidate, a legal aid worker and climate advocate named Megan Leslie won. When the result was announced, Alexa whispered in MacDonald's ear, "'It would be a wonderful thing if you make it unanimous,'" MacDonald recalled. "I had no experience with a contested nomination at that point, so I hadn't realized I should do that." She did. And the next day, she and Alexa campaigned for Leslie. The torch had been passed.[74]

Alexa McDonough meets with students during her time as interim president
of Mount Saint Vincent University from 2009 to 2010

(courtesy of Mount Saint Vincent University)

THERE'S LIFE AFTER POLITICS

1

Janet MacMillan, the chair of the board of governors at Halifax's Mount Saint Vincent University, and Catherine Woodman, her soon-to-be successor, weren't sure what to expect when they arrived at Alexa McDonough's condo on a Monday in the late spring of 2009. It was their second visit in just three days.

They'd initially met the previous Friday, only telling Alexa they wanted to discuss something to do with the university. MacMillan and Woodman had done their best to keep their desperation to themselves. A few weeks earlier, the university's president, Kathryn Laurin, unexpectedly resigned in the middle of her first term. The two women needed to find an interim president — and yesterday — to step into the role, be accepted by an always finicky university community, and lead the university for at least a year while the board conducted a national search to find a permanent replacement.

Alexa greeted them that first day, MacMillan remembered, "dressed casually, as one would be in their home in the afternoon, pants and a blouse." She was "gracious and open and chatty." She got them tea. After some small talk, they got to the point: would Alexa consider becoming interim president of Atlantic Canada's historic women's university?

Alexa had lots of questions "because that's Alexa — inquisitive mind, absolutely interested and knowledgeable about Mount Saint Vincent," MacMillan said. But she thought Alexa was simply being polite. After more than an hour's conversation, "there was no commitment whatsoever."

So they weren't sure what to expect when they returned to continue the conversation. "Alexa opened the front door," Woodman recalled with a laugh, "and she's dressed in a navy blue suit. And she had her binder." There was no tea, no chit-chat. "Out came the questions and the specifics and the follow-ups.... I think we both knew the minute she opened the door dressed in that navy suit and we saw the work she'd compiled with her questions. . . she had committed."

Alexa told the women she'd spent the weekend consulting with two people she trusted whenever she needed to make "really important decisions"—her son Justin and her friend Betty Muggah.

The actual negotiations were easy—and surprising. MacMillan, whose day job was co-owner of one of Atlantic Canada's largest PR firms, had done her share of negotiating, but it was the first time she'd ever negotiated with someone who wanted less than she'd offered. "I would say, 'Here's what we're prepared to offer you.' And she would say, 'I think that's too much.' And then she countered, offering to donate a portion of her salary towards different projects." MacMillan paused. "It was never about the money."

It wasn't. "I think for Alexa, a lot of it was in the values of Mount Saint Vincent University, to which she felt very much aligned, to the history of the university as well as its place in our province to the focus on women," MacMillan theorized, adding, "This was the ideal job for her. She could never achieve what she wanted to achieve as a partisan. She could convince people she had integrity and she was all of these wonderful things, but she could never get enough of them to vote for her, whereas in this job, the partisan stuff didn't come in and she was able to be the person she always was. It was the right place for her."

•

Johann LeBlanc had been the executive assistant to the president of Mount Saint Vincent University, widely known as the Mount, for only a few months when her first boss resigned. LeBlanc had arrived at the Mount after five years as executive assistant to Dr. Ken Rockwood, the director of the Geriatric Medicine Research unit at Dalhousie University. While she'd loved the work—LeBlanc had a certificate in gerontology—she had two young children and wanted a more stable position with regular hours.

Now, she would have to figure out how to work with a new boss. She knew who Alexa McDonough was, of course, and "was enamoured of her as a woman," even though she herself wasn't political. "I always thought she was this strong, big woman. But she comes in and she's very petite…and she's very humble." But she was, it quickly became clear, also a let's-get-things-done new broom.

Alexa arrived to a pile of faculty grievances. Thanks in part to budget cuts and threats to programs, the faculty had become frustrated, and the university roiled in continuing unhappiness. Alexa scooped up the grievances. "Let me make a few phone calls," she told LeBlanc.

"And she went into the office…and the grievances went away," marvelled LeBlanc. "I was gob-smacked. That was when I knew it was going to work really, really well. That was probably two hours into her job.

"One of her biggest lessons for me," LeBlanc added, "was to take the 'I' out of your conversation and say 'we.' Together we can do things."

Alexa may have been an interim president, but she had no intention of being a placeholder. During orientation week, LeBlanc said, she wore the frosh T-shirt, welcomed students, mixed and mingled. She'd often stop in her car to pick up students walking to campus. "She was just so happy to be around people all the time. That's what she thrived on, and figuring out how she could help them."

Having quickly won over faculty and students, Alexa reached out to the Sisters of Charity, the founders of the university. Though the Mount was no longer a religious institution, members of the order still lived in the Mother House on campus and even had representation on the university board. In the 1980s, Alexa had run afoul of the Roman Catholic hierarchy and the Mount's then president after some NDP supporters sold pro-choice buttons and copies of a biography of Dr. Henry Morgentaler during a party convention at the university. But now, "Alexa picked up the phone and called the head sister and we had a meeting," LeBlanc said.

LeBlanc was constantly astounded at Alexa's networks of connections. "I never knew who was going to call. I'd be answering the phone and it would be a senator, or it would be a political leader, or it'd be an international person. I'm like, 'Oh my god. I think I just talked to…' It was really, really neat to see all the lives she impacted and how they all stayed connected with her." As Alexa's assistant, one event particularly resonated with her. "She invited the 'troops' back in. I think every assistant she ever worked with showed up. I thought, 'What is this?' Everyone had stayed connected."

•

"Let's do a peace conference," Alexa announced one morning shortly after she'd become president.

"What do you mean, let's do a peace conference?" LeBlanc replied. "Like twenty people, thirty people?"

"No, no. We're going to get a few hundred people here."

During the planning for the conference, LeBlanc remembered, she, Alexa, and Macha MacKay, a peace-advocate friend of Alexa's who also happened to be Peter MacKay's mother, travelled to Pugwash, Nova Scotia, to meet with peace conference organizers there to see how they might work together. "That was the best road trip of my life," LeBlanc laughed. After their meetings, the women ended up staying overnight at "The Donut"—which is what Alexa called her son Travis's condo in the exclusive Fox Harb'r Resort developed by Tim Hortons co-founder Ron Joyce. There was wine. "They talked about everything, and I just sat there listening to these powerful women who were change-makers, just talking. . . . I didn't want to go to sleep because I just wanted to capture this moment that was surreal for me."

More than one hundred people ultimately attended the four-day conference, "Being the Change: Building a Culture of Peace," which took place at the Mount in July 2010 and featured speakers from around the world. The conference brought welcome new awareness to the Mount, but the conference themes also showcased Alexa's personal passions, including peace education, women's activism, and the disarmament movement.

"She brought in the world to the Mount, and she got the students involved in it, and political leaders," LeBlanc said. "There were receptions, and it was all about dialogue with the goal to build a culture of peace in our classrooms, our communities, and our world. It was amazing."

•

During those intense months of planning for the conference, however, LeBlanc began to sense "something was up" with her boss. "I was sitting in meetings and I noticed she started to repeat herself a lot. I started to watch the reaction of people with her—her peace friends, the goers, the doers, the grannies—and they all had a lot of respect for her, but I saw they were kind of starting to notice too."

LeBlanc looked for reasons for it not to be what she feared it might be. "We did a lot of late nights and I thought, 'Well maybe she's just tired,' or 'maybe she's not eating.' I'd have to remind her to go eat because busy people work through lunch and supper and sometimes we would be there till eleven at night. . . ." Social isolation? "It wasn't social isolation because she's very social, but maybe there's just a lot on her plate."

For years, Johnann LeBlanc had worked closely with Dr. Rockwood, one of Canada's most respected Alzheimer's researchers. She'd spent time in nursing homes, working with dementia patients. "Am I being paranoid?" she wondered. But she'd also volunteered with Alexa's brother, Robbie, at the provincial Alzheimer Society, so she knew about the Shaw family's history with the disease.

She struggled with what she should do, or say. Finally, one afternoon, after everyone had left for the day, she went into Alexa's office and sat down. "Alexa, I've got to ask you something," she began. "I'm just . . . I'm noticing something here and I don't want you to be uncomfortable, but I'm noticing you're repeating yourself a lot and you're asking me to do the same thing a couple of times. It hasn't just happened once, it's happened . . . it's been happening. And I'm just worried for you. . . . If you don't mind, I can call Dr. Rockwood and explain to him what I'm noticing and maybe he can get you in to see him."

Recalling the conversation close to a decade later, Johnann LeBlanc teared up. "It was a tough conversation," she said. "But she was stellar. She didn't waver. She said, 'Yes. Let's get this done. Let's get on this.'"

Soon after, given their family history, Alexa and Robbie agreed to see Rockwood, who'd been their father's geriatrician. The test results showed Robbie did not have the disease. But Alexa did. She was just sixty-six years old.

2

George Elliott Clarke didn't hear the message until he arrived at his office that Monday morning in 2012. "Hi, George. It's Alexa McDonough calling." It had been close to fifty years since Alexa did her university student placement at the preschool run by Clarke's mother. Today, Clarke was one of the country's most celebrated writers, a Governor General's Award–winning poet, a playwright, and a novelist. His day job was as a professor of English at the University of Toronto.

Although the two hadn't been close, their paths occasionally crossed. In 2009, for example, Alexa had attended a reading he gave. After the event, Alexa, by then officially retired from politics, "asked me if I would consider being a candidate for the NDP in the next election. She said she had spoken to Jack Layton and he was supportive." Clarke demurred, but he was flattered to have been asked. It reminded him of the conversation they'd had back in 1979, when Alexa first ran for office and had tried, unsuccessfully, to convince a radicalized young Clarke to campaign for her. "We had a very nice conversation."

The next year, when Clarke's opera, *Trudeau: Long March, Shining Path*, about the late former prime minister got its first and only live production—a five-day run at the Sir James Dunn Theatre at Dalhousie—Alexa was in the audience. More than that, Clarke explained, she'd made a financial contribution to help stage the production.

When she left the message on Clarke's answering machine, Alexa McDonough had just finished reading his weekly column on books, writing, politics, and life in the Halifax *Chronicle-Herald*. His column that day had focused on Omar Khadr, the Canadian child soldier who'd been taken to Afghanistan by his father, an al Qaeda supporter, was captured in a 2002 firefight with US forces, and spent nearly a decade in prison at Guantanamo Bay. Under pressure, he'd agreed to plead guilty to "murder in violation of the laws of war" in hopes of being transferred to Canada to serve the rest of his eight-year sentence. That had just happened when Clarke wrote his column.

"I loved your article today," Alexa said. "It is a continuing horror that he is continuing to be in prison." But that wasn't really why she was calling. Whenever she read his column, she told him, "I just think of how proud your mom and dad would be—and what wonderful, wonderful human beings they were. And it is amazing that you—smart, saucy little kid with a huge sense of humour from a young age—have turned into such a worldly figure and philosopher-king. And I just want you to know I loved your parents, and I just think of them every Sunday morning with mostly a big smile and, just as often, a tear or two.

"As I say, no reason to return my call. I just wanted to let you know that. Why think it and not pass it along? Take care."

George Elliott Clarke shed a tear or two listening to the message, which he has never erased from his machine.

•

The idea for the Alexa McDonough Institute for Women, Gender and Social Justice at Mount Saint Vincent University emerged from a series of conversations between Alexa's brother, Robbie, and Ramona Lumpkin, Alexa's successor as president of the university.

One of Lumpkin's first big projects at the Mount was to raise funds for a new academic building dedicated to honouring women. Lumpkin wanted to rename the Mount's Institute for Women, Gender and Social Justice, which was to be housed there, after Alexa. "She had been quite an idol of mine before I met her, and even more after." But she needed to raise $250,000 to make it a reality. And Alexa was not "a buddy-buddy, rub-shoulders-with-the-rich-and-the-well-endowed. So Robbie came up with the idea of introducing me to Les Holloway."[1]

"Robbie called me up one day and asked if we could have a cup of coffee," Holloway remembered. "He wondered if I might be willing to help in arranging union contributions for the institute. Of course I would. I'd do anything for Alexa. I told him I'd do my best."

Together, they decided on the ask: $25,000 per union from ten unions. "Les would come pick me up in his little red Jeep," Lumpkin recalled, "and we would go visit the unions to tell them about the project. I got to listen to him make the pitch. He was wonderful at that. He would tell them how if he had Alexa in the car with him and they were going somewhere, they would never pass a picket line without her saying, 'Stop, stop, stop the car!' And they would get out and join the picket line." By the time Holloway finished pitching, he had raised $265,000. Lumpkin laughed. "It was in many ways some of the easiest money we raised."

Lumpkin wanted to make the 2013 naming announcement a surprise for Alexa, who hadn't been aware of the fundraising. But they worried Alexa, who'd recently been diagnosed with breast cancer, might beg off, thinking she was just being invited to another party. So Lumpkin came up with a ruse. She told Alexa the party was for Brian Jessop, the Mount's vice-president of administration, one of Alexa's favourite colleagues at the university. "We're going to make him an honorary feminist!" she told Alexa. Jessop—whom Lumpkin called "a guy's guy, an athlete, an engineer, and a feminist, although I don't think he would ever use that word about himself"—agreed to play along.

It worked. When she arrived, "everyone jumped out. 'Surprise!' She finally realized this wasn't about Brian; it was about her. It was a wonderful moment."

Today, the Alexa McDonough Institute—which won a 2016 Nova Scotia Human Rights Award for its annual Girls Conference, which brings together girls and young women to discuss human rights, social justice, and other issues—has become a "hub of feminist energy, action, and research."

"It is just a fitting tribute to the woman Alexa has been," declared Lumpkin.

•

Despite her retirement from politics and her Alzheimer's diagnosis—which still wasn't obvious to most casual acquaintances and which she herself had never publicly acknowledged—Alexa continued to attend NDP events, including the 2014 provincial convention in Halifax.

It was the first convention following the defeat of the Dexter NDP government, but Alexa—as always—chose to excavate the best from the worst. "This is such a mature, grown-up party compared to the rookie bunch we used to be," she told Pat Kipping, a friend and broadcaster who had recently begun to document Alexa's memories. "We are dealing with this massive loss, but nobody was dwelling on it, nobody was looking back. Everybody was busy trying to lend their experience and expertise to how do we go forward. I came away very inspired and impressed and exhilarated."

During one session, Alexa sat at a round table with other party members. As she looked around, she realized one of her tablemates—wearing a face-shielding baseball cap and slouched over as if he did not want to be recognized—was Bob Levy, her former fellow MLA whose election-eve resignation to accept a judgeship in 1988 had triggered one of the worst chapters in Alexa McDonough's political career.

The two had not spoken in twenty-six years.

Levy had retired from the bench in 2008—the same year Alexa quit politics—and quietly rejoined the party, working behind the scenes for the party during the 2013 campaign.

When the session broke up, Alexa recalled later, "I went over and said, 'Well Bob, it's really nice to see you here. Does anyone else know you're here?'"

"I don't want anyone else to know I'm here."

"Well, I'm sure people would love to know you're here."

"I don't think so." He added almost plaintively, "Do you know how much courage it took for me to come here? Please don't make it any harder for me."

"I thought, 'OK, I respect that," Alexa said later. "What an honest, reasonable plea.'" So she didn't ask that Levy's presence as a former MLA, a key member of the party during the 1980s, be acknowledged from the podium.

Instead, the two exchanged a few more awkward pleasantries. "I thought of all the things I wanted to say," Levy would say later, "But I didn't. And it was never resolved."

•

Harold Crowell, Alexa's former boss in the social planning department during the late 1960s, was now in his eighties, suffering from Parkinson's disease and living at Parkland, an assisted living facility near Alexa's Halifax condo. Alexa and two other former colleagues from the department took turns visiting him. Sometimes, they would read to him from a book, sometimes from the daily newspaper. "He loved to hear the news," Alexa remembered. If she missed a word or made a mistake reading, he would stop her. "Read that again, Alexa. That didn't make sense."

After a while, the first of their former colleagues died. And then the second. "It was just Harold and me." Alexa continued to read to Crowell until he too died in the fall of 2017.

He wasn't the only person from her past Alexa reconnected with in retirement. Carolyn MacGregor and her then husband, Peter, had been part of the McDonough social circle during the mid-seventies. Like Alexa and Peter, Carolyn and her husband had divorced. She later married publisher Jim Lorimer and became "a passionate environmentalist, feminist and a lifelong learner." But now she was suffering from dementia and living, like Harold Crowell, in Parkland. Alexa would often go for walks with her until she too died in the summer of 2019.

•

In 1998, five years after her father died of Alzheimer's and more than a decade before she herself would be diagnosed with the disease, Alexa McDonough spoke to a Canadian Alzheimer Society meeting in Vancouver.[2]

At one level, she spoke as the leader of the federal New Democratic Party fighting to convince Ottawa to restore the $3.5 billion Paul Martin had cut from the general health-care budget and, more specifically, to expand vital supports like home care for those struggling to cope with the impact of Alzheimer's in their families. "We can't claim in all honesty to have a universal health-care system," Alexa declared, "as long as home care isn't included in Medicare."

But she was also there as someone who had personally experienced the ravages of the disease in her own family. When Lloyd began to exhibit the warning signs of Alzheimer's, she told her audience, the family had approached her father's doctor, "a respected and experienced GP. He was adamant these were the usual, normal signs of aging." When the family suggested Lloyd be referred for a geriatric assessment, "he dismissed it out of hand. I remember his exact words: 'Why would you want to know whether he has Alzheimer's anyway? There's nothing you can do about it.'"

Alexa went on to talk about the important role family members and caregivers play in forcing governments to understand the need for more research and better family support. "That's why your human stories are so important," she told them. "That's why I'm happy to be among you sharing my family's stories."

She shared a number of stories that day, including one about her mother's reaction after Alexa had appeared on a TV interview show in which she'd discussed their family's experience with Alzheimer's. She had struggled whether to tell her mother about the interview in advance, she said, "because I wasn't sure how she'd react. I decided not to tell her." It turned out her mother had seen the interview anyway. Her response, Alexa allowed, was telling: "'You will never know how much it meant to me for you to acknowledge the guilt involved in struggling with your dad's Alzheimer's.' . . . There was a lesson in that for me, perhaps for all of us."

Ironically, it was not a lesson Alexa McDonough seemed inclined to follow. She had lived much of her life in the public fishbowl, been open about her private life and loves, even discussing her own personal health issues. In 2013, for example, two years after her Alzheimer's diagnosis, she disclosed she was undergoing treatment for breast cancer. "I'm speaking out because early diagnosis is often the key to survival," she explained.[3]

But she rarely, if ever, spoke about her struggles with Alzheimer's, even among her closest friends and family members. "She has never really talked about her diagnosis," Robbie said. "She would talk about her memory and how she couldn't remember things as well as she once did, but she never said the word 'Alzheimer's.'" Both Robbie and Alexa's oldest son, Justin, had served as president of the Nova Scotia Alzheimer Society, and Alexa herself had been featured in a public service announcement for the organization, but she'd spoken only about her family's experiences with the illness, not her own situation.

Why? It's impossible to know for certain, of course, but the answer may lie in her own relentless optimism, her ability to scope out hope no one else could see. Alzheimer's, she knew from the current state of the science and her own sad experiences, offered no happy ending. So she chose to ignore its looming spectre for as long as she could and, in the process, managed to keep the effects of the disease at bay for far longer than anyone, including her doctors, expected. She remained active.

After the 2011 federal election, for example, she travelled to Ottawa for a national tribute to Jack Layton, the late NDP leader who had died of cancer. She then stuck around for orientation sessions for newly elected MPs from all parties, helping the newcomers come to grips with issues "ranging from office management to how to avoid temptations like the endless supply of booze at Hill functions."[4]

She canvassed for the NDP during elections. "She insisted on going to the end of a small, dimly lit street where there was no sign of life," Alia Saied, the coordinator of the party's Nova Scotia caucus office, recalled of one door-knocking adventure during the 2017 provincial election. "She knocked on a door and then banged again. Finally, a man opened up, but he was not really interested in talking politics." She laughed. "Well! Not only did Alexa convince him to vote for the NDP, she even went to the polling station with him! . . . Her strength is really her tenacity."[5]

That said, her outings became less frequent as the years went on. In February 2019, Phyllis Larsen accompanied Alexa on a flight to Ottawa for the funeral of Paul Dewar, an NDP MP whose time in Parliament had overlapped with Alexa's. "We were in the airport waiting for our flight," Larsen recalled, "and she would ask, 'Is that our flight?' Two seconds later, she'd ask the same question. When I'd say you just asked me that, she'd make a joke of it, laugh it off."

But it was becoming more difficult to laugh off.

•

An aside. In the summer of 2020, when Alexa's sons understood I would be writing about their mother's Alzheimer's—a decision they understood and supported—they knew they needed to have "that conversation" with her. Was Alexa comfortable with this finally becoming public? It turned out she was. She even gave her long-time geriatrician, Ken Rockwood, permission to talk with me about her case.

Why, I wondered? Noting that Alexa had functioned well for far longer than anyone might have expected, Rockwood suggested she was now "keen" to share that good news with others. "She has long been careful about her privacy," he allowed, "but she realizes there's a point where the better thing is to talk about it. But what's driving that—this is what I find very, very impressive—is her feeling people will benefit if they get to see the example of someone who's had dementia for years and is still functioning very well."

3

It was Monday, September 23, 2019, and Alexa McDonough was having one of her "good days." These days, not all her days were good. Few understood that better than Betty Muggah. She and Alexa had been friends for nearly sixty years and shared more than a lifetime's worth of confidences, laughs and tears, through good times and bad. But Muggah was also a trained social worker who'd supported families managing care for aging loved ones with dementia.

In November 2018, Muggah and another of their childhood friends, Catherine Fry, flew to Halifax to spend a week with Alexa. It was a standard-issue friends' visit but also an opportunity for them, as women who'd "known

Alexa when," to gauge their friend's current state of health. "Everyone —
family, friends — knew Alexa had been losing her short-term memory for
the last three to four years." The question was what, if anything, to do about
that now.

After returning to Ontario, Muggah put her concerns "on paper in a note,
under various headings and including my own observations, as well as what
I'd been hearing from her friends and family," and sent it to Alexa's brother,
Robbie, and sons, Justin and Travis. Later, with their permission, she shared
it with Alexa's closest friends.

"The bottom line," she wrote: "our dear friend may no longer be able to
manage on her own." She recalled, laughing, "That sparked conversation."

Everyone understood Alexa would resist the prospect of moving into a
seniors' residence. But Alexa, a private person in spite of her public persona,
also wouldn't want professional caregivers, strangers she didn't know,
working, maybe living in her condo.

Alexa wasn't the only one who pushed back. Some of her friends worried
any such move might undermine her fragile sense of self-confidence and
independence. That argument also resonated with Justin, the eldest son.

So, in March 2019, Muggah returned to Halifax to help talk the family,
and Alexa, through to their decision. "I was clear in my own mind what
needed to be done, but it was tough for me as a friend, tough for the family,"
she allowed. "I knew I had to play a professional role in this case rather than
think about my personal relationship with Alexa."

One of the most difficult obstacles to overcome, she remembered, was
for Alexa's sons to accept the time had come for them to take charge. Their
mother had been so strong, so competent, for so long, but they could no
longer defer to her judgment. She walked Justin and Travis through the "very
specific conversation" they needed to have with their mother. They rehearsed.
"What if she pushes back?" they asked. "Stay the course," Muggah advised.
"Make it clear that you're worried, that you can't continue to live with the
worry of her living on her own." It was true, but also calculated. The two
old friends had had those discussions long before Alexa's dementia. "I knew
Alexa. She would not ever want to be a burden to her sons."

But even with that, of course, there was convincing Alexa herself the time
had come for her to move. In the end, that was not as difficult as anticipated.

While in Halifax, she and Alexa would go for walks. "Let's stop in for a visit at Parkland," Muggah would suggest. Or they would decide to go out for lunch. "Let's get something to eat at Parkland."

Parkland at the Gardens, a luxurious, modern seniors' complex in the heart of familiar South End Halifax, was just a few blocks from Alexa's condo. It had been home to many Haligonians Alexa had known in various times and places in her life, including Harold Crowell and Carolyn MacGregor. "As soon as we entered the lobby, she'd see people she knew," Muggah said. "She'd very quickly end up in the lounge, talking with people she knew. It provided a comfort level."

For her family, there was comfort in knowing Parkland offered "a full continuum of service," from entry-level, "beautifully appointed 'All-Inclusive Lifestyle' suites for those who want an active lifestyle without the bother of daily chores" to what Parkland's marketing people decorously referred to as "'Memory Care'... for those requiring assistance due to Alzheimer's or other dementias."

The move itself was a "complete success." In June 2019, soon after Alexa moved into a two-bedroom assisted living suite in Parkland, Muggah and Alexa's sister-in-law, Jean, organized a small reception to "celebrate Alexa's indomitable positive spirit, her new home at Parkland, the teamwork that has made the transition possible and (relatively!) hassle-free, and all the friends and family who surround her with so much love."

As the author of her forthcoming biography, I was among those invited. I couldn't help but notice just how diminished, almost lost Alexa now seemed. During the previous winter, we'd met almost weekly for interview sessions in her condo, which sometimes lasted several hours. While she occasionally had difficulty remembering names or recalling recent events and sometimes repeated the same stories, she'd seemed mostly engaged and connected to the larger world. Today, however, as she stood off to one side, watching her brother, sons, grandchildren, friends, and former colleagues extol her virtues and laugh about her foibles through stories and good humour, she seemed to struggle to follow all that was being said.

Finally, it was Alexa's turn to speak. She stepped into the centre of the gathering and the transformation was stunning, as if she'd reached deep inside herself to find the Alexa she had been. "I'm very happy to be here," she began, her familiar voice no longer small, filling the room, commanding the attention of everyone. "This is a wonderful place and I'm so pleased to be here," she explained, but then quickly segued—ever the politician, always the woman out to make the world a better place—to her pointed point. "But, you know, I can't help thinking about all of those seniors out there who also need a place like this, but can't afford it."

•

As is common with those with dementia, Alexa's rise-to-the-occasion moments became briefer and less frequent. During the summer, Muggah spent more time with her, both at Parkland and at Betty's cottage in Baddeck where they'd enjoyed a week together. "This nasty disease seems to be advancing more quickly," she wrote me in an email in early September.

Now, nearing the end of September, Muggah and her husband had returned to spend a few more days with Alexa. Coincidentally, Betty had seen on the news that morning that the current NDP leader, Jagmeet Singh, would be in Halifax for a late-afternoon town hall meeting as part of the 2019 federal election campaign.

Since this seemed to be one of Alexa's good days, Muggah had an idea. "Would you like to go?" Alexa would. Muggah helped her dress for the occasion in some new clothes she'd brought back for Alexa after a recent trip to France. Phyllis Larsen, who often accompanied Alexa to NDP events, joined them. "We fluffed her hair and off we went."

Despite the fact the decision to attend had been last minute, Alexa's name, still revered in party circles, was immediately added to the media schedule as a "notable" attendee: "Alexa McDonough, Past NDP Leader."

But that message didn't reach Lisa Roberts, one of the province's current NDP MLAs, who was charged with introducing Jagmeet and "anyone in the room who needed to be introduced." As soon she saw the province's first female NDP leader seated in the front row, however, Roberts understood McDonough "needed to be introduced," even if she also knew she needed no introduction. She had attended enough NDP conventions to have seen "the huge cheers that go up for Alexa whenever she shows up. People love her." When Roberts first ran in a by-election in 2016, she had been a beneficiary of funding from the Women in The Legislature Fund, whose creation Alexa had helped spearhead more than thirty years earlier.

When Roberts singled out McDonough, reminding an audience that didn't need reminding she had been the first woman leader of the NDP in Nova Scotia, the most successful woman leader of the NDP in federal politics, a "trailblazer," there was sustained, spontaneous applause.

Jagmeet Singh picked up on that theme when he began his own speech. "Alexa was a little bit shocked by the love," Singh told the audience, "but she shouldn't be shocked. She was, she is, a trailblazer. She has inspired a lot of people. And if I can be honest with you, I wouldn't be the leader I am today if it wasn't for people like Alexa that broke barriers.... Thank you, you're awesome!" he offered, and then proceeded to stride over to her front row seat as the applause continued. "ALEXA MCDONOUGH!" he boomed as she rose to greet him. He held her hand aloft and they embraced as the crowd, in the words of *Star Metro Halifax* reporter Yvette d'Entremont, "went wild."

After the event, Jérôme Labbé, a young reporter from Radio Canada, approached Alexa. Labbé was too young to know much about McDonough's history — "I had to Google her later" — and certainly not her medical condition. But he'd seen the reaction of the crowd and thought an interview might add a bit of colour to his reporting.

"Are you sure you're OK with doing this?" Larsen asked Alexa.

She was.

"First of all," Labbé began in English, "let me ask you how you've been?"

McDonough responded, with some hesitation, in French. "Oh, je vais bien, merci. Je suis très, très heureuse avec l'énergie dans le parti et nous avons un leader fantastique, je pense, très, très spéciale."

She apologized to him later for her French, saying she hadn't had much opportunity to practise and confessed to a larger truth of her federal political career: "I made efforts, but it was never easy for me."

Labbé was kinder. "She was as good/bad in French as she was when she was NDP leader," he told me. "To be honest," he added in a way that was more reassuring than distressing, "she sounded... well, just like any politician: sure of herself, not expressing any forms of doubt about the outcome of this election and the choice [of leader] that had been made in the last years."

Alexa McDonough was still Alexa. Always.

TRAILBLAZER

On December 7, 1970, while a twenty-six-year-old Alexa McDonough tried to wrap her head around where she should go with her growing disillusionment with politics as practised by the Liberal Party of Nova Scotia, a federal Royal Commission on the Status of Women in Canada published its final report.

Prime Minister Lester Pearson had established the commission in 1967 after intense lobbying from women's groups. Its purpose was "to inquire into and report on the status of women in Canada."[1] The seminal 488-page report included 167 recommendations on everything from abortion to alimony, pay equity to family law, all clustered around the principle that "equality between men and women in Canada was possible, desirable and ethically necessary." But as the commissioners themselves also noted pointedly at the time: "No country can make a claim to having equal status for women so long as its government lies entirely in the hands of men."

Although she could not have known it then, that quest for equal political status would become the north star of Alexa McDonough's political career.

When the royal commission published its report, women in Canada had had the vote for fifty years, but in 1970 only one woman — Grace MacInnis, soon to be one of Alexa's role models — sat in the 264-seat House of Commons. Eleven years later, when Alexa won her seat in the Nova Scotia legislature, she was not just the lone woman in the House but only the third female MLA in the province's long history, as well as the first woman in all of Canada to lead a recognized political party.

Today, close to one-third of Nova Scotia's MLAs are women, and women make up close to 30 per cent of our federal Parliament. That's still nowhere near "equal status," of course, but the percentages of women in politics does finally hover in the neighbourhood many social scientists consider a necessary "critical mass" for women to have a significant impact on policy. Statistically, the numbers mean that this critical mass is self-sustaining.

While her own political career ended before the equal-status objective could be realized, much of the credit for pushing Canada toward that goal line must go to the tireless work and example of Alexa. She would demur, of course, making the case she was the inheritor and passer-along of the work of generations of feminist political women who went before. She'd cite Grace MacInnis and Rosemary Brown, personal political exemplars who fed Alexa's evolving socialist perspectives as well as the feminism that became ingrained into her world view. And she'd point at all those other women over the years, in all political parties, who'd sacrificed, often more than she had, to run for political office and who had encouraged other women to follow in their footsteps.

She would be right, of course. But she would be wrong too.

Alexa Ann Shaw McDonough is a singular trailblazer—as a feminist, as a politician, and, perhaps most significantly, as a feminist politician. But more than that.

She remained, from the beginning to the end of her political career, a person of principle in an often unprincipled world, a woman committed to and driven by the desire to help shape a better, fairer, more equal world for everyone. She never wavered on this, either in her determination or her optimism that the goal was attainable.

For Alexa, feminism was not an end itself but, more importantly, the means to an even better end. As she declared in a speech prepared for a 2002 Canadian Labour Congress convention, "If we can't enforce a confrontation on poverty, on our thinking about war, about pollution, about the exploitation of our fellow human beings and about the need to respect each other and the environment . . . if we do not challenge the concept that might is right, and that competition is the basis for survival, then there really is not much point to women's participation in political life."

Although Alexa would attribute those words in her speech to the "Rosemary Brown Creed," the reality, as her former NDP colleague Judy Wasylycia-Leis told me, is that the themes were "Alexa all over. That's where Alexa came from, the understanding that there's not much point to women's participation in political life unless it is to deal with poverty in our midst and the environmental crisis and so on. Her example then influenced people like me and so many other women who followed in her footsteps. That's why, when I think of Alexa McDonough, I think of her as a true trailblazer for women."

Alexa herself ruminated on what drove her in a 2014 interview about her career with *Halifax Magazine*'s Marjorie Simmins. "You're not just speaking for yourself, that's what's interesting about it," she explained. "It is challenging, a bit daunting, but it's also very rewarding. You're not doing this for yourself; you're doing it to help break down barriers or pave new pathways."

Alexa McDonough. Feminist. Politician. Trailblazer.

ACKNOWLEDGEMENTS

First of all, I want to thank Alexa McDonough, not only for agreeing to allow me to rummage through the back pages of her life but also for patiently sitting through countless hours of questions and interviews even as she struggled with the impact on her own memory of a difficult and debilitating disease. She was—as she has always been—relentlessly upbeat and invariably helpful.

Alexa's sons, Justin and Travis, and her brother, Robbie, commissioned this biography and then not only allowed but also encouraged me to go wherever the story led. An author can't ask for more.

This biography builds on earlier in-depth interviews conducted by Pat Kipping and Barbara Jack, and I thank them for generously sharing the recordings and transcripts with me. I'm also grateful to Joanne Lamey, the unofficial historian and keeper of the Nova Scotia NDP's memorabilia and ephemera. Amy Fredericks, the keeper of a Shaw family tree, kindly shared with me as well.

Alexa's tight-knit groups of women friends—led by the indefatigable Pamela Whelan and Betty Muggah—have been a continuing source of support and encouragement, allowing themselves to be interviewed, often multiple times, suggesting the names of others who just *had* to be interviewed, leading me to documents, answering my questions, and all the questions that followed those answers.

I got lucky. When Alexa and I first began to talk, I remember asking if she'd kept any personal papers beyond those in archives. She said she'd be happy to share whatever she had but she was certain she'd culled most of them in her various moves over the years. She was wrong. After she moved out of her Halifax condo, her son Justin alerted me to dozens of boxes and bins full of unsorted letters, documents, and photos, all stored and forgotten in a basement locker. Those materials provided a treasure trove for the biographer, offering of-the-times context that help explain her evolution as a person and a feminist.

I got lucky too when I went off in search of the records of Alexa's grandparents' divorce, which I understood from family lore had been a significant milestone in

Alexa's mother's life and consequently in her own. The court records had been misfiled in the public archives and, despite the best efforts of many in various archives and court offices — thank you Karen White, Hannah Steeves, Jennifer Stewart, Kim Myatt — refused to be found. Finally, having given up on getting specifics, I decided to read up on academic writing about the issue of cruelty as a ground for divorce in the early twentieth century and stumbled on a specific reference to the case, complete with detailed citation. Thank goodness for academic sourcing. Problem solved. Records found. They were worth finding.

During my research many others also generously agreed to share their stories and memories. I thank them all: Bill Beverley, Hugh Blakeney, Nancy Bowes, Ed Broadbent, Robert Chisholm, James Clancy, George Elliott Clarke, Patricia Dale, Linda Davidson, Yvette d'Entremont, Nancy (Hagen) Dickson, John Duckworth, Brian Flemming, Janice (Merritt) Flemming, Sharon Fraser, Catherine (Isnor) Fry, Colin Gabelmann, Joann Griffin, Skip Hambling, Les Holloway, Ron Johnson, Michael Kirby, Jérôme Labbé, Ray Larkin, Stephen Lewis, Alexis MacDonald, David MacDonald, Margie MacDonald, Sine MacKinnon, Monia Mazigh, Lawrence McBrearty, Peter McDonough, Matthew Morgan, Mary Morison, Henry Muggah, Dan O'Connor, Jean Shaw, Brenda Taylor, Dennis Theman, Gail Thompson, Jim Vibert, Duff Waddell, Rick Williams, Paul Withers, and Jane Wright.

On the writerly side, thanks, as always to my agent, Hilary McMahon, and the wonderful team at Goose Lane: Susanne Alexander, Alan Sheppard, and Julie Scriver. I'm especially grateful to my editor Susan Renouf, who is not only an astute editor knowledgeable in the ways and wiles of both publishing and Nova Scotia politics, but she is also, as I discovered in the process, a close but distant relative in that who's-your-father Nova Scotia way. Thanks also to copy-editor Paula Sarson, whose careful reading flagged enough errors to make me blush, wrangled my occasionally inconsistent usage into a consistent style, and made me realize, again, just how important editors are.

Finally, as always, I thank my wife, Jeanie, and my children and grandchildren for putting up with my life-consuming writing obsession.

Halifax
October 2020

ENDNOTES

PROLOGUE

1 Stephen Kimber, "Why They Played the Game," *Today*, March 20, 1980.

BEFORE

1 Divorce records, MacKinnon v. MacKinnon, August 11, 1922. C-292, RG 39 D, Public Archives of Nova Scotia, Halifax.

2 Associated Press, "Carnegie Award for Harvard Hero," *Boston Globe*, April 26, 1934.

3 The choice of location seemed fitting. The bridge had been the backdrop for a dramatic moment in William Faulkner's classic novel *The Sound and The Fury*, which had been published four years earlier and found a cult following among nearby Harvard English majors. One of the book's central characters, a doomed depressive nineteen-year-old named Quentin Compson, had walked to the centre of the arch bridge, placed a suicide note and his grandfather's pocket watch on the ground, tied two flatirons to his feet, and plunged into the Charles River where he was "swallowed by the New England night."

4 "'Anybody's Game' Presented in Belmont," *Boston Globe*, January 13, 1934.

5 "Belmont High Graduates 239," *Boston Globe*, June 16, 1934.

6 Jean MacKinnon, letter to Lloyd Shaw, May 2, 1937.

7 Jean to Lloyd, January 15, 1939.

8 Jean to Lloyd, January 30, 1937.

9 Jean to Lloyd, April 5, 1937.

10 L.E. Shaw, *My Life in the Brick Industry* (privately published, 1955).

11 Jean to Lloyd, January 15, 1939.

12 H. Blair Neatby and Don McEown, *Creating Carleton: The Shaping of a University* (Montreal and Kingston: McGill-Queen's University Press, 2002), 5.

13 In Ottawa at the time, noted the authors of *Creating Carleton*, "the divisions between Protestants and Catholics seemed as significant as those between rich and poor." Although Carleton was intended to be non-sectarian, its first chair of the board joked that the school's unofficial motto was "to hell with the Pope."

14 "Splendid New Opportunity Provided for Youth of Capital and Employees in Wartime Work to Advance Status," *Ottawa Citizen*, September 12, 1942.

15 David Lewis, *The Good Fight* (Toronto: Macmillan of Canada, 1981), 234.

16 "Research Chief Here for CCF," *Vancouver Sun*, September 9, 1943.

17 "Who Gets Insurance Profits?" *Vancouver Sun*, January 13, 1944.

18 "Autocrats Always Thin Skinned," *Lethbridge Herald*, January 18, 1944.

19 Letter from Harry Brumpton to Alexa McDonough, April 20, 1999.

20 Silver Donald Cameron, "The Socialist Chairman of the Board," *Vancouver Sun*, February 26, 1977.

21 "Concise Encyclopedia of Tufts History," Tufts Digital Library, https://dl.tufts.edu/teiviewer/parent/f1881x54h/chapter/D00008.

22 Alexa Payan obituary, *New York Times*, February 20, 2014, https://www.legacy.com/obituaries/nytimes/obituary.aspx?n=alexa-mackinnon-de-payan&pid=169771810.

23 David Lewis, *The Good Fight* (Toronto: Macmillan of Canada, 1981), 304.

24 Dean E. McHenry, *The Third Force in Canada* (Manhattan: Praeger, 1976).

25 Silver Donald Cameron, "The Socialist Chairman of the Board," *Vancouver Sun*, February 26, 1977.

26 "Halifax Woman Wins Prize 'Search for Talent' Contest," *Halifax Daily Star*, November 6, 1945.

COMING OF AGE IN AN AGE

1 Jury Gotshalks and his wife, Irene Apinée, were among the first arrivals, landing at Halifax's Pier 21 aboard the *Aquitania* on October 5, 1947. Both trained at the Latvian National Ballet School, they were befriended in Halifax by eager-for-culture local citizens, including the Shaws. Despite knowing neither the language nor the city, they soon set up their own ballet school, as well as Gotshalks Halifax Company. Three years later, Celia Franca, the legendary co-founder of the National Ballet of Canada, would lure them to Toronto to become founding members of her new company. But by then, there were others. First, Gunter Buchta, a German who'd used dance therapy to help him recover from a leg wound suffered on the Russian front, then employed his new-found skill to transition into a career as a dance instructor. In 1951, he founded the Ballroom Dancing Club of Halifax. Three years later, Mirdza Dambergs, a prima ballerina with the Latvian National Opera, arrived with her husband, mother-in-law, and three small children after too many harrowing years as refugees in Germany and France. Thanks to a glowing recommendation from the Gotshalks, Dambergs was hired to teach dance at the Halifax Conservatory of Music. Soon after, she too launched her own school, Mme. Dambergs School of Ballet. Alexa danced with all of them.

2 Lloyd became president of the company in 1967, after his older brother Ron was named chairman. L.E. Shaw died in 1960, of Alzheimer's disease.

3 "Address on 'Africville Project' to the Women's Auxiliary of First Baptist Church" by Jean Shaw, October 17, 1961.

4 Letter from Garnet Colwell to Alexa Shaw, June 28, 1961.

5 "Two-Week Project a Big Success" by Alexa Shaw, Halifax *Mail-Star*, July 18, 1963.

6 Letter from H.M. DeWolfe to Alexa Shaw, January 19, 1962

7 In an October 13, 1963, letter to her parents from Queen's University, she lamented: "From all past experience (right from Cornwallis [Junior High] thru QEH, Solebury and now Queen's), 'my year' has always been *the* worst."

8 "City Ballet Students Present Annual Show," Halifax *Mail-Star*, June 1, 1961.

9 Alexa Shaw, school essay, October 25, 1961.

10 In 2017, a Bucks County, PA, grand jury issued a forty-nine-page report documenting what it described as a five-decades'-long cover-up of sexual relationships between faculty and students at the school. One of the nine adults it said had been credibly accused was Pop Shaw, who'd had a two-year affair with a student in the early 1950s. He died in 1982. The school has since

removed his name and portrait from the campus.

11 Pat had been such a standout in a student production of *The Glass Menagerie* that Arthur Kennedy, an award-winning movie and Broadway actor—and the father of another Solebury student—approached her backstage after her performance. "He told me, 'If you ever decide to go into theatre, look me up,' and he gave me his card." Pat did become an actress but found it difficult to land roles because of what Alexa remembers as her height. "She was six-feet tall." Pat eventually switched to theatre publicity and owned her own Broadway press agency.

12 Letter from Bill Berkeley to Alexa Shaw, November 17, 1962.

13 Duncan McDowall, *Queen's University, Volume 3, 1961-2004: Testing Tradition* (Montreal and Kingston: McGill-Queen's University Press, 2016).

14 Law would go into a successful professional sports career in the Canadian Football League.

15 During one such trip, she broke her leg. "Almost at the very point when I was thinking to myself that I was really skiing for the first time and wasn't it just the most wonderful feeling in the world," she wrote to her parents, "CRUNCH!" She ended up on her back with one leg facing uphill and the other down. Her safety harness hadn't released quickly enough. "Gad, what a sound!"

16 Ruth is a pseudonym.

17 In a December 1983 article in *Chatelaine,* Alexa described her two years at Queen's, "having a good time and not taking advantage of the opportunities to learn about economics or political science," as her "greatest regret." But, she added, "I don't regret having a good time."

18 In 1976, she married the actor Sidney Poitier.

19 Clarke, whom her son George Elliott describes as "*the* local pioneer in early childhood education" would go on to found two more daycare centres, including the Centre for Exceptional Children.

20 The Shaws lived at 16 Armview Avenue in Shore Acres, a tony residential neighbourhood in South End Halifax, which had been developed in the 1940s by L.E., both to showcase the possibilities of brick housing for Haligonians and also to serve as a kind of Shaw family compound.

21 Letter from Peter McDonough to Alexa Shaw, August 9, 1965.

22 Much of the correspondence between Alexa and Peter during this period is undated beyond the day of the week.

23 Alexa to Peter, July 21, 1965.

24 Alexa to Peter, June 27, 1965.

25 Wasserman quit Smith and moved to England in 1967 after the CIA began rummaging around in his anti-Vietnam war views. He spent the rest of his career teaching in Britain.

RUNNING FROM HOUNDS

1 Peter B. Levy, *The Great Uprising: Race Riots in Urban America during the 1960s* (Cambridge: Cambridge University Press, 2018), n.p.

2 "The Four Days in 1968 that Reshaped D.C.," *Washington Post*, March 27, 2018. https://www.washingtonpost.com/graphics/2018/local/dc-riots-1968/.

3 "NDP Hopes to Shake Up Ottawa," *Globe and Mail*, April 14, 1997.

4 Letter from Alexa McDonough to her parents, June 30, 1968.

5 "Trudeau Leads Liberals to Canada Election Win," *Reno Gazette-Journal*, June 26, 1968.

6 City Manager's Files, Ex-Africville Residents, 1969-70, 102-4A.129.2, Halifax Municipal Archives https://www.halifax.ca/sites/default/files/documents/about-the-city/archives/102-4A.129.2_0.pdf.

7 Stephen Kimber, *"NOT GUILTY": The Trial of Gerald Regan* (Toronto: Stoddart, 1999), 96.

8   John Edward Belliveau, *The Headliners: Behind the Scenes Memoirs* (Hantsport: Lancelot Press, 1984).

9   Peter would later serve as vice-president of the Halifax Cornwallis Liberal Association.

10 McDonough says she never personally experienced Gerald Regan's darker side — he was credibly accused of sexual attacks on more than three dozen women — but she knew several women who claimed he'd assaulted them.

11 "Alexa's Second Wind," Halifax *Chronicle-Herald*, November 17, 1990.

12 Many years later, when Alexa and her son Justin attended Mamie Penny's funeral in Ste. Anne du Ruisseau, the tiny Acadian community on the southern tip of Nova Scotia where Mamie had grown up, she recalled, "We were greeted like old friends because she'd talked about us so often."

13 Lloyd and Jean had built their own new house on the property, while Robbie and Jean acquired an adjacent lot for their own summer cottage.

14 "Socialist Soul-Search Updates Party Position," Regina *Leader-Post,* December 14, 1973.

15 United Press International, May 10, 1969.

16 Bryony House, the first such transition house in Nova Scotia, continues to operate more than forty years later.

17 Wasylycia-Leis would not only go on to serve as a cabinet minister in Howard Pawley's Manitoba NDP government, but she would also become one of the national organizers of Alexa's 1995 leadership campaign and a member of the federal NDP caucus from 1997 to 2010.

18 "Why They Played the Game," Stephen Kimber, *Today*, March 29, 1980.

19 "They Never Did Blow It," *Ottawa Citizen*, June 23, 1979.

20 In the 1979 federal election, Alexa was one of 218 female candidates, of whom just 14 were ultimately elected.

21 "Fewer Women Up Front but More Become Backroom Boys," *National Post*, April 28, 1979.

22 "Trudeauburgers Most Popular but Will that Count at the Ballot Box?" Regina *Leader-Post*, May 15, 1979.

23 Tory premier John Buchanan named him director of inter-governmental affairs, a deputy minister–level job that, according to *Globe and Mail* columnist Barbara Yaffe (January 17, 1981) came complete with "private bathroom, a forest of rented plants and a magnificent view of Citadel Hill."

24 "Void Facing NS New Democrats," *Globe and Mail*, May 19, 1980.

25 "If Akerman Goes, What Next for the NDP," *Atlantic Insight*, May 1980, 10.

26 J. Murray Beck, *Politics of Nova Scotia 1896-1988* (Tantallon: Four East Publications, 1988), 316.

27 "Void Facing NS New Democrats," *Globe and Mail*, May 19, 1980.

28 Letter from Paul MacEwan to Alexa McDonough, December 10, 1980.

29 "Behind the MacEwan–NDP Battle," Ian Thompson, *Halifax Magazine*, October 1980, 9.

30 Letter from Paul MacEwan to Bob Levy, May 7, 1980.

31 It turned out that both Akerman's and federal party leader Broadbent's office subscribed to the publication.

32 Barbara Yaffe, "Talking Back: Why Akerman Finally Called It Quits," *Globe and Mail*, January 17, 1981.

33 Paul MacEwan, *The Akerman Years: Jeremy Akerman and the Nova Scotia NDP* (Halifax: Formac Publishing, 1980).

34 "New Waterford Loses Two Former MLAs," *Cape Breton Post*, June 17, 2018.

35 Helen MacDonald, an NDP MLA, who served briefly as provincial party leader from 2000-2001.

36 Jim Vibert, "Alexa McDonough in NDP Race," Halifax *Chronicle-Herald*, September 26, 1980.

37 Letter from Alexa McDonough to Reeves Matheson, September 30, 1980.

38 "Alexa Leads Race," *Calgary Herald*, November 10, 1980.

39 "She Offers Nova Scotia Voters a Real Alternative," *Vancouver Province*, November 17, 1980.

40 Letter from Paul MacEwan to Alexa McDonough, October 2, 1980, and November 7, 1980.

41 "'Party is Dead' says Nova MLA," *Cape Breton Post*, December 31, 1980.

BELLY OF THE BEAST

1 "Campaign for Own Seat Crucial for Nova Scotia NDP Leader," Regina *Leader-Post*, October 2, 1981.

2 The NDP candidate in 1978, by contrast, had managed to take just 14 per cent of the popular vote in a three-way contest.

3 "NDP Chief Picks Tough Crowd to Wrestle for her NS Seat," *Globe and Mail,* September 12, 1981.

4 "NDP's New Leader Faces Daunting Task," Southam News, *Montreal Gazette,* September 9, 1981.

5 "NDP's New Leader Faces Daunting Task," Southam News, *Montreal Gazette,* September 9, 1981.

6 During the course of the next twenty-seven years, Alexa would win nine elections in Halifax, four provincial and five federal, never once losing an election.

7 "NDP's New Leader Faces Daunting Task," Southam News, *Montreal Gazette,* September 9, 1981.

8 "Nova Scotia NDP Leader Shakes Up Political Scene," *Ottawa Citizen*, June 25, 1981.

9 "Strike Poses a Dilemma for NDP," *Calgary Herald*, September 17, 1981.

10 "Official Party Status Lost; NDP Leader Faces Lonely Road," *Globe and Mail*, October 20, 1981.

11 "Campaign for Own Seat Crucial for Nova Scotia NDP Leader," Regina *Leader-Post*, October 2, 1981.

12 "Official Party Status Lost; NDP Leader Faces Lonely Road," *Globe and Mail*, October 20, 1981.

13 "Official Party Status Lost; NDP Leader Faces Lonely Road," *Globe and Mail*, October 20, 1981.

14 Harry Bruce, "The Fiery Baptism of Alexa McDonough," *Atlantic Insight*, November 1982.

15 House of Assembly Debates, March 1, 1982.

16 After Bruce died in 1984, Maxine Cochran succeeded him as MLA and, in 1985, became Nova Scotia's first female cabinet minister.

17 House of Assembly Debates, February 22, 1982.

18 Alexa McDonough's personal files.

19 "Government Job for ex-MLA Rapist Upsets Opposition," *Globe and Mail*, February 27, 1982.

20 She told the *Globe and Mail*'s Michael Harris (February 27, 1981) her office had received a "continual flood" of calls from "old, young, male, female, local and long-distance callers" protesting the appointment.

21 House of Assembly Debates, February 25, 1982.

22 "Patronage, No Matter What," *Globe and Mail*, March 1, 1982.

23 "Family Hardship Cited, Ousted Lawyer, Rapist Quits N.S. Liquor Post," *Globe and Mail*, March 2, 1982.

24 "Alexa's Second Wind," Halifax *Chronicle-Herald*, November 17, 1990.

25 Bruce, "The Fiery Baptism of Alexa McDonough," *Atlantic Insight*, November 1982, 21.

26 House of Assembly Debates, February 25, 1982.

27 House of Assembly Debates, March 1, 1982.

28 Bruce, "The Fiery Baptism of Alexa McDonough," *Atlantic Insight*, November 1982, 23.

29 House of Assembly Debates, March 1, 1982.

30 Personal files, Alexa McDonough.

31 House of Assembly Debates, March 1, 1982.

32   Interestingly, on the day the committee began its hearings, Alexa—who was not a member—focused on more pressing public issues, introducing two resolutions, one calling on the Attorney General to step up prosecution of domestic abuse allegations even if judges "rarely impose prison sentences," and the second urging the government to "show some leadership" by pegging the pensions of retired public servants to the consumer price index.

33   "Shaw Family Stands Up to Millwood Allegations," Canadian Press, May 13, 1982.

34   "Shaw Firm's Profit $19,530, Committee Told," Halifax *Mail Star*, May 13, 1982.

35   Bruce, "The Fiery Baptism of Alexa McDonough," *Atlantic Insight*, November 1982, 21.

36   Brother Robbie would later marvel at his sister's ability to "let criticism and false information from foes, and unfair and sometimes vicious commentary from media and other sources...just roll off her back. I had intended to run for MLA when I stepped down from the premier's office, but found I was absolutely not able to let criticism roll off my back at all!"

37   "Digby's Three Years of Bitterness," *Globe and Mail*, July 2, 1982.

38   The strike finally ended on April 1, 1983, after many of the most recalcitrant school board members had been defeated in local elections. The workers got their jobs back, some retroactive pay, and a wage boost that brought them closer— but not yet equal to—what drivers in the neighbouring county earned.

39   "Canadians Hold Vigils for Man Serving Time for NJ Slaying," Associated Press, January 20, 1985.

40   Although those appeals were eventually rejected, Curtis was repatriated to Canada in May 1988 to serve out the rest of his sentence. He was granted day parole in 1989, and full parole a year later. He later completed university and became a genome researcher in Halifax.

41   David Hayes, *No Easy Answers: The Trial and Conviction of Bruce Curtis* (Toronto: Viking, 1986), 282.

42   The Curtis family ultimately declined the offer because Bruce's case was just a month away from an appeal hearing and they were nervous about "changing horses in midstream."

43   The best and most complete version of Marshall's story can be found in Michael Harris's book *Justice Denied: The Law versus Donald Marshall* (Toronto: Macmillan of Canada, 1986).

44   Stephen Aronson had been driven so far into debt working to free Marshall, he'd had to give up his legal practice.

45   In 1990, Thornhill was charged with fraud in connection with his bank loans, but the charges were dropped a year later. In 1986, MacLean pleaded guilty to charges involving fraud and forging expense documents and was expelled from the legislature after refusing to quit.

46   "McDonough is Breaking the Old Boys' Rules," Parker Donham, *Kentville Advertiser,* April 20, 1983.

47   "Woman MLA Eyes NS NDP Leadership," *Ottawa Citizen*, January 29, 1983.

48   In 1985, the province's Auditor General accused MacKay—who had been defeated in his Sackville riding in the 1984 general election by the NDP's John Holm—of using a false address to claim MLA expenses. He paid back $7,000.

49   "Woman MLA Eyes NS NDP Leadership," *Ottawa Citizen*, January 29, 1983.

50   "NDP Voice Silenced by Illness," *Globe and Mail*, May 28, 1983.

51   "Alexa's Second Wind," Halifax *Chronicle-Herald*, November 17, 1990.

52   According to her brother, Robbie, Alexa always had "an amazing ability to sleep soundly anywhere any time. It enabled her to sleep fewer hours at night and not get exhausted to the point where she was ineffective. The minute an airplane's wheels were up, or a bus or a car started, she was out like a light."

53 Dickinson, who would eventually manage close to thirty political campaigns during his long career, claimed he "once barged into a household of five people who had promised to vote for the New Democratic Party, stuffed their dinner back into the oven, and drove them to the polling station to cast their ballots just minutes before the deadline. 'And, without a word of a lie, we won that poll by four votes,'" he told the *Globe and Mail* in a June 8, 1995, story.

54 "NDP's Leader Knows the Score in NS Election," *Globe and Mail*, November 5, 1984.

55 "Buchanan Exploits Mulroney Connection in Opening NS Tory Election Campaign," *Globe and Mail*, October 3, 1984.

56 J. Murray Beck, *Politics of Nova Scotia: 1896-1988* (Tantallon: Four East Publications, 1988.)

57 "The Other Day, Sandy Cameron, the Nova Scotia Liberal leader, Said…" *Globe and Mail*, October 29, 1984.

58 "NDP's Leader Knows the Score in N.S. Election," *Globe and Mail*, November 5, 1984.

59 "NDP's Leader Knows the Score in N.S. Election," *Globe and Mail*, November 5, 1984.

60 "NDP 'Victory' in NS may be More of a Defeat," Southam News, November 12, 1984.

61 Deborah Jones, "Rewarding a Down-Home Style," *Maclean's*, November 19, 1984.

62 Ian MacKay, "In Conversation with Alexa McDonough," *New Maritimes*, July–August 1984.

63 Williams, who went on to become the deputy minister in the office of Policy Priorities in the first NDP government in the province's history in 2009, now says the "biggest source of failure for the Dexter government" was that it failed to learn the lessons of the 1985 policy conference and "got back into steel plants and electrification."

64 Surprisingly—or perhaps not so surprisingly—economic policies discussed at the conference got little media attention. Instead, the press focused on two peripheral issues. One involved a booth set up in the hallway outside the meeting room that featured pro-choice buttons and pamphlets, as well as a biography of Dr. Henry Morgentaler, the Montréal abortion crusader. Both Roman Catholic Archbishop James Hayes and Mount Saint Vincent University president Margaret Fulton criticized the presence of such a display at a Roman Catholic women's university founded by the Sisters of Charity. (Alexa herself later served as the Mount's president.) The second issue of media note was a joke resolution calling on the party to "enjoy itself more." "I'm not opposed to fun," said trade union delegate Chester Sanford, "but I think it makes us look a little ridiculous."

65 "NDP on Abortion: Courageous or Foolhardy," Berwick *Register*, August 27, 1986.

66 "Pro-choice 'Best' Consensus," Halifax *Mail-Star*, August 18, 1986.

67 "Abortion: NDP Takes a Stand," Halifax *Chronicle-Herald*, August 19, 1986.

68 Katrina Ackerman, "A Region at Odds: Abortion Politics in the Maritime Provinces, 1969-1988" (PhD thesis, University of Waterloo, 2015), 201.

69 "NS Minister Takes Blame in Expense Claim Controversy," *Globe and Mail*, April 12, 1988.

70 House of Assembly Debates, October 30, 1986.

71 The courts later ruled the law unconstitutional. MacLean ran as an independent in the subsequent by-election. He won.

72 "Justice System Delivers Knockout Blow to MLA," *Calgary Herald*, February 15, 1988.

73 "Scandal Forces NS Deputy Premier to Resign," Regina *Leader-Post*, April 13, 1998.

74 "Marshall Inquiry Revelations Jolt Legal Establishment," *Globe and Mail*, July 2, 1988.

75 "Why Does Mr. Morris Infuriate Her So Much," *Pandora*, September–December 1987.

76 Sexual orientation was finally added as a protected category in the Nova Scotia Human Rights Act in 1991.

77 "NS to Implement Public, Private Sector Pay Equity Programs," *Ottawa Citizen*, February 2, 1988.

78 This reconstruction of their conversation is based on interviews with both Alexa McDonough and Bob Levy, as well as the accounts of others who spoke with them in the immediate aftermath.

79 House of Assembly Debates, May 28, 1988.

80 Canadian Press, "Critic Ignores His own Advice." *Edmonton Journal*, July 31, 1988.

81 "How the Mixed News Came to Halifax," *Globe and Mail*, September 8, 1988.

82 "Nova Scotia NDP Leader Scorns Patronage," *Calgary Herald*, August 3, 1988.

83 "'Uncle John' Buchanan Canada's Longest Reigning Premier," *Globe and Mail*, September 7, 1988.

84 *CBC TV News*, August 29, 1988.

85 "Alexa's Second Wind," Halifax *Chronicle-Herald*, November 17, 1990.

86 "'Uncle John' Buchanan Canada's Longest Reigning Premier," *Globe and Mail*, September 7, 1988.

87 "Alexa's Second Wind," Halifax *Chronicle-Herald*, November 17, 1990.

NEW BEGINNINGS

1 "Mr. Alexa Keeps his Roles in Perspective," Halifax *Mail-Star*, September 3, 1988.

2 "Alexa McDonough: Fiercely Competitive Spirit Pilots Province's NDP," Halifax *Chronicle-Herald*, May 21, 1993.

3 Paul Withers, "Why John Buchanan Was an Era-Ending Politician," *CBC News*, October 4, 2019, https://www.cbc.ca/news/canada/nova-scotia/paul-withers-john-buchanan-obituary-legacy-1.5293657.

4 "Making Atlantic Waves," *Maclean's*, January 21, 1991.

5 "The Buchanan Legacy," *Ottawa Citizen*, August 26, 1991.

6 "NS Government's Fate Hangs on By-election," *Montreal Gazette*, August 7, 1991.

7 Although he generally sided with his former colleagues, Thornhill had voted against the Cameron government's budget as too draconian.

8 "Premier gets First Taste of Public Anger," *Vancouver Sun*, May 13, 1992.

9 Mr. Justice K. Peter Richard, *The Westray Story: A Predictable Path to Disaster, Report of the Westray Mine Public Inquiry*, Government of Nova Scotia, 1997.

10 Dean Jobb, *Calculated Risk: Greed, Politics, and the Westray Tragedy* (Halifax: Nimbus 1994), 68.

11 C.G. "Giff" Gifford, a close friend of her father's and one of her "stalwarts in the five previous elections," had died since the 1988 campaign.

12 "Liberals Post Major Win in Nova Scotia," Regina *Leader-Post*, May 26, 1993.

13 "Loyalties out the Window in NS," *National Post*, May 7, 1993.

14 "PCs Sink, NDP Soars in Popularity Poll," Halifax *Daily News*, October 17, 1990.

15 "Pundits Predict Liberal Government," *Montreal Gazette*, May 25, 1993.

16 "That Darn Alexa Myth," Halifax *Daily News*, December 5, 1994.

17 "Fiercely Competitive Spirit Pilots Province's NDP," Halifax *Mail-Star*, May 21, 1993.

18 Speech to the Canadian Alzheimer Society, Vancouver, BC, April 24, 1998.

19 "Time was Right—Alexa," Halifax *Chronicle-Herald*, November 21, 1994.

20 "That Darn Alexa Myth," Halifax *Daily News*, December 5, 1994.
21 "McDonough Won't be Hanging Up Her Guns," Halifax *Chronicle-Herald*, November 22, 1994.
22 "That Darn Alexa Myth," Halifax *Daily News*, December 5, 1994.
23 "McDonough Starts Life on the Backbench," Halifax *Daily News*, November 22, 1994.
24 "McDonough Won't be Hanging Up Her Guns," Halifax *Chronicle-Herald*, November 22, 1994.

THE NATIONAL STAGE

1 Letter from McDonough to McGill, January 30, 1995.
2 "Finding the Button for Stephen Lewis," *Globe and Mail*, May 10, 1989.
3 "NDP Honours Alexa," Halifax *Mail-Star*, April 10, 1995.
4 "New Democrats Search for a Leader," *Toronto Star*, October 12, 1995.
5 "Nova Scotia's McDonough Taking a Run at NDP Leadership," *Globe and Mail*, May 31, 1995.
6 "An NDP Historian's Handicap of the Race," *Vancouver Sun*, October 13, 1995.
7 "McDonough Captures Leadership of NDP," *Globe and Mail*, October 16, 1995.
8 Herschel Hardin, a Vancouver-based author and Canadian nationalist, also ran for the leadership but didn't make the primaries' cut.
9 "McDonough Captures Leadership of NDP," *Globe and Mail*, October 16, 1995.
10 Graham Truelove, *Svend Robinson: A Life in Politics* (Vancouver: New Star, 2013) 192.
11 "McDonough Captures Leadership of NDP," *Globe and Mail*, October 16, 1995.
12 Graham Truelove, *Svend Robinson: A Life in Politics* (Vancouver: New Star, 2013) 192.
13 "Party Elite Defeats Robinson," *Toronto Sun*, October 16, 1995.
14 The description of Alexa's first meeting with David MacDonald comes from interviews with both Alexa and MacDonald, as well as various media accounts, including "The Prime of Ms. Alexa McDonough" by Silver Donald Cameron in the November/December issue of *Homemaker's*; "It's Love," by the *Ottawa Citizen*'s Juliet O'Neill in the Halifax *Daily News*; and "Love Among the Policy Ruins" by Linda Frum in the *National Post*, February 6, 1999.
15 "Still the Outsider," Halifax *Daily News*, April 23, 1996.
16 "McDonough Lectures NDP," Halifax *Daily News*, May 31, 1995.
17 "Mellower Robinson No Less of a Threat to McDonough," *Ottawa Citizen*, August 11, 1996.
18 "McDonough talks tough: PM following Reform's lead, says new head of federal NDP," Halifax *Daily News*, October 16, 1995.
19 "Mixed Emotions: McDonough says Farewell to Legislature, MacEwan," Halifax *Daily News*, October 21, 1995.
20 "High Hopes: Profile of Alexa McDonough," *Our Times*, March–April 1997.
21 "Wallflower Chief Bad for NDP," Saskatoon *StarPhoenix*, May 13, 1996.
22 "Are There Still Smoky Backrooms on Parliament Hill?" Regina *Leader-Post*, November 2, 1996.
23 "Speaking of Resignation," *Ottawa Citizen*, April 2, 1997.
24 Salloum moved to Ottawa to become Alexa's communications assistant following the 2000 federal election.
25 "McDonough Sports a New Image—and Romance," *Toronto Star*, February 18, 1997.
26 "McDonough, NDP Started Strong but now They're Fizzling across Canada," *Vancouver Sun*, May 24, 1997.
27 "High Hopes: Profile of Alexa McDonough," *Our Times*, March–April 1997, 18.
28 "McDonough, NDP Started Strong but now They're Fizzling across Canada," *Vancouver Sun*, May 24, 1997.

29 "McDonough's Call for Jobs is Cheered in Cape Breton," *Montreal Gazette*, June 2, 1997.

30 "NDP Rides Atlantic Wave, McDonough Sweeps Halifax Area, Rebuilds Base in West," *Toronto Star*, June 3, 1997.

31 "McDonough Expected It: NDP Leader Wasn't Surprised by Party's Rising Atlantic Tide," Halifax *Daily News*, June 4, 1997.

32 "Joy! Honest John's City Belongs to McDonough," Halifax *Daily News*, June 3, 1997.

33 "NDP's Defectors Lay Blame at Rae's Feet," *Toronto Star*, June 9, 1997.

34 O'Connor soon moved back to Halifax, where he became chief of staff to the new Nova Scotia NDP leader, Robert Chisholm. In 1998, the year after Alexa piloted the NDP to its federal triumph in Nova Scotia, Chisholm would lead the provincial party to its best showing ever, tied for first place in seats with the Liberals, who barely managed to hang on to form a minority government with the help of the Conservatives.

35 "NDP's McDonough Hopes to be Like Blair," *National Post*, December 21, 1998.

36 "NDP Reaches Out to Business," *Montreal Gazette*, September 1, 1998.

37 "NDP's Embrace of Business has Pitfalls," Regina *Leader-Post*, September 12, 1998.

38 "Finally, a Refreshing Political Voice on Globalization," *Vancouver Sun*, September 29, 1998.

39 "Buzz Hargrove's Labour Lost," *Ottawa Citizen*, December 6, 1998.

40 "UK Politics: What is the Third Way?" *BBC News*, September 27, 1999, http://news.bbc.co.uk/2/hi/458626.stm.

41 "NDP-Labour Rift in Vision for Party's Future," Saskatoon *StarPhoenix*, January 8, 1999.

42 "Fiscal Realist Takes Top Job for Federal NDP," *National Post*, January 15, 1999.

43 There were also the usual sideshows. In June, Alexa had removed Svend Robinson from his front-row House of Commons seat for violating party policy by introducing a resolution to remove any reference to God in Canada's constitution. The timing was awkward to say the least; New Democrats in both Manitoba and Saskatchewan, provinces where religion still mattered, were gearing up for provincial elections. Robinson's punishment was mild and largely symbolic—she allowed him to remain as the party's foreign affairs critic—and he had initially appeared to accept her decision. But then, a few days later, he wrote a letter to party officials, protesting his treatment, only to pivot again a few days after that when he "hugged McDonough on a public stage and said the matter was over." Some of his supporters were not so forgiving, and there were two resolutions on the convention agenda protesting McDonough's decision.

44 "Move to Centre Won't Sacrifice Values: McDonough," *National Post*, August 28, 1999.

45 "McDonough Plays Down Hargrove's Dire Predictions," *Ottawa Citizen*, October 17, 2000.

46 "McDonough Hopes Party Fate after Election is Power Broker," *Globe and Mail*, November 25, 2000.

47 "PM to Atlantic Canada: Don't Waste your Vote," *Ottawa Citizen*, October 27, 2000.

48 "NDP Leader Insists Party not Headed for Oblivion," *Ottawa Citizen*, October 17, 2000.

49 "McDonough's Sons Follow Tory Lead, Add More Political Eye Candy to the Campaign Trail," *National Post*, November 20, 2000.

50 "Sound Bites," *Vancouver Province*, November 19, 2000.

51 "McDonough's Secret: Eyeliner Tattoos," *National Post*, November 25, 2000.

52 "Losses Don't Deter McDonough," Halifax *Mail-Star*, November 29, 2000.

53 "The History of the New Politics Initiative: Movement and Party, Then and Now," rabble.ca, November 29, 2011, https://rabble.ca/news/2011/11/history-npi-movement-and-party-then-and-now.

54 "NDP Spars over Renewal," *Montreal Gazette*, November 24, 2001.

55 The NPI "continued to organize local consultations and other activities for a couple of years," Jim Stanford noted in "The History of the New Politics Initiative," November 29, 2011, "but the focus of its work was not clear, and the political environment was becoming more hostile (in the wake of the 9/11 attacks and the subsequent decline of anti-globalization struggles)." The movement formally dissolved in 2004, following Jack Layton's election as NDP leader.

56 Alexander Thomson Houston, "The Perfect Storm: Using Pinard and Irving to Explain the Canadian 2011 Election 'Orange Crush'" (master's thesis, Acadia University, 2015).

57 "Alexa Calls it Quits," Halifax *Chronicle-Herald*, June 6, 2002.

58 "McDonough's Mother Remembered as a Fighter for Social Justice," Halifax *Chronicle-Herald*, June 12, 2002.

59 "The Case of Maher Arar," Amnesty International, March 6, 2017, https://www.amnesty.ca/legal-brief/case-maher-arar.

60 "Leader Lauded in House," Halifax *Chronicle-Herald*, December 13, 2002.

61 Monia Mazigh, *Hope and Despair: My Struggle to Free My Husband, Maher Arar* (Toronto: McClelland & Stewart, 2008), 9.

62 Anthony Depalma, "THREATS AND RESPONSES: DETAINEE; Canadian Immigrant Arrested at JFK is Deported to Syria," *New York Times*, October 12, 2002.

63 "US Deports Canadian to Syria," *Ottawa Citizen*, October 12, 2002.

64 Monia Mazigh, *Hope and Despair: My Struggle to Free My Husband, Maher Arar* (Toronto: McClelland & Stewart, 2008), 62.

65 "Alexa's Adieu," *National Post*, January 25, 2003.

66 Monia Mazigh, who was courted by both the NDP and the Liberals, did run for the NDP, unsuccessfully, in Ottawa South in the June 28, 2004, federal election. Two months later, she joined the NDP's Caucus Research Bureau as a researcher.

67 The inquiry concluded "categorically that there is no evidence to indicate that Mr. Arar has committed an offence or that his activities constitute a threat to the security of Canada." In 2007, Ottawa formally apologized and paid him $10 million in compensation.

68 During a radio debate in that campaign, Alexa McDonough and Peter MacKay got into a sparring match. After MacKay criticized the quality of some NDP candidates, Alexa pointed to how well Alexis MacDonald seemed to be doing against him. MacKay fired back, "I think you better stick to your knitting and win your own riding." McDonough jumped on his words to accuse him of a "sexist slur." Although he insisted it was a common term for minding your own business, MacKay apologized. Years later, when MacKay's son was born, Alexa sent him a gift: a pair of mittens and knitting needles. MacKay admitted, "I thought it was kind of cute."

69 David's and Alexa's relationship—as had been the case with other men in Alexa's life—eventually survived the end of their romance and David's 2005 marriage to Deborah Sinclair. In 2012, MacDonald recalled, the three of them even attended together the NDP leadership convention that elected Tom Mulcair. "We'd be sitting around at the convention centre, and people would say, 'Isn't that Alexa and David together?'," he remembered with a laugh. "'Who's that other one?' 'Well, that's his wife.'" MacDonald said the trio "caucused together, and we decided who we'd support in each of the ballots, and we agreed right through the final vote."

70 Travis and his young family were still living in Ireland at the time. There are now seven grandchildren.

71 "Halifax MP Alexa McDonough Announces Retirement," *CBC News*, June 2, 2008, https://www.cbc.ca/

news/canada/nova-scotia/halifax-mp-alexa-mcdonough-announces-retirement-1.703579.

72 "Reactions to Retirement," *Metro Halifax*, June 3, 2008.

73 "After 29 Years in Politics, McDonough Eyes Time with Family," Halifax *Chronicle-Herald*, June 3, 2008.

74 Leslie won, and was re-elected in 2011. She became one of the youngest MPs ever chosen as a deputy leader of the official opposition. She was defeated in the 2015 federal election.

THERE'S LIFE AFTER POLITICS

1 Despite their romantic breakup, Alexa and Holloway remained friends. Once, when I was interviewing her, Alexa told me she had to cut off our conversation early because Holloway would be arriving to pick her up. They were attending an event at the Mount together.

2 Speech to the Canadian Alzheimer Society, April 24, 1998.

3 "McDonough Treated for Breast Cancer," Canadian Press, May 4, 2013.

4 "The First Day Back and Two MPs' Messy Breakup," *Maclean's*, September 26, 2011.

5 Jérôme Labbé, "Alexa McDonough, l'infatigable militante néo-démocrate," Radio Canada, September 24, 2019, https://ici.radio-canada.ca/nouvelle/1314267/nouveau-parti-democratique-npd-jagmeet-singh-campagne-elections-canada-2019.

TRAILBLAZER

1 Cerise Morris, "Royal Commission on the Status of Women," *Canadian Encyclopedia*, March 22, 2016, https://www.thecanadianencyclopedia.ca/en/article/royal-commission-on-the-status-of-women-in-canada.

INDEX

References in bold refer to images.